Passage to Power

Harvard East Asian Series 91
The Council on East Asian Studies at Harvard University,
through the Fairbank Center for East Asian Research,
administers research projects designed to further
scholarly understanding of China, Japan, Korea, Vietnam,
Inner Asia, and adjacent areas.

Passage to Power

K'ang-hsi and His
Heir Apparent, 1661-1722

Silas H. L. Wu

HARVARD UNIVERSITY PRESS
Cambridge, Massachusetts
and London, England 1979

Library of Congress Cataloging in Publication Data

Wu, Silas H   L   1929-
    Passage to power.

    (Harvard East Asian series; 91)
    Bibliography: p.
    Includes index.
    1. Ch'ing Sheng-tsu, Emperor of China, 1654-1722.
2.   China—History—K'ang-hsi, 1662-1722.
I Title. II. Series.
DS754.4.C53W8   951'.03'0924 [B]   79-4191
ISBN 0-674-65625-3

For Beatrix, Christopher, and Melinda

Preface

THIS book is about a conflict between a father and son. Since the father is the Emperor K'ang-hsi of China, who reigned from 1661 to 1722, and the son his heir, Yin-jeng, it is also a story of the murderous power struggle that took place for succession to the ancient Chinese throne. The personal history is intertwined with the larger history of the dynasty and of the court of K'ang-hsi during the formative years of Ch'ing rule in China. I have used the father-son drama as a focal point in relating the events that followed the Manchu conquest; the context of the political culture within which the power struggle occurred serves as the stage.

I have chosen to write this story from the point of view of the father. The Emperor K'ang-hsi was a paradoxical man, psychologically complex and therefore an interesting subject. He was an absolute monarch, whose every action affected the lives of his people and the course of history in China. He was also inconsistent and full of mysterious fears. He was the most powerful person in China, yet often very timid and reluctant to use that power; a man capable of disinheriting and jailing his heir, but only after participating in a twenty-year cover-up of this same son's crimes.

In order to throw light upon the motives of the key actors, as well as the social and political characteristics of their times, I have drawn upon the accumulated evidence of the workings of the Ch'ing court—its politics, culture, administrative organization, and communications system—utilizing the exhaustive records kept by the court. I have relied heavily on many personal documents, which, according to modern psychological research, are important sources for the reconstruction of a historical personality. These documents include letters, diaries, and, most important, the "palace memorials." Devised by K'ang-hsi for information gathering and secret communication with his officials, the palace memorials resemble confidential letters, but are much more than that: their contents are so rich that their value often surpasses that of letters, diaries, and autobiographical references combined. These memorials and the records of the emperor's pronouncements (which, when given orally, were recorded in the *Imperial Diary*) constituted the two sources for the official chronicles, such as the *Veritable Records*. (For more discussion of sources, see my bibliographical note.) Despite this richness of documentation, however, the Ch'ing records offer only scanty information about a person's childhood. Hence my reconstruction of the father's and son's childhoods is based largely on K'ang-hsi's recollections.

Although this book is the product of one man's research, it reflects the wisdom of several colleagues in the Ch'ing field. John Shrecker and Alexander Woodside bravely read a rough draft with meticulous care; they each offered a wealth of insightful suggestions. John K. Fairbank, who encouraged this undertaking when it was originally conceived, made critical comments on the first three chapters. Jonathan Spence kindly read the final draft and shared with me his aesthetic views concerning the general format of a book.

I benefited greatly from discussions with Olive Holmes about how to make historical writing interesting for the general reader as well as for the scholar. Cornelia Levine worked on the manuscript in its initial form. And Anna Laura Rosow helped smooth the remaining rough spots in the final draft.

This study was aided by generous grants from the American Council of Learned Societies (1970) and the Social Science Research Council (1974), as well as a Distinguished Fulbright Scholar grant (1977); these made possible my travel and research in Taiwan and Japan. Further financial assistance was provided by Boston College and the John K. Fairbank Center for East Asian Research at Harvard University. Special thanks go to the director and the archivists of the National Palace Museum in Taiwan, who opened the entire K'ang-hsi/Yung-cheng archives for my project. I should also like to thank the staff members at Harvard-Yenching Library for their help in facilitating my research.

Finally, I am grateful to my wife and children for their patience and understanding during the many years of research and writing of this book, and I affectionately dedicate it to them.

Contents

Passage to Power

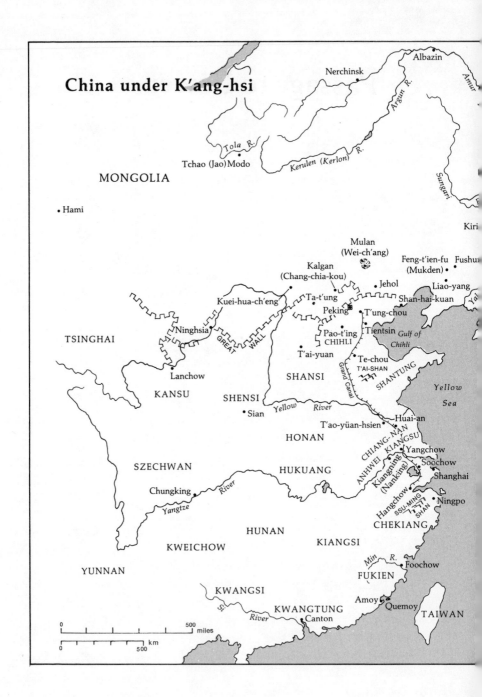

China under K'ang-hsi

Albazin

Nerchinsk

Amur R.

Argun R.

Sungari

MONGOLIA

Tola R.

Tchao (Jao) Modo

Kerulen (Kerlon) R.

Kiri

Hami

Mulan
(Wei-ch'ang)

Feng-t'ien-fu   Fushu
(Mukden)

Kalgan
(Chang-chia-kou)   Jehol   Liao-yang

Kuei-hua-ch'eng   Ta-t'ung   Shan-hai-kuan

Peking   T'ung-chou

Ninghsia   Pao-t'ing   Tientsin   Gulf of
CHIHLI   Chihli

GREAT   WALL   T'ai-yuan   Te-chou
T'AI-SHAN   SHANTUNG

TSINGHAI   Lanchow   SHANSI   Grand Canal   Yellow
Sea

KANSU   SHENSI   Yellow   River   Huai-an

Sian   T'ao-yüan-hsien   CHIANG-NAN   KIANGSU

HONAN   ANHWEI   Yangchow

SZECHWAN   HUKUANG   Kiangning   Soochow
(Nanking)   Shanghai

Chungking   River   Hangchow   Ningpo
SSU-MING
Yangtze   SHAN

HUNAN   CHEKIANG

KWEICHOW   KIANGSI

YUNNAN   Min   R.   Foochow

FUKIEN

KWANGSI

KWANGTUNG   Amoy   Quemoy
St.   Canton   TAIWAN
River

0   500
miles

0   500
km

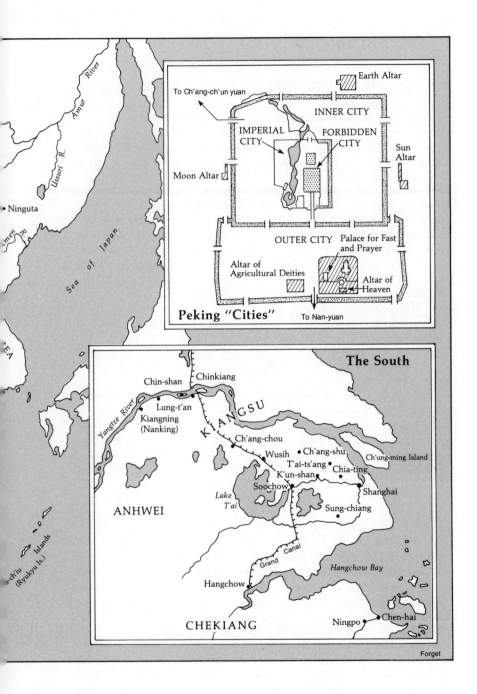

Amur River

Ussuri R.

Sea of Japan

Ninguta

Peking "Cities"

To Ch'ang-ch'un yuan

Earth Altar

INNER CITY

IMPERIAL
CITY

FORBIDDEN
CITY

Sun
Altar

Moon Altar

OUTER CITY   Palace for Fast
and Prayer

Altar of
Agricultural Deities

Altar of
Heaven

To Nan-yuan

The South

Chin-shan   Chinkiang

Yangtze River

Lung-t'an
Kiangning
(Nanking)

KIANGSU

Ch'ang-chou

Wusih   Ch'ang-shu

T'ai-ts'ang   Ch'ung-ming Island

K'un-shan   Chia-ting

Soochow   Shanghai

ANHWEI

Lake
T'ai

Sung-chiang

u-ch'iu Islands
(Ryukyu Is.)

Grand Canal   Hangchow Bay

Hangchow

CHEKIANG   Ningpo   Chen-hai

Forget

Explanatory Note

Languages. The Manchus originally had only an oral language and depended on Mongolian for written communication. In 1599, however, a Manchu script was devised from a modified Mongolian alphabet. By 1632, when the new system was perfected, Manchu and Chinese were used side by side within the government; Mongolian was retained primarily for dealing with the Mongol population. By the middle of the K'ang-hsi period (1661-1722), Sinification had progressed sufficiently that intragovernmental communication was predominantly in Chinese and few Manchus could command their written language. Although Manchu was still used at times by the imperial family and by Manchu officials, Chinese was the main language for memorials and edicts. Major governmental compilations (such as the *Veritable Records*, the *Imperial Diary*, and the *Collected Statutes*) were written in Chinese, then translated into Manchu and Mongolian. By the end of the eighteenth century Manchus were speaking and writing mostly in Chinese. Thus, among the references cited in this study, fewer Manchu than Chinese sources appear.

Names. In the Chinese custom, I have used an emperor's reign title as if it were his personal name; hence "K'ang-hsi," "Emperor K'ang-hsi," and "the Emperor K'ang-hsi" all denote the K'ang-hsi emperor. Chinese names are romanized according to the Wade-Giles system; personal name follows family name without a hyphen between the two (Li Kuang-ti, T'ang Pin). Some Manchu names are romanized according to the Wade-Giles system, with a hyphen between all syllables (Fu-ch'üan, Te-ko-le); others, particularly those of well-known Manchus who appear in Arthur W. Hummel's *Eminent Chinese of the Ch'ing Period, 1644-1912*, are written in accordance with Manchu pronunciation, without syllable separation or hyphenation (Songgotu, Mingju, Tohoci). Some Manchu names are spelled in the official chronicle, *Ta-Ch'ing shih-lu* ("Veritable Records of the Ch'ing Dynasty"), with Chinese characters different from those used in the original documents (Tohoci's name in memorials is T'ao-ho-ch'i; in the official chronicle, T'o-ho-ch'i). Manchus often assumed Chinese-like names, which were treated by their contemporaries like conventional Chinese names. Although, for example, our romanization system makes it clear that Hsü-yüan-meng is a Manchu name, the man was actually referred to as "Yüan-meng," as if this had been his personal name, or as "Mr. Hsü." Manchus in fact used only personal names; they had clan names but no family names. Kinship connections therefore are not revealed by names. (Soni's sons, for example, include Gabula, Songgotu, Hsin-yü, and Fa-pao).

Dates. Chinese dates are used in the notes primarily to identify documents and occasionally are given in the text with their Gregorian counterparts because of the additional information they convey. Since they derive from the emperor's reign, Chinese dates enable the reader to determine when during the K'ang-hsi reign a particular event occurred. As an example, the twenty-eighth day of the sixth month of the thirty-second year of the K'ang-hsi reign would read KH 32/6/28; since K'ang-hsi reigned for sixty-one years, this is a date in the middle of his reign.

Ages. The Chinese unit of age is the *sui*, roughly equivalent to the Western year. Use of the term can be misleading, however, for a Chinese is one sui at birth and he becomes a sui older every lunar New Year. Thus, a baby born on the eve of a new year is two sui the next morning, whereas by Western count he is only two days old. The ages given in this book are approximations of Western years; in general, the number of years is at least one less than the number of sui.

Prologue

O N October 17, 1708, Emperor K'ang-hsi, at his hunting camp in Inner Mongolia, performed an unusual act that shocked the entire East Asian world. He ordered that his thirty-five-year-old heir apparent, Yin-jeng, be brought to him in chains and, in front of all the Manchu and Chinese dignitaries gathered there, he angrily denounced his son for unfilialness and cruelty. He claimed that Yin-jeng had broken into his tent the previous night and attempted to take his life. He then announced his decision to depose Yin-jeng from his position as heir apparent and ordered him transferred to Peking for permanent confinement.

To justify his drastic decision to his people, K'ang-hsi made astonishing revelations about Yin-jeng's many evil acts and his immorality—extravagance, sexual perversion, sadism—and, most serious of all, his repeated attempts to usurp the throne and his attempted assassination. The enraged emperor was convinced that Yin-jeng was simply insane.

Soon after the solemn proclamation was made, however, K'ang-hsi began to see bad omens, to dream strange dreams, and to believe that the whole situation was the working of ghosts who had possessed Yin-jeng, causing him to appear insane. For this and other reasons, he reinstated his son early in the spring of the year, following Yin-jeng's supposed exorcism. Three years later, however, in 1712, K'ang-hsi was forced to depose Yin-jeng once again—this time permanently—because Yin-jeng was deemed indeed mad, absolutely unfit to succeed in the rule of one of the largest empires in the world.

Yin-jeng's deposition was merely the climactic point in one of the

longest succession struggles in China's three thousand years of imperial rule. It was preceded by a series of nerve-racking confronta-
tions between father and son, which had built up tensions over a
period of more than twenty years; it was followed by another series
of even more vicious and intense struggles for the vacated heirship
among the imperial children. When the struggles were abruptly terminated by K'ang-hsi's death, in 1722, a new round of rivalries
between the losers and the new emperor, Yung-cheng, was begun,
which lasted for several years until Yung-cheng finally liquidated
all his brothers who had conspired to undermine his rule. Before
the new emperor accomplished this, by about 1730, rivalry had
dominated the headlines of the first half of his reign (one of the
shortest in China's imperial history, lasting from 1723 to 1735).

This episode of human tragedy not only had a strong impact on
contemporary court politics and on major segments of the Manchu-
Chinese society, but also left an imprint on the imperial system as it
evolved in modern Chinese history. The modern history indeed of
all of East Asia would have been quite different had Yin-jeng been
allowed to succeed K'ang-hsi on the throne.

Of course our interest in the story is not based on what might
have been, but on what actually happened. The story is compelling
both because of its illumination of human experience and because
of its significance in world history. It teaches many lessons about
the peculiarities of imperial politics, which must impress us with
their aspect of modernity and similarity to contemporary Peking
politics. It has become increasingly clear that the political culture
and behavior of imperial China were so dominant as to play a
major role in the Chinese political heritage, with impact not only
on the Republican era but also on post-1949 revolutionary China.
Our study, therefore, of one of the most prolonged and complex
succession struggles of the largest empire in the East Asian world
will no doubt enhance our comprehension of present-day Chinese
politics.

The story is only part of a much larger one, involving two peo-
ples and the encounter of two cultures—that of the Manchus and
that of the Chinese. It vividly demonstrates the advantages and pit-
falls of the assimilation of the culturally superior Chinese by the
militarily superior Manchus. It reveals tensions, not only between
the two traditions, but also within the tradition of the Manchu ruling class—the Manchus sometimes agreeing on the adoption of certain elements of Chinese culture, yet disagreeing irreconcilably on
others.

How should we begin? Since the story takes place at a "nodal point" in modern Chinese history—the Manchu conquest of China —it may best be related against this important setting.

LIKE THE HIGHLY civilized Mediterranean world in the West, the Chinese people had been conquered many times, partially and sometimes totally by northern barbarians. The Mongols were the first to achieve complete conquest of the Chinese; they established the Yuan dynasty, which lasted from 1260 to 1368. Under the dynastic title Ch'ing (1644-1911), the Manchus were the second— and final—barbarian tribe to gain the imperial throne in Peking, claiming the "Mandate of Heaven" to rule all China. Despite their small number (Manchus made up less than two percent of the population of the empire) the Manchus were much more successful than the Mongols at maintaining control over the Chinese, an accomplishment historians generally attribute to the early Manchu rulers' policy of governing the Chinese in the Chinese way. From the beginning of their conquest, the Manchus absorbed Chinese moral values and political ideology and institutions, and they used Chinese literati to staff their government. This process of Sinification evolved for nearly a century before the final structure of Manchu rule crystallized. The K'ang-hsi reign (1661-1722) constituted a decisive period within the process; as an example, K'ang-hsi copied from the defunct Ming dynasty (1368-1643) the system of establishing an heir apparent. His conflict with his son occurred within this broad context of cultural assimilation, during the Manchus' search for dynastic legitimation and an effective political structure.

K'ang-hsi's ancestors were of the Jurched tribe from the frontier region of southern Manchuria. They had been subject to Chinese influence long before they developed any ambition for Chinese imperial power. Nurhaci (1559-1626), founding father of the Manchu state, had intimate contact with the Chinese from his youth and thus was familiar with Chinese ways of life and the Chinese mentality.[1] He was able, within a short period of time, to conquer rival tribes in Manchuria and establish a semicentralized bureaucracy. During his lifetime he developed a social organization based on the original Manchu clan structure, the Eight Banners, a system devised for both social and military control. It was a centralized feudal structure with a strong element of slavery.

Nurhaci's successors speeded the process of political concentration. During the reign of T'ai-tsung (Hong Taiji, 1592-1643, r. 1627-1643),[2] certain elements of the Chinese political system were grafted onto the surface of the developing Manchu ruling structure. Then, under the reign of Shun-chih (r. 1644-1661), a full-fledged Chinese system was instituted. During the regency of Shun-chih's uncle Dorgon, the process of assimilation was selective, but when Shun-chih took over the reins of government after Dorgon's death, in 1650, he began the wholesale copying of the Ming system; this included the reintroduction of the eunuch agency, a powerful organ within the palace that had dominated the latter half of Ming rule and which had been banned during Dorgon's time. After Shun-chih's death, in 1661, the Manchu ruling elite expressed their strong disapproval of his policy of indiscriminate Sinification.

When the seven-year-old Hsüan-yeh was designated heir by his dying father, Shun-chih, he was entrusted to a four-man regency dominated by the Manchu strong man Oboi. The regency systematically dismantled the Chinese elements within the political structure and even went so far as to have all official titles changed back to the Manchu language—many of the Manchu aristocrats still resented Chinese influence and disliked the presence of the Chinese literati in the imperial court.

After Hsüan-yeh, now the K'ang-hsi Emperor, was of age to assume real power, in 1668, he eliminated the Oboi faction and soon discovered that the Manchu regime was far from secure, that Manchu conquest was not yet complete: Taiwan was in the hands of Ming loyalists; many provinces from the southeast to the southwest were still under the autonomous rule of the Chinese military lords known as the Three Feudatories; and anti-Manchu resistance in the South, a region encompassing major cities in the lower Yangtze delta—notably, Yangchow, Hangchow, and Soochow—remained strong and potentially explosive. (The Southerners' memory of the massacres committed by the marauding Manchus during the Shun-chih years was still fresh. In Yangchow alone, Manchu horsemen raped women en masse and slaughtered three-quarters of a million Chinese within ten days; other cities suffered similar fates at the hands of the Manchu conquerors.)[3] It was against this background that K'ang-hsi initiated his policy of full-scale Sinification to accomplish the unfinished process of Manchu conquest and to lay a solid foundation of government for the Manchu rule in China.

Manchu conquest and K'ang-hsi's policy are important factors in our understanding of the father-son story. But in order to comprehend many of the peculiar features of the story, we also need to be acquainted with the political and cultural environment of late-seventeenth- and early-eighteenth-century China.

Of foremost importance was the cultural tension between the North and South. If the Great Wall on China's northern frontier forever symbolizes her sorrows and difficulties with the barbarians, the Grand Canal that links Peking and the South represents the northern conquerors' problem of maintaining political control over the Chinese South. The problem was how to draw upon the human and economic resources of the South without falling under its nearly irresistible spell.[4]

The Chinese South had developed a distinct culture as early as the last quarter of the sixth century. The Chinese who had migrated to this region from the North during the centuries of political dis-union (220-589)—when northern barbarians moving into North China compelled them to escape—had created a life-style that was more leisurely, elegant, and sensual than that of the North. The rise and fall of subsequent dynasties, Chinese or alien, had not altered the distinctive features of this culture.

Yangchow epitomized the Southern culture.[5] Strategically situated at the confluence of the Grand Canal and the Yangtze and Huai rivers, the city was the nerve center of domestic trade. The early-Ch'ing policy of tapping Southern economic resources contributed to the rise in the late seventeenth and eighteenth centuries of a new economic class. This class gave the Yangchow area added economic significance. The Imperial Household (*Nei-wu fu*) gave the salt monopoly to wealthy merchants in exchange for their service as salt-tax collectors; these merchants functioned as the economic arm of the emperor's private bureaucracy and were referred to as the "merchants of the Imperial Household." Many were relatives of influential Chinese Banner officials or retainers of powerful Manchu court ministers. Such "merchant aristocrats" set the high style of life in the South and "vied with one another in extravagance." Some spent "ten thousand taels of silver in a single day"; some "threw down gold foil" like crazy men from the tower on top of the Golden Hill (Chin-shan) just for fun; one "erected wooden nude female statues in front of his inner halls, and controlled them mechanically so as to tease and surprise his guests"; and they "vied with one another in novelties and eccentricities that were too numerous to describe in full."[6]

Not all the new rich were vulgar eccentrics. Refined salt merchants patronized scholars and poets and cultivated expensive hobbies as bibliophiles and art connoisseurs. A great many famous Southern scholars, including incumbent and retired high officials from the K'ang-hsi court, at one time or another visited Yangchow and participated in the Southern way of life; some were closely connected with rich and powerful salt merchants.

It was in their taste in women that these two modes of life, the vulgar and the refined, converged. Yangchow women were renowned for their delicate, bound feet; neighboring Soochow women were admired for their elaborate hairdos. Local scholars and visit-

ing bureaucrats competed with wealthy merchants for Yangchow
concubines and patronized elegant courtesans. In the last days of
the Ming, the Chinese general Wu San-kuei, who was guarding the
strategic Shan-hai Pass between Manchuria and China proper,
"welcomed" the Manchu forces entering China partly as a form of
revenge on the bandit leader Li Tzu-ch'eng, who had abducted
Wu's mistress, Ch'en Yuan-yuan, a former courtesan of national
renown. Another famous Southern courtesan was Li Hsiang-chün,
whose unswerving fidelity to Hou Fang-yü—celebrated poet and
high official of the fugitive Ming court in the South—made her the
heroine of K'ung Shang-jen's famous tragedy *The Peach Flower Fan*
(*T'ao-hua shan*); the play became *de rigueur* in the K'ang-hsi court
after the emperor showed his patronage by holding its debut at the
palace.[7] Other scholar-officials also took great pride in their concubines, boasting that the women were of the "Yangchow brand."[8]

K'ang-hsi's affection for Southern culture enhanced the tendency
of the Manchu court to admire the Southern way of life. Powerful
Manchu ministers, such as Mingju, hired Southern literati as resident tutors and purchased Southern youngsters as servants because
of their sensitivity, charm, and fair looks.[9] The ministers themselves became connoisseurs of rare books and collectors of Sung
and Ming paintings, and they whetted the appetite of the Manchu
elite for Southern theater and Soochow cuisine. Southern literati
were recruited into imperial service and vied with the Manchu
courtiers for imperial favor (indeed, they were the cause of the
fierce factional struggles that plagued the first half of the K'ang-hsi
reign).

The South's natural beauty so impressed K'ang-hsi during his
first tour, in 1683, that he decided to build a suburban villa, to the
west of Peking, that would remind him of the region.[10] The design
evoked Southern rivers and hills, and it was here that he spent most
of his days, leaving the imperial palaces in Peking for ceremonial
use. Nevertheless, the strong and disciplined K'ang-hsi was able to
resist the sensual elements of Southern culture, which not all in his
retinue were able to do. When they accompanied him down the
Grand Canal to the South on his many inspection tours some members of his party succumbed to the South's voluptuous lure.

Just as the cultural disparity at times created tensions between
the South and the North, sociopolitical tensions deriving from that
disparity existed within the Manchu ruling elite. Such tensions were
inevitable given the Manchu rulers' desire to adapt the Chinese
political structure to the Manchu Banner system. The Chinese imperial institution was based on the Confucian ideology of "one
ruler under heaven" and placed absolute power in the hands of the

emperor. The banner system, on the other hand, was a centralized feudal structure in which the feudal lords (the banner nobility) regarded their retainers as personal slaves—at least nominally—and exacted their loyalty. In some cases, even when a retainer (particularly a *pao-i*, bond servant) was enlisted to serve as high-ranking official in the emperor's court, his lord still maintained the authority to control his social life. The lord had the right to apply physical punishment to a retainer and many were beaten to death under false pretenses—the lord might appropriate the retainer's wife after torturing the man to death under such charges as alleged drunkenness.[11]

The banner loyalty system obviously conflicted with the imperial demand for direct and exclusive allegiance to the throne. Throughout the early decades of Manchu rule, imperial power steadily increased at the expense of hereditary power. The conflict of loyalties made for continual tension within the Manchu power structure.[12] In general, K'ang-hsi demonstrated a greater capacity than his successors for tolerating the existence of the dual loyalties. This policy had serious political ramifications during his reign, and dualism was eliminated only during the Yung-cheng period.[13]

Slavery within the banners intertwined with Chinese slavery practices in the early Ch'ing, causing more complexities within the entire slavery system. Although the purchasing of slaves was legal, there were also numerous slave volunteers, Chinese who for economic security gave up their freedom to be owned by a Manchu family, or who sold their young boys and girls to theatrical troupes belonging to wealthy Chinese or Manchus. Furthermore, the banner system contained a slave system within a slave system. Whereas most bannermen were only nominal slaves, the *pao-i*—bond servants—were actual slaves of a Manchu prince or of the emperor himself. These *pao-i* either were captives from battles—Mongols, Chinese, or Koreans—or were the relatives of condemned criminals; others had voluntarily become slaves because of impoverishment or separation from their families.

Pao-i at the disposal of the emperor formed the basis of his private bureaucracy, the Imperial Household Department. In conjunction with eunuchs and female attendants, they saw to the various personal needs and functions of the emperor: food, clothing, housing, travel, and security. They could be sent by the department to take up official assignments outside Peking, as a textile commissioner in the South, for example, and they could even be appointed to positions in the imperial government itself.[14]

Below the *pao-i* were the *Sin jeku* (or in Chinese, *Hsin-che-k'u*: slaves who received rations under the Office of the Overseers), who

constituted the lowest social stratum among the Imperial Household personnel. Slaves under this office were descendants of criminals in the early days of the Manchu conquest, or relatives of convicted high officials (Chinese and Manchu alike) who had been
deprived of their regular "citizen's status," so to speak. Their duty
was to perform all sorts of menial tasks within the Imperial Household. One of the ways for this group of slaves to change their status
was to have their daughters be selected first as ladies-in-waiting and
then as imperial concubines; the mother of K'ang-hsi's eighth son,
Yin-ssu, was from a *Sin jeku* Family (conflict between status and
ability would prove an important factor when Yin-ssu entered the
succession race).[15]

  BOTH CULTURAL AND sociopolitical tensions were important
precipitating factors in the political struggle in the K'ang-hsi court.
But the struggle also involved paradoxical behavior on the part of
the key actors that in order to understand one must go beyond outside influences to the inner orientation of these personalities. Starting with a generational conflict, familiar to us today, between
parent and child, we must then consider abnormal psychology:
K'ang-hsi's exceptional compassion and indulgence of the son bordered on the obsessive; Yin-jeng's emotional disturbances and craving for power drove him to insanity. The parapsychological also
plays a role, in the form of ghosts and strange dreams; whether or
not we believe in these things is not the issue. What is relevant is the
effect of such matters on the participants' feelings and behavior.
  This, then, leads us to the question of human motivation. Since
psychological studies of Chinese historical figures are still lacking,
there is no way to present a complete theory of Chinese psychology. But on the assumption that a theoretical framework is needed
to guide the narrative and analysis of my story, I herewith offer a
few facts concerning human motivation that will enable us better to
understand the characteristics and problems of the father-son relationship. This is what has been known among social scientists as
the value approach.[16]
  The value approach to human behavior is not new in the West,
but we have only just observed its beginning in Chinese scholarship. The single factor that most affected imperial succession undoubtedly was power. But political agents in history have demonstrated varying attitudes toward power; it is a common phenome-
non that some people have power but do not value it. "The playing
of a role in politics," as the political scientist Harold D. Lasswell
puts it, "does not have the same meaning to different persons."[17]
One man voluntarily abandoned his royal position "for the woman

I love"; others have neglected their imperial duties and assigned exclusive importance to artistic pursuits (such as the T'ang emperor Hsüan-tsung [Ming Huang], of the eighth century, and the Sung emperor Hui-tsung, of the twelfth century). In contrast, there have been rulers who clung to power to the point of provoking assassination; and there have been people without power who were so power-crazed that they attempted coups d'état. Of the 180 succession cases during China's imperial age, 118 involved violence and murder.[18]

Most crises of succession undoubtedly involved other factors as well. And the crisis during K'ang-hsi's reign contained paradoxes. For example, K'ang-hsi valued imperial power so little that while still young and strong he wanted to abdicate; but later, in old age, he held on to it tenaciously, even when he was dying. His clinging to power during the last decade of his reign caused intense struggles in court and even exposed him to the threat of assassination.

One major factor that explains such a paradox—as well as many other elements in the story that may seem baffling to the Western reader—is that of *hsiao*, or filial piety. In the heart of K'ang-hsi this term stood for an intensely felt emotional commitment, not merely some cliché out of a Confucian handbook: when K'ang-hsi praised someone for having *hsiao*, or attacked that person for lacking it, he was not making a casual comment but rather delivering a profound value judgment. Similarly, when he himself felt intense love and respect for someone—as, for example, for his grandmother, the Great Dowager Empress Hsiao-chuang—he expressed these feelings in terms of filial piety. His emotion ran so deep that it affected his subconscious, as became clear when the tensions with his son Yin-jeng grew unbearable. Hence, we must begin our search for K'ang-hsi's inner orientation with his formative years, when *hsiao* first took root.

Like a musician playing his concertina, I have stretched the backdrop of our story wide, to its cultural and sociopolitical dimensions, then pressed it back to the very center of human motives. My approach will be repeated throughout the book in order that the human drama and political history may unfold in harmony.

PART I

Filial Piety

1
The Grandmother

THE vernal equinox in 1663 visited the imperial capital, Peking, on the eleventh day of the second lunar month during the second year of the K'ang-hsi Emperor's sixty-one-year reign (1661-1722). This was the day that concluded the first half of spring, throughout China a time of joyous, carefree celebration.

Normally, the emperor and the imperial family would have shared in the rejoicing of the people throughout the season. But the year 1663 was an exception. Within the imperial palaces sadness and anxiety prevailed.

For many days now, the slight figure of the nine-year-old K'ang-hsi had been shuttling between two palaces. His mother, only twenty-three years of age, was seriously ill. His forty-nine-year-old grandmother was greatly concerned; she was extremely fond of her daughter-in-law. The boy split his days between the palaces of the two women in his family.

The boy emperor was of medium height and slender. Under a high, broad forehead his eyebrows were short, thick, and curved slightly downward; his nose was large; his mouth and chin firm; and he had large, pronounced "jug ears." His face was pockmarked. (As will be explained, this was an auspicious sign. Similarly, the Chinese believed that the high forehead and protruding big ears were marks of special intelligence.) The impression this face gave was one of vitality, intelligence, and maturity. But today the usually healthy face was haggard, showing the effects of too little sleep and lack of food.[1]

For three months his mother, the Dowager Empress Hsiao-k'ang, had been ill and steadily deteriorating. The boy emperor had at-

13

tended her in such a dedicated fashion that he insisted on (as the
official chronicle puts it) "personally tasting the bitter broth of the
Chinese herbal medicine; he never allowed his eyelashes to cross;
and he never loosened his waistband while sleeping beside her."
When his mother's illness took a turn for the worse, he became
"haggard from grief and anxiety, and seriously neglected eating and
sleeping, and lost much weight." He refused to listen to the urging
of the regents and close palace attendants that he take at least a
brief rest.

During this period of vigilance K'ang-hsi had nevertheless managed to pay repeated visits to the Palace of Loving Kindness and
Tranquility (Tz'u-ning kung), the residence of his paternal grandmother, the Great Dowager Empress Hsiao-chuang, in order to inquire about *her* health. So that he might offer comfort to this beloved relative, he forced himself to "suppress his sad countenance
and put on a show of calm while in the grandmother's presence"—
he broke into tears only when he had retreated from her presence.[2]

K'ang-hsi's mother died the evening of the vernal equinox. The
day already had particular significance for the boy: in 1651, in
honor of the equinox, his father, the late Emperor Shun-chih, had
ordered a sun altar constructed in the eastern suburb of the capital
city; this act was to promote harmony with Heaven and bring
blessings on his family and empire.[3] What an irony that Heaven
should take away the life of K'ang-hsi's mother on this special day.
The boy reacted by "beating his breast, stamping his feet, and wail-
ing with deep grief"; he was so distressed that he did not eat and refused to "sip a drop of water."

K'ang-hsi's behavior illustrates his characteristic filial piety.[4] But
there is also evidence that his sorrow was perhaps compounded by
frustration.

The empress's death was hastened, if not exactly caused, by
social pressures from Manchu diehards who still advocated the tradition of *hsün-tsang* (being buried, after suicide, with one's deceased husband)—an inhumane custom that the Chinese had long
abandoned but which persisted in the Manchu feudal society.
Hsün-tsang was considered an essential act for imperial consorts
who were dearly loved by the emperor or who wished to demonstrate eternal fidelity.[5] Pressure on the empress to comply with this
custom was strong, but she was persuaded that she was needed to
assist her son, the new emperor, who was still in his minority.[6]
Although it is probably true, as claimed in the official records, that
K'ang-hsi's young mother died of illness, the fact that her death
occurred only two and a half months before the expiration of the
twenty-seven-month mourning period observed for Shun-chih does

arouse suspicion of unnatural death.[7] For Hsiao-k'ang came from an influential Chinese family, and her presence threatened the reactionary Manchu nobles.

Coupled with the knowledge of his mother's possibly unnatural death was the fact that K'ang-hsi had largely been neglected by her. It is therefore conceivable that his grief when she died derived as much from anger over her death as from any strong affection. As he would later testify sadly about his relationship with his parents, "Not even for a single day did I ever enjoy my parents' affection by being around them."[8]

But one should not doubt K'ang-hsi's extraordinary devotion to his grandmother. Not only during her lifetime but even after her death, in 1688, K'ang-hsi's filial devotion to her remained a dominant force in his behavior, both within his family and in court politics.[9] What were the origins of this special bond that elicited such unusual self-control from a nine-year-old?

THE GREAT DOWAGER Empress Hsiao-chuang was a descendant of a brother of Chinghis Khan.[10] She was taken by Hong Taiji, the Emperor T'ai-tsung (r. 1627-1643), as an imperial concubine in 1624, the reigning empress then being Hsiao-tuan, her aunt (her father's sister), who had married Hong Taiji in 1614 but had borne no sons. In 1638 Hsiao-chuang gave birth to Fu-lin (1638-1661), who at the age of six was made emperor of the Ch'ing dynasty, with the reign title Shun-chih (r. 1644-1661). With Fu-lin's enthronement Hsiao-chuang's status was elevated to that of dowager empress. During the first seven years of his reign, Shun-chih's government was under the autocratic rule of his regent uncle, Dorgon;[11] but after the death of the senior dowager empress, Hsiao-tuan, in 1649, Hsiao-chuang became the sole dowager empress and the imperial family came under her full control.

Hsiao-chuang's strong personality led her largely to dominate her son, and her assertiveness at times strained their relations. The choice of an empress was the crux of their disagreement. Probably under the influence of Dorgon, Hsiao-chuang arranged for the young emperor to marry her niece, the daughter of her brother Wu-k'o-shan, and make her his empress. Shun-chih disliked this girl so intensely that in 1653, at the age of fifteen, he decided, against his mother's will, to deprive this wife of the empress-ship, and so demoted her.

In spite of this disagreement, Hsiao-chuang was again able to persuade Shun-chih to marry, this time her grandniece, known as Empress Hsiao-hui. No affection developed between Shun-chih and his new empress. Instead, two years later, in 1656, he became in-

fatuated with his new concubine *née* Donggo.[12] This woman was
actually the wife of Bombogar, Shun-chih's youngest half brother.
According to an eyewitness Jesuit account, she had first become
Shun-chih's lover—causing the helpless Bombogar to commit suicide out of "shame and frustration"—and a month later she was
taken into the imperial harem for her "virtuous character"—as
stated in the official chronicle. Donggo bore Shun-chi a son, whom
he undoubtedly would have made his successor had the boy not
died in infancy (Shun-chih posthumously conferred on him the
highest princely title to show his special affection.) When Donggo
died a few years later, in 1660, Shun-chih ordered thirty of her
maids and favorite eunuchs to commit suicide so as to accompany
her spirit to the next world. Until his death the following year, at
age twenty-four, Shun-chih evinced little affection for any other
woman in his harem. K'ang-hsi's mother (1640-1663), a mere consort, was made the Empress Hsiao-k'ang only after her son, Hsüan-
yeh, had become the K'ang-hsi Emperor.

K'ang-hsi had few happy recollections of his early childhood,
which was spent in isolation from his parents. At his birth his
mother was fifteen, his father seventeen. The inability of very
young consorts to produce sufficient milk to feed their babies had
made the wet nurse a necessary participant in the nurturing of royal
children.[13] An imperial decree of 1661 institutionalized the practice:
whenever a wet nurse was needed, the chief eunuchs notified the
captains and overseers of the *pao-i* (bond servant) bannermen in
the Imperial Household Department, ordering them to select candidates from among their wives. Once an imperial wet nurse was
chosen, the Imperial Household would hire another wet nurse, at a
price of no more than eighty taels of silver, to breast-feed the imperial wet nurse's own baby.

There was another reason for the prolonged separation of parents and child. In seventeenth-century China, as in other parts of
the world, smallpox epidemics were responsible for many childhood deaths. Following an ancient Chinese method, children were
inoculated to gain immunity: either pus from the natural pustule of
a patient or a powder made from the scabs of the pustules was
blown into a nostril of the child, the left nostril for a boy, right for
a girl. If the reaction was positive (that is, an initial fever, followed
by a mild outbreak of pustules), the child would then be cared for
as if he or she were suffering from the disease itself, thus minimizing
complications caused by erroneous diagnosis or a resultant cold,
which actually were the major causes of mortality among child suf-
ferers of smallpox. In a letter of 1726, P. D'Entrecolles, a French
Jesuit resident in Peking, reported on these methods in great de-

tail.[14] He obviously was strongly impressed, which is understandable when one considers that in the West the first successful inoculation against smallpox, by Edward Jenner, did not take place until seventy years later, in 1796.

Not all inoculations, however, resulted in positive reactions. K'ang-hsi was one of those who failed to react to the inoculation and so was vulnerable to a natural smallpox attack. The only protection available was to shield the child from contacts with the disease, and he was accordingly quarantined in a Buddhist temple in the western suburb of Peking, where he spent lonely, parentless days.[15] Nevertheless, during an epidemic he did contract smallpox, which left his face scarred for life. These scars bore witness not only to his immunity to further smallpox attacks but also to his being specially favored by Heaven and the functionaries in the popular Buddhist pantheon—the goddess of smallpox and the like—whom the Manchus believed to be ultimately responsible for his recovery.

During his period of isolation, K'ang-hsi remained largely under the care of two nurses, both of whom figured prominently in his later reign.[16] One was a Chinese woman, Mrs. Ts'ao, mother of the celebrated Ts'ao Yin, a bond servant of the Imperial Household who was to serve the emperor in the South as a trusted informant in his extrabureaucratic control system. K'ang-hsi referred affectionately to Mrs. Ts'ao as "that old lady in my household." His other nurse was a Manchu woman, the mother of Gali (Gali was later notorious for his corruption, but K'ang-hsi nevertheless appointed him to many prominent positions, including the governor-generalship of Chiang-nan and Kiangsi).

K'ang-hsi's grandmother Hsiao-chuang took a special interest in him even during these early days. While his father never seemed very close to the boy, Hsiao-chuang filled the need for parental affection in this critical period in his life. As K'ang-hsi later testified, his grandmother took great pains to educate him from infancy onward. She enforced strict discipline to ensure the development of K'ang-hsi's mind and body. He recalled: "Since I was a toddler just learning to speak, I received my grandmother's kind discipline: in eating, in walking, and in speaking, she encouraged me to behave in the proper manner. She taught me to practice those manners even while alone. If I failed slightly to obey, she immediately corrected me and even punished me. I credit her with the accomplishments of my entire career."[17]

Among the graces that his grandmother taught K'ang-hsi was the art of diplomatic speech. This was useful especially when he had to converse with his hot-tempered father. The latter, in a tantrum, was said to have mutilated one of his thrones with a sword; as his trusted Chinese Buddhist mentor described, "he cannot control his dragon temper, and frequently subjects people around him to whipping."[18]

In 1659 Hsiao-chuang brought K'ang-hsi and two of his surviving half brothers, Fu-ch'üan (the eldest) and Ch'ang-ning (the second youngest), to greet their father, probably at a time when Shun-chih was ill. The question of succession was naturally on the emperor's mind. On this occasion he asked about the boys' respective ambitions. Ch'ang-ning, only about three, was too young to reply. Fu-ch'uan, six, answered, "I would like to become a worthy prince." K'ang-hsi, five, said, "When I grow up, I want to emulate my imperial father." The Shun-chih Emperor, according to the official record, was pleased with this reply and decided to make K'ang-hsi his successor.[19]

Unofficial sources suggest that the grandmother had coached K'ang-hsi in this flattering response before taking him to his father.[20] She seemed to have begun cultivating the future emperor's image in Shun-chih's mind even before K'ang-hsi's birth, because of her particular affection for the child's mother. One day, the story goes, after K'ang-hsi's mother had been to the grandmother's palace to visit her, Hsiao-chuang beheld a vision of dragons coiling around the young woman's garment. The grandmother marveled at this sign and asked her daughter-in-law what it meant. The young woman then announced her pregnancy. The grandmother said that when she had conceived the Shun-chih Emperor the same extraordinary sign had occurred. She thereupon predicted that her daughter-in-law's future child, if it were a boy, would be "blessed with great blessings," a phrase that meant "become an emperor."[21] Apocryphal though the tale is, it does suggest Hsiao-chuang's predisposition toward K'ang-hsi from the earliest possible time.

On February 5, 1661, shortly before his death from smallpox, Shun-chih announced his decision to designate his seven-year-old son, Hsüan-yeh, as his heir apparent.[22] Hsüan-yeh was duly enthroned as the K'ang-hsi Emperor, to be assisted by four Manchu regents appointed by his dying father. But the government soon become dominated by Oboi, strongest of the four regents.[23]

K'ANG-HSI'S ACCESSION to the throne of China introduced numerous challenges for the boy. During the first six years of his reign these challenges came largely from Manchu dignitaries— especially from Oboi and his faction. They resented the increasing Chinese influence that seemed to threaten to supplant Manchu tradition as well as Manchu nobles in the imperial power structure. As mentioned earlier, the untimely death of K'ang-hsi's mother—

member of an influential Chinese family—might well have been the work of this reactionary force, which, in the name of Manchu tradition, perhaps compelled her to accompany the late Shun-chih Emperor to his grave. To terminate the reigning dowager empress's life this way would prevent political control by a Chinese family; it would also be a blow aimed at the great dowager empress, who had been fond of her Chinese daughter-in-law.

To face these challenges, K'ang-hsi profited from his grandmother's skillful guidance. She must have realized that in order to assure a lasting victory in the power contest she needed to enlist people in court who were loyal to the throne; she also needed time to train her grandson to assume the burden of being ruler of all China. During these trying years under Oboi's domination, she taught K'ang-hsi many of the principles of government as she understood them. The values and ideals that she instilled in the youngster provide important clues in understanding the emperor's adult behavior.

The foremost principle of government Hsiao-chuang taught was to maintain the status quo. In 1661, soon after his enthronement, the grandmother was said to have asked K'ang-hsi about his ambition as a ruler. He answered, "I have no desires except that I wish the nation to enjoy peace and order, the people to be content with their own occupations, so that all will be able to live together in grand harmony." She was immensely pleased. Policies adopted by K'ang-hsi in later years amply attest to these early goals.[24]

K'ang-hsi described Hsiao-chuang's role in his education in his own Family Instructions, given to his children in 1722, the year of his death. He there related:

> As soon as I succeeded my father to the throne, my sacred grandmother cautioned me with the following instructions: "Since ancient times it has been a very difficult task to be a ruler. The emperor, alone, must rule the great masses of the people, who are always eagerly looking to the emperor for food and livelihood. You must give thought to the matter of winning their support, for only then can you be said to have grasped the way of government. By doing so, you will be able to bring peace and prosperity to all people within the four seas for countless generations."[25]

IN THE CHINESE culture, it is required that a sense of indebtedness toward one's parents, or parental surrogates, be manifested in the pattern of behavior known as *hsiao*. Such filial piety is characterized by unconditional submission and infinite obligation. How true this was in the case of K'ang-hsi. The French Jesuit Joachim

Bouvet wrote in the 1690s that the emperor "had obeyed his grand-mother's will in all matters." If Bouvet perhaps exaggerated K'ang-hsi's other virtues, this testimony to his uncommon affection for his grandmother was borne out both by the ruler's private letters and by Chinese sources.[26]

But in some cases filial submission to the grandmother who had taught him to work toward the status quo violated the principle of not rocking the boat. Early in his reign, K'ang-hsi's acceptance of the great dowager empress's selection of his empress brought on the first major struggle between the grandmother and the Manchu opposition.

2
The First Empress

K'ANG-HSI'S Great Matrimony[1]—as the wedding of a Chinese emperor was called—was set for the eighth day of the ninth month of the fourth year of his reign (October 16, 1665), when he was eleven. The girl chosen as K'ang-hsi's empress, also eleven, was the granddaughter of the regent Soni and the daughter of Gabula,[2] chamberlain of the Imperial Bodyguard Division.

The rituals were performed almost exactly according to the Chinese traditon, with certain Manchu adaptations—notably, the emphasis on horses and saddles among the gifts in the *na-ts'ai* (presents sent to the bride's home as part of the betrothal ceremony). On an auspicious day chosen by the imperial astronomers sometime before the wedding, the emperor sent a delegation—led by the ministers of the Imperial Household Department and of the Board of Rites—of three imperial sisters, three wives of regents, chamberlains, and the Imperial Bodyguard to deliver presents to the bride's house. These consisted of ten horses, equipped with saddles, ten sets of armor with helmets, a hundred rolls of satin, and two hundred rolls of other fine cloth.

The entourage was met by the girl's father, Gabula, with her grandfather Soni leading the male members of the family and Soni's wife leading the female members. The family lined up on two sides of the courtyard and performed the Three Kneelings and Nine Prostrations, facing north (the emperor's throne faced south), to thank the emperor for this extraordinary honor.

On the seventh day of the ninth month, one day before the Great Matrimony, the emperor sent high Manchu officials to perform sacrifices at the Altars of Heaven and Earth, at the Imperial Ances-

tral Temple (*t'ai-miao*), and to the gods of soil and grain at the
Altar of Agricultural Dieties. At the same time, an imperial delegation was sent to the bride's house to offer her parents the Great
Dowry (*ta-cheng*), which included: "two thousand *liang* [Chinese
ounces] of gold, ten thousand *liang* of silver, one golden tea canis-
ter, two silver tea canisters, two silver chests, one thousand rolls of
satin, twenty saddles, twenty military saddles for camels, and forty
horses." The ceremony was completed with a thanksgiving ritual
identical with that performed on the occasion of the delivery of
presents.

The eighth day of the month was the Great Matrimony. Early in
the morning Emperor K'ang-hsi ascended his throne at the Hall of
Grand Harmony (T'ai-ho tien), where he viewed the Imperial Patent certifying the establishment of the Empress Hsiao-ch'eng and
her golden seal. The emperor then handed the two emblems to the
imperial envoys, who, carrying the Imperial Scepter at the head of
an impressive procession, delivered the emblems to the empress's
house.

After the empress had accepted the emblems and performed
thanksgiving kneelings and prostrations, she was carried to the
palace in a palanquin. The procession began with four ministers'
wives leading the palanquin and seven following it, all mounted—
women on horseback being a conspicuous feature of the old Manchu tradition. This cortege was flanked by imperial bodyguards
and their chamberlains. The empress's entourage was given the
privilege of walking on the imperial roadway that led directly to
the Central Palace (*chung-kung*, a term synonymous with "empress," since she resided there, while all imperial concubines lived
in palaces on either side of it).

Meanwhile, K'ang-hsi, dressed in imperial wedding garb, paid
visits to the great dowager empress and the dowager empress, his
stepmother Hsiao-hui, at their respective palaces, in order to thank
them for their kind arrangements. He then served as host at a banquet at the Hall of Grand Harmony for the empress's relatives (the
empress remained in her palace), as well as for princes and ministers. While this was going on, the dowager empress led the wives of
certain ministers and of the regents to the great dowager empress's
palace, where an elaborate banquet was held in honor of the new
empress's mother and the mother's relatives. At about six in the
evening the Great Matrimony was concluded with the traditional
Chinese banquet of Nuptial Cup (*ho-chin yen*), to which the noble
wives were invited, after which the emperor and empress were left
alone in the Central Palace.

The following day, the emperor instructed the Board of Rites to research Chinese precedents on the addition of honorific characters to the titles of the great dowager empress and the dowager empress to thank them for "having selected the wise and virtuous to be Our help-mate." On the same day, the empress paid homage to the great dowager empress and the dowager empress. And on the third day, the emperor held a special audience at the Hall of Grand Harmony, so that princes and high officials might present their memorials of congratulations. A decree was subsequently issued to the entire empire proclaiming the completion of the Great Matrimony. The decree defined the significance of the Great Matrimony as a means of securing an empress who would establish a legitimate position and line of succession, and assist the emperor in carrying out filial obligations toward his grandmother and stepmother.[3]

THE GREAT MATRIMONY indeed signified a grand act of filial piety, as the young K'ang-hsi had willingly accepted his grandmother's choice of an empress.[4] In submitting to his grandmother, K'ang-hsi intensified the rivalry between the dominating regent Oboi and the great dowager empress. To understand the dispute, it is necessary to see the relationship between the position of the empress and the process of imperial succession, a process that had become a problem in the course of Manchu Sinification.

In the old Manchu tradition, a successor to the ruler was elected by powerful princes choosing among all the sons born to the former ruler and a plurality of his *amba fujin* (Chinese: *ta fu-chin*; legitimate wives). Succession was flexible, to say the least, and led to infighting among the contenders. In the Ming system, only the sons born of the empress—the lone legitimate wife of a reigning emperor —could be designated heir apparent, with the firstborn enjoying priority; sons born of imperial concubines could be designated heir apparent only when the reigning empress had no sons. In the latter case the status of the mother and the seniority of her son would determine the order of priority in the succession system: for instance, the eldest son of the imperial concubine of the first rank— the next highest ranking imperial consort below the empress— would have precedence. This system, of course, often transposed the focus of the power struggle from the selection of an heir apparent to the selection of an empress.

At the time of Nurhaci, founding father of the Manchu regime, the hierarchical structure already betrayed some Chinese influence. Because of death or deposition, Nurhaci had established in his lifetime a total of four *amba fujin*. At first, he had named the eldest son, Cuyen, of his first *amba fujin* as his successor, but he later deposed and had Cuyen executed for treason, and when Nurhaci died, in 1626, he left no heir designate. His son Hong Taiji—whose mother, Ula Nara, was an *amba fujin* whom Nurhaci had dearly loved—emerged from an angry contest as the Emperor T'ai-tsung, illustrating the fluidity of the Manchu succession system. T'ai-tsung adopted the Chinese hierarchical titles for various members of his harem, including the title empress for his sole *amba fujin*. This woman, the Empress Hsiao-tuan, bore him no sons, and the five-year-old Fu-lin, born of an imperial concubine of the first rank, was elected the Shun-chih Emperor, as a compromise following another round of infighting among the contenders. Fu-lin's mother, Hsiao-chuang, was given the title dowager empress only after his accession. From the time of the Shun-chih reign, the Ming tradition for imperial succession was fully adopted by the Manchus, and the status of the empress was firmly linked with the legitimate heir to the throne.[5]

The Ch'ing system, however, contained details that distinguished it from the Ming: the Ming imperial house sometimes selected empresses from among women of dubious origins, whereas Manchu imperial-family tradition required that an empress come from a "renowned" family.[6] At the time that K'ang-hsi's empress was selected, 1665, there appear to have been at least two such candidates for the position, from the families of two regents, Ebilun and Soni. Oboi apparently supported the candidacy of the daughter of Ebilun (later, in 1677, she would become Empress Hsiao-chao)—Ebilun was a strong adherent of the Oboi faction—and K'ang-hsi's grandmother favored the daughter of Gabula, son of Soni. Though the official record fails to name Ebilun's daughter as the other contender for the empress-ship, there is enough evidence to support this assumption.[7]

The grandmother's choice of an empress from the Soni family was eminently justified in view of the Soni family's splendid record of service to the imperial house. They had been meritorious in many military campaigns under Nurhaci and Hong Taiji, and Soni had served Shun-chih with unswerving loyalty. Among the major posts he had held were minister of the Imperial Household Department and member of the Council of Deliberative Princes and Ministers—highest in the Manchu hierarchy. During the regency, he resisted the usurpation of power by Oboi and loyally sided with K'ang-hsi's grandmother in safeguarding K'ang-hsi's imperial prerogatives.

K'ang-hsi was proud that his empress came from the Soni family. Though both were eleven when they were married, the empress was slightly older and was described as very mature for her age. She probably acted as much the older sister (or mother substitute) as she did the young bride. K'ang-hsi had uncommon affection for his empress.

For Oboi, the Great Matrimony of K'ang-hsi meant defeat and humiliation. He resented the grandmother's uncontested influence on the emperor. K'ang-hsi now followed a filial routine of daily greeting his grandmother in person, and when separated from her, of sending greetings through ministers and messengers. On one occasion, K'ang-hsi was at the Nan-yuan Park, a hunting ground in the southern suburbs of the capital. He asked Oboi to convey greetings to his grandmother; Oboi refused by saying "Why don't you do it yourself?"[8] When the emperor turned to Ebilun, the latter likewise refused to comply with the imperial request. Personal grievances and animosities such as these were by no means trivial; many of the family troubles that seriously affected court politics in the later years of the K'ang-hsi reign could be traced back to these early skirmishes of jealousy and power plays resulting from the choice of an empress.

The Oboi threat in the political realm was the first challenge the young emperor had to meet. In addition to having to learn patience, the emperor and his grandmother needed to broaden support in court circles and build a stronger power base to remove Oboi's domination. A few courtiers who had sided with the emperor and his grandmother—and for whose loyalty and support the emperor became deeply indebted—played leading roles in shaping the pattern of court politics in later years.

Three of these officials figured prominently in the power contest with Oboi. The first was Songgotu (?-1703), son of the regent Soni (who died of old age in 1667) and uncle of the Empress Hsiao-ch'eng. The second was Mingju (1635-1708), also a Manchu, whose family was closely related to the imperial house by marriage: his great-grandaunt was the mother of Hong Taiji, K'ang-hsi's grandfather, and he himself had married a daughter of K'ang-hsi's grand-uncle Ajige.[9] The third was Hsiung Tz'u-li (1635-1709), a prominent Chinese Confucianist from southern China.[10]

It was owing to the concerted efforts of these loyal courtiers that K'ang-hsi and his grandmother were able first to meet Oboi's threat and eventually to eliminate him, in 1669. Songgotu had requested imperial permission to be allowed, while a vice-president in the central bureaucracy, to serve as an imperial bodyguard, with the ostensible intention of protecting the young emperor. In fact, Songgotu was K'ang-hsi's chief strategist; it was he who suggested how to put Oboi under arrest by using trickery that resulted in Oboi's execution. Songgotu was made grand secretary immediately following Oboi's death.[11] Mingju, an able bureaucrat, was a shrewd military strategist. His role during the Oboi period was marginal, but later he rose to power surpassing even Songgotu's. Hsiung Tz'u-li was outspoken and critical of Oboi for usurping imperial power. He assisted the young emperor in dealing with Oboi by serving as K'ang-hsi's chief representative in soliciting loyalty from the Chinese literati.[12] Oboi having dismantled many of the Chinese institutions introduced to the Ch'ing court during the Shun-chih period, Hsiung was primarily responsible for persuading the young K'ang-hsi to go all out in restoring them, even while Oboi still held power. As an imperial tutor, Hsiung was the first person to introduce the young emperor to Confucian learning, which the emperor acknowledged in later years.[13]

THE YEAR 1669 HAD special significance for the fifteen-year-old emperor. With the death of Oboi, K'ang-hsi finally achieved the full imperial power the regents had officially turned over to him two years earlier. A few months later, the empress bore her first child. This son was given the "infant name"—a sort of intimate nickname—Ch'eng-hu, meaning "recipient of abundant blessing."[14] The year must have been taken by K'ang-hsi and his beloved empress as a propitious one, since it ended a period of severe tests in court and saw the birth of their child. From then on, along with having matured socially and physically, K'ang-hsi began to rule as well as to reign.

But hopes for happiness were soon dashed. In 1671 the "abundant blessing" did not materialize: Ch'eng-hu died. Over the next three years four other of the six sons so far born to K'ang-hsi (children of concubines) also died. But despite the great sadness felt by the emperor, he made a show in public of being more concerned with his grandmother's feelings than with his own. When he went to see her, he "talked with her joyously as if nothing had happened!"[15] Both the great dowager empress and the empress became ill after Ch'eng-hu's death, which made K'ang-hsi so anxious that his own health deteriorated.[16]

The year 1674 brought not only the birth of the empress's second son, Yin-jeng (June 6),[17] but also the outbreak of a dangerous civil war and the death of the empress.

The threat of the Rebellion of the Three Feudatories (1673-1681), led by Wu San-kuei (1612-1678),[18] had already been felt by the court by June 1673. Originally a Ming general, Wu had defected to the Ch'ing in 1643 and welcomed K'ang-hsi's father, Shun-chih, to Peking to be emperor of China. Shun-chih made him a lord, vested with autonomous power in one of the Three Feudatories in the

southwestern region of China. By June 1673, Wu ostensibly "petitioned" K'ang-hsi to be released from his feudal duties and powers
so that he might retire to his native Liao-tung, in southern Manchuria. The petition was, in fact, a double-edged threat: Wu would
retain his power if the request were denied; or he would rebel with
a legitimate excuse if approved. Court opinions were divided:
Songgotu advocated appeasement; Mingju argued for confrontation; the grandmother advised K'ang-hsi to take Mingju's suggestion. K'ang-hsi granted Wu San-kuei permission to retire to his
home.[19] On December 28, 1673, Wu San-kuei rebelled against the
Ch'ing court and declared himself emperor of the Chou dynasty.

A month later an assassination attempt was made in the capital
on the life of the emperor; the would-be assassin, Yang Ch'i-lung,
claimed to be the Chu San T'ai-tzu (third heir apparent of the Ming
house). The accompanying insurrection was quelled, but Yang
escaped. By early May, the lord who controlled the southeastern
coastal province of Fukien also rebelled. And Taiwan, located only
110 miles across the sea from Fukien, was still in the hands of Ming
loyalists, who threatened a counterattack on the mainland. Before
long, the rebel forces from Fukien had approached the Yangtze and
were poised to invade Nanking, Southern capital under the Ming
and a city of great political and strategic significance in the South.
K'ang-hsi was scared; at times he became faint-hearted.[20]

By June, the empress anxiously approached the birth of her second child. According to Confucian precepts, failing to produce a
male heir at this critical juncture could be taken as "the greatest
breach of filial piety." (Only a couple of weeks earlier, on May 21,
Lady Jung, a favorite concubine of K'ang-hsi, had given birth to a
son who had died.) The empress had strong reasons for hoping for
a healthy boy.

On June 6, at about ten in the morning, the empress fulfilled her
last filial obligation in presenting K'ang-hsi with a male heir. The
infant name given the baby, Pao-ch'eng ("success guaranteed"),[21]
reflected the imperial family's high hopes for the child. By four
o'clock that afternoon the empress had died. K'ang-hsi's joy over
the timely arrival of a son was obliterated by his wife's sudden
death.

The emperor's grief was boundless. Following the Ming tradition, he suspended court audiences for five days straight. At the
memorial held a month after her death, he poured libations before
the casket of the deceased empress, to show his great affection. He
publicly commended Hsiao-ch'eng for her "filiality" toward the
dowager empress and the great dowager empress, her "kindness

toward palace servants," and the assistance she had rendered to him in "handling the many domestic affairs in the imperial family— respectfully, diligently, and frugally."[22]

K'ang-hsi's feelings toward his new son were, understandably, ambivalent. On the one hand, he blamed the baby for the empress's death—he later was to charge Yin-jeng with "having caused his mother's death" as the first act of "unfilialness." On the other hand, he seemed in some ways to identify with Yin-jeng, since he too had suffered the early loss of his mother. Moreover, Yin-jeng perhaps served as a focus for K'ang-hsi's displaced love for the empress.[23] Whatever his mixture of feelings, the father tended to be permissive and overindulgent with this child.

PART II

Longing

3
The Heir

ON January 27, 1676, K'ang-hsi announced his decision to name the eighteen-month-old Yin-jeng crown prince.[1] Politically, it made very sound sense. During the ten-month period before the move was announced, imperial forces had suffered serious setbacks at the hands of rebels in the south and the west; a Mongol chieftain had also started an uprising north of China. In order to meet the challenge, K'ang-hsi had accepted suggestions from his Chinese ministers, such as Hsiung Tz'u-li, to accelerate the process of Sinification of the Manchu regime by wholesale adoption of Chinese institutions,[2] and the establishment of a crown prince was an important institution K'ang-hsi copied from the defeated Ming.

As an initial pious gesture to muster Chinese support, K'ang-hsi paid a visit to the Ming Imperial Tomb, in the Ch'ang-p'ing district north of Peking, and he sent officials to pour libations at other tombs of Ming rulers. Most important, he made a special trip to the Tombs of Filiality, where he reported the grievous political situation to the spirit of his late father;[3] he knew it would be the greatest act of unfiliality if he lost the empire. And as the military situation worsened, K'ang-hsi and his grandmother must have thought of the need for a successor.

The naming of an heir apparent had a dual objective: political stability and legitimacy in succession. The imperial edict establishing the crown prince stated that the decision was intended "to consolidate the people's hearts within the four seas" and "to set right the legitimate line of imperial succession for ten thousand years."[4]

Specifications for the education of both a crown prince and an emperor were set down, and the Supervisorate of Imperial Instruction, directing the crown prince's education, was instituted. For the emperor, Daily Lectures (*jih-chiang*) were to be held to study Confucian classics, the Daily Lecturers (*jih-chiang kuan*) functioning both as "expositors" and as "diarists" (*ch'i-chü-chu kuan*), to record the emperor's daily movements and utterances.

(Just as the plans for imperial education were being drawn up, the urgency of the establishment of the heir apparent was intensified by news of serious defeats in the southeast: the rebels in Kwangtung were gaining, and the forces led by Cheng Ching, son of the Ming loyalist Cheng Ch'eng-kung, had successfully established strong bases on the Fukien coast and recaptured the key coastal city of Chang-chou, near Amoy.)[5]

In addition to its being politically inspired, K'ang-hsi's naming of a crown prince was an act of filial piety. As stated in the same edict, he made Yin-jeng heir apparent "in obedience to the order of the Great Dowager Empress."[6]

There were probably also emotional elements motivating K'ang-hsi. The psychological mechanism of transferring affection from mother to child is well stated in an ancient Confucian saying: "When one loves a person, he extends that love to the crows of the latter's roof." K'ang-hsi himself testified in 1708 that he "cherished [Yin-jeng] with genial warmth" because he "was born of the Empress."[7]

The investiture of the heir apparent took place on the thirteenth day of the twelfth month of the fourteenth year of K'ang-hsi's reign (January 27, 1676), when the emperor was twenty-one.[8]

At dawn, all the Manchu princes, ministers of state, and nobles gathered in the huge courtyard in front of the Hall of Grand Harmony, where the emperor granted audiences on solemn occasions. The weather in Peking at this time would have been frosty, but everyone sat in the open, cross-legged on fur cushions, reverently awaiting the emperor. In front of the throne a table had been placed, on which the grand secretary and president of the Board of Rites had set the Imperial Scepter, the Imperial Patent, and the Golden Seal. On each side of the throne was a large japanned screen with figure designs.[9]

Upon entering the hall, the young emperor cursorily examined the patent and seal before seating himself on the throne. Court etiquette was precisely defined for such audiences: As the Scottish physician John Bell witnessed it on another occasion, K'ang-hsi would be dressed in a "short loose coat of sable, having the fur outward, lined with lamb-skin." Under the coat would be a "long tunic of yellow silk, interwoven with figures of golden dragons with five claws"—the five-toed dragon motif was an imperial symbol and could be used only by the emperor's family. "On his head was a little round cap, faced with black fox-skin," ornamented with only a beautiful pear-shaped pearl; below the pearl hung a red silk tassel.

After the emperor was seated, court music was played and fireworks were set off to create a jubilant atmosphere. Then, following the spoken commands of the master of ceremonies, the gathering saluted the emperor with three kneelings and nine prostrations according to the "Kneel! Prostrate! Prostrate again! And again!" rhythm of the master of ceremonies.

The formal appointment procedure began when the Imperial Decree was read to the imperial envoys: "On this thirteenth day of the twelfth month of the fourteenth year of the K'ang-hsi reign, We have decided to appoint Yin-jeng, my second son born to the Empress, to be the Heir Apparent to my throne. We have therefore solemnly commissioned you, Our ministers, to carry out the necessary rites with this scepter."[10] The chief grand secretary handed the scepter to the envoys; the Manchu princes were conducted to the hall, where tea from His Majesty's table was served in their honor. After this, the emperor returned to his palace.

So far, the whole ceremony had followed the Ming form closely. But modifications had to be made for the remainder of the exercise because of the heir apparent's age. After the imperial envoys arrived at the Ching-jen Palace, residence of Yin-jeng and the late empress, they first placed the scepter, patent, and seal upon a yellow-silk-covered table in front of the palace. The heir apparent was too young to perform the required rituals and his wet nurse, who knelt in front of the table holding the prince in her arms, was authorized to accept the emblems. After three kneelings and nine prostrations in front of the scepter to thank the emperor for the appointment on behalf of the prince, she carried the heir apparent out, following the eunuchs who held the emblems. The imperial envoys returned the scepter to the emperor's palace, and reported the completion of the ceremony to His Majesty.

Subsequently, the emperor led all the Manchu princes and grandees to the palaces of the great dowager empress and the dowager empress to show his respect for their sagacious guidance in this solemn act.

The following day, the emperor again met his court at the Hall of Grand Harmony to accept their congratulations, and a proclamation was issued through the nationwide horse-express post system to the entire empire informing his subjects of this most important decision. Included in the proclamation were thirty-three imperial favors granted to the people—lifting of taxes, forgiveness of criminals awaiting capital punishment, and many others.[11]

The significance of naming an heir apparent was heavily documented; but as to the role K'ang-hsi played in raising his child, the records, unfortunately, provide little information. There is no doubt that K'ang-hsi had unusual affection for his son, and he surely was interested in Yin-jeng's development, but because of the political situation of the time, K'ang-hsi's interaction with Yin-jeng during his early childhood was probably minimal. To win the civil war, K'ang-hsi needed to give his complete attention to the urgent decisions required of him every day and every hour (in Father Bouvet's biography of K'ang-hsi, he wrote, "Day and night the emperor's time was occupied by conferences with his ministers").[12] In later recollections, the emperor testified to his tense and hectic life during these years.[13] The rebellions had made such an impact on his psyche that in his Family Instructions he repeatedly referred to them, more indeed than to any other facet of his experience, except for his relationship with his grandmother and his problems with raising an heir. (It appears that in K'ang-hsi's heart these three seemingly unrelated matters were actually intertwined: civil war, the great dowager empress, and Yin-jeng, the heir apparent.)

If K'ang-hsi was not able to give the young child adequate attention, who, then, did influence Yin-jeng in his earliest years? Since his mother had died giving birth to him, Yin-jeng was left in the care of a nurse,[14] with whom he developed close ties, as with her husband, Ling-p'u (the names of nurses seldom appear in old records). The nurse could not be expected to exercise the same authority as a parent; she was understandably indulgent, for the status gap between nurse and future emperor was even greater than in the usual servant-master relationship—her rank within the Manchu feudal hierarchy was "bond servant of the Imperial Household Department," the lowest category except for those in the *Sin jeku*. There must have been, therefore, a reversed authority relationship between the nurse and the child, which produced the spoiled brat —self-indulgent, selfish, and aggressive—that the heir apparent later proved to be.

Rather than mitigating the problem, the nurse's husband enhanced it, in the effect he had as a role model. He was later described by K'ang-hsi as "the most covetous man in the imperial court, hated by his fellow bond servants in the Imperial Household Department."[15] Yin-jeng as an adult duplicated Ling-p'u's insatiable craving for money.

Songgotu, a maternal granduncle, was another person who must have had close contact with Yin-jeng during his early years, since in his culture the ties between a child and its mother's family were usually much closer than the ties with paternal relations. Songgotu, as we shall see, was a cruel and extremely arrogant man. Yin-jeng's later fondness for sadistic violence was very reminiscent of Song-gotu's viciousness.[16]

Of the two female influences in his family, the great dowager empress—aging, frequently ill,[17] and devoted to K'ang-hsi's efforts to quell the rebellion—probably had little effect on Yin-jeng. The other available female influence was the dowager empress, Hsiao-hui.

Hsiao-hui seems to have been an unpopular member of the court. K'ang-hsi made a curious reference to her in his old age,[18] which suggests his hidden displeasure at her handling of his children while he was young. In an opposite vein to the repeated tribute to the grandmother for her contributions to his early character building, K'ang-hsi rebuts some criticism for not having visited the step-mother frequently enough (he maintained that it was not frequency but sincerity that counted for genuine filial piety). In another reference to her, K'ang-hsi said that his eldest son, Yin-shih, "might want to have people executed by citing authorization from the Dowager Empress."[19] And there was an anecdote passed down to the eighteenth century about Hsiao-hui and the notorious Chang Feng-yang. A bond servant from the house of Prince Chieh-shu, Chang became a confidant in the dowager empress's palace and wielded evil influence in court during the first half of the K'ang-hsi reign, his power supposedly deriving from Hsiao-hui herself! Chang's influence was considered even greater than that of Songgotu and Ming-ju. As a popular saying put it:

> Go to Songgotu—if you seek an official position;
> Go to Mingju—if you need special consideration;
> But go to Chang Feng-yang—if you need to know
> how long you can stay in your position.[20]

On one occasion, Chang was bold enough to ransack the house of an important Manchu prince who was close to Prince Chieh-shu. Only after petitioning K'ang-hsi could Chieh-shu use his feudal power to have Chang flogged to death. Shortly after the punishment was carried out, a decree arrived—too late—from the dowager empress, ordering Chang set free (everyone in Peking was of course glad about the action taken against Chang).[21] Though the anecdote undoubtedly was dramatized, it at least indicates how the dowager empress interfered in court politics.

Hsiao-hui's character may be inferred from an earlier incident. Soon after she was made Shun-chih's empress, she was openly denounced by him for her "lack of filial piety" toward his mother, the

Dowager Empress Hsiao-chuang,[22] and was punished by having
her imperial prerogatives curtailed for two months. She was either
barren or shunned by Shun-chih, for she never bore a child; she did
maintain close contact with the palace nurses,[23] and so her influence on Yin-jeng and her other stepgrandsons was probably considerable, and very likely negative.

During his childhood, Yin-jeng might have felt that his special
status as heir apparent was a burden, for his father seemed at times
to favor other sons and their mothers. In this Yin-jeng perhaps
feared that K'ang-hsi was re-creating his own childhood situation,
when he had felt threatened by Shun-chih's infatuation with the
concubine Donggo. Let us examine K'ang-hsi's relationship with his
consorts during Yin-jeng's childhood—say, before 1686, when Yin-
jeng was twelve—and Yin-jeng's relationship with his ten half
brothers born by 1686 who survived to become his potential rivals.
The young Te-fei seems to have been K'ang-hsi's favorite of all the
imperial concubines after Yin-jeng's mother's death. From 1678 to
1688, she produced more children for the K'ang-hsi Emperor—
three sons and three daughters—than any other consort. The first
of her children, Yin-chen (the future Yung-cheng Emperor), was the
only child, K'ang-hsi once said, whom he had "personally raised."
This was probably why Yin-jeng was particularly hostile toward
this fourth brother.[24] Yin-chen was born in 1678, which suggests
that K'ang-hsi probably began relations with Yin-chen's mother in
1677, the year after Yin-jeng was named heir apparent and two
years after Yin-jeng's mother had died.[25] Te-fei originally was a
lady-in-waiting from the Uya clan, whose father, Wei-wu, was a
colonel in the Manchu Banner hierarchy. As with other ladies-in-
waiting,[26] it was the emperor's prerogative to initiate relations with
her without a formal ceremony. Only fifteen when Yin-chen was
born, she was rewarded with the elevation of her status from lady-
in-waiting to imperial concubine of the lowest rank.

Yin-jeng's hostility toward his other brothers might well have
stemmed from feeling similarly threatened. Yin-shih, eldest among
the brothers, was the son of another of the favored concubines.
Sibling rivalry in childhood would result in Yin-shih's becoming
Yin-jeng's archenemy in later years.

Among the remaining eight brothers, Yin-chih (the third son)
was the only one who was friendly with Yin-jeng—later he, too,
would betray a lack of filial piety. The fifth son, Yin-ch'i, was
rather an exception, for although he was raised by Hsiao-hui, there
is no evidence that he had any serious personality problems. The
sixth son, Yin-tso, died at age five, and the seventh, Yin-yu, was
born deformed and was friendly with all his brothers. Yin-ssu, the

eighth son, Yin-t'ang, the ninth, and Yin-o, the tenth, later became the strongest anti-Yin-jeng group in the struggle for succession. Of the last three sons, Yin-tzu, the eleventh, died at eleven, and Yin-t'ao, the twelfth, and Yin-hsiang, the thirteenth—aged only one by 1686—could hardly have had much contact with Yin-jeng during his childhood.

Knowing that Yin-jeng's adulthood friends were found primarily among people of low morality, including eunuchs and low-status personnel from the Imperial Household Department—such as bond servants from the Imperial Buttery and Tea House—as well as his bodyguards, one can infer that favorable influences from such characters during Yin-jeng's childhood were quite minimal.

In 1681, when K'ang-hsi was twenty-eight and his heir apparent seven, the emperor finally brought the eight-year-old civil war to a triumphant conclusion. Two years later, he conquered Taiwan, the last stronghold of Ming resistance, thus completing the unification —and the Manchu conquest—of China. Though in ensuing years K'ang-hsi continued to feel threatened on the northern frontier by the Western Mongols and their possible collusion with Czarist Russia, the degree of political stability that followed the civil war permitted him to turn to some long-term projects for internal consolidation. This included the education of his crown prince.

We know that K'ang-hsi was able to play a much more active role in Yin-jeng's late childhood than in his early years; however, the record is thin on the precise father-son interaction during this period of Yin-jeng's life. In particular, we lack information about the personalities K'ang-hsi brought into the picture. We know, for example, that K'ang-hsi appointed a respectable Southern scholar named Chang Ying to tutor the crown prince,[27] but we do not know the names of the boy's other tutors at this time, though logically there must have been some. We also know that in 1684 Yin-jeng, aged ten, finished reading the Confucian primer called *The Four Books* (*Analects, Mencius, Doctrine of Mean,* and *Great Learning*), but we do not know in detail the rest of his curriculum. Later K'ang-hsi spoke of Yin-jeng's accomplishments in both intellectual pursuits and military skills, such as archery (at nine Yin-jeng's bow brought down a tiger in a hunting exercise), and the father praised him for facility in all three official languages—Manchu, Chinese, and Mongolian—but there is little information as to who Yin-jeng's military instructors or language tutors were. We do know that the prince studied mathematics and medicine with his father's Jesuit advisers.[28]

A poem that the emperor composed in 1684 upon receiving ten-year-old Yin-jeng's report on the completion of *The Four Books* be-

trays a good deal of pride in the young prince, and even more in his
own concepts of educating the child:

> All ancient worthies had their family instructions;
> Poetry and proprieties are the subjects of study.
> Be it for the state or for the family,
> There is only one principle governing the matters of learning.
> When I arrived at the eastern bank of the River,
> Three thousand *li* away from the capital,
> I gazed into the sky beyond the northern cloud,
> To pour out my longings and my concern.
> Early this morning, I opened my mail;
> I found some sheets full of characters:
> Each word was from an innocent heart,
> Declaring that he had completed *The Four Books.*
> So young, he earnestly pursues learning,
> This indeed should please the heart of his father.
> Nevertheless, one ought to make still greater progress
>   day by day,
> Without thinking to stop even for a moment.
> The Great King Yü valued every inch of his time;
> Today, one should cherish even one-tenth of it.
> Whenever one opens a volume to admire the ancient worthies,
> Immediately one is touched by the profound truth.
> Thus, when your heart is gladdened as the days go by,
> Naturally, you will find delight in Principle and
>   Righteousness.[29]

Many years later, K'ang-hsi proudly referred to Yin-jeng's pre-
cocity, saying, "in literature and in archery, Yin-jeng was second to
no one."[30] A rare piece of paired verses that the heir apparent wrote
in his teens (probably in 1689) seems to substantiate his father's
praise:

> In the pavilion, the bright moon heightened my inebriation;
> On the river, the evening glow deepened my poetic vision.[31]

The allusion to drink, it must be noted, should not be taken as
mere metaphor borrowed by Yin-jeng from the T'ang poets: Wang
Shih-chen, who recorded these verses, was later dismissed by
K'ang-hsi for indulging excessively in wine with Yin-jeng. But perhaps overwhelmed by his son's intellectual accomplishment, K'ang-
hsi did not seem to realize that the crown prince might already be
troubled by inner frustrations.

4
The Southern Literati

K'ANG-HSI'S enthusiasm for intellectual achievement brought him only mixed blessings. On the one hand, his close association with the Southern literati helped broaden his Chinese learning and enabled him to project the image of an exemplary Confucian monarch loyally supported by his Chinese subjects. But intellectual achievement does not guarantee moral excellence, and some of the Chinese literati K'ang-hsi had brought to serve in court—as imperial tutors and concurrently as high-ranking officials—formed factions for selfish purposes. Their corrupt behavior not only severely demoralized the imperial bureaucracy, but also contributed to the failure of the emperor's efforts to educate the Heir Apparent Yin-jeng. A review of the notorious figures among the literati will enhance our understanding of the part they played in the deterioration of the heir apparent's character. It will also shed light on the growing tensions between father and son as Yin-jeng entered adolescence.[1]

Hsiung Tz'u-li was the most important intellectual influence on K'ang-hsi during his early reigning years. As mentioned earlier, Hsiung was a prominent figure in the restoration of Chinese institutions after the downfall of Oboi. But soon after this, he became a target of Songgotu's resentment, perhaps owing to jealousy of Hsiung's position, high in imperial favor. In 1676 Hsiung Tz'u-li was found guilty of falsifying evidence and betraying a colleague in the Grand Secretariat in order to cover up a mistake he himself had committed. Songgotu seized the opportunity to engineer Hsiung's dismissal as grand secretary, and had him ordered to return to his home in the South.[2] (Twelve years later, when called back to Peking in 1688, Hsiung would again exert considerable influence over K'ang-hsi.)

Hsiung's departure from the emperor's counsel created an opportunity for other Chinese intellectuals to assume domination of the inner palace. In 1677, a year after Hsiung's dismissal, K'ang-hsi appointed some of his tutors and literary assistants to the permanent staff of his new South Library, also known as the Imperial Study.[3] In the emperor's view, the creation of the South Library was an integral part of the Confucianization of his bureaucracy for both political and personal purposes.

The Library was not institutionalized until early 1678, yet its roots extended back to the post-Oboi years, when court factions had emerged. Songgotu had engaged in a power struggle not only with Hsiung Tz'u-li but even more so with his Manchu colleague, Mingju, and Songgotu's influence on K'ang-hsi had suffered a setback at the beginning of the civil war, when his appeasement policy toward Wu San-kuei was rejected in favor of the strategy of confrontation advocated by Mingju and the great dowager empress. In 1680 he would be dismissed as a grand secretary, thereafter losing much of his influence at court.[4]

In 1678, however, Songgotu's influence was still such as to permit him to place his own man in the center of the imperial power structure. This man was Kao Shih-ch'i, one of the two Chinese first appointed to the permanent staff of the South Library. Kao's subsequent rise to uncommon favor in the K'ang-hsi court enlightens us as to the emperor's personal needs and illustrates the workings of court politics.

Kao was born in the Northern province of Chihli (Peking's province),[5] but was brought up in the Southern city of Hangchow—he designated Hangchow as his native place when he registered for the civil-service examination. The examination system consisted of three levels, district, provincial, and metropolitan, and generally, only after one had passed the last and obtained the highest degree, *chin-shih*, could one expect to receive regular official appointments. Because of his poverty, the young Kao had received only enough education to achieve the first level, *sheng-yüan*, a licentiate, which was locally prestigious but did not qualify one for an official post.

Kao was, however, both a conscientious student and a skillful writer. In 1663, when he was eighteen, he was so poor that he decided to travel north to Peking to seek his fortune. In the Pao-kuo Temple, a popular spot for religious and social gatherings, he produced and sold calligraphy and literary pieces to earn a meager living.

Kao's elegant penmanship attracted the attention of a powerful bond servant of Songgotu's, who was then managing his master's household affairs. The bond servant invited Kao to become his bookkeeper and personal secretary. Impressed by Kao's talent, Songgotu appointed him his special assistant. Thus favored by his connection with Songgotu, Kao was able to join the bureaucracy through the "irregular route," that is, without an advanced degree. He entered the Imperial Academy as a student, and after graduation, in 1671, he was made a clerk in the Hanlin Academy (similar to a Western postdoctoral institution). The position was so insignificant that advancement to higher positions would normally have been difficult. But four years later (1675), Kao was transferred to a clerkship in the Supervisorate of Imperial Instruction. This office, as previously mentioned, was in charge of the education of the crown prince, although at that time the heir apparent was only a baby, not yet two. Because of his rare talents in calligraphy, and aided by Songgotu's patronage, Kao soon gained recognition in the inner-court service.

In 1676 Hsiung Tz'u-li was dismissed, and K'ang-hsi lost a trusted tutor and literary assistant. Meanwhile, the grave situation of the civil war had spurred the emperor to adopt the Ming system of appointing a crown prince, and had also increased the emperor's incentive to learn the Confucian principles of government in order to cultivate his image as a Confucian monarch. He therefore needed talented literati to serve as tutors, calligraphers, and editors to polish his literary works and pronouncements—tasks performed today by public-relations experts and speech writers.

The Ming system for imperial Confucian education was copied exactly. Under that system there were two institutions to continue the process of imperial education. The first was the Imperial Seminars on Classics (*Ching-yen*), which were held twice a year, one in the spring and the other in autumn; the spring session was normally held in the second month of the lunar calendar and the autumn session in the eighth month. The second institution was Daily Lectures; despite the name, these were not held every day, but generally on alternate days.[6] Daily Lectures followed the spring session of the Seminar on Classics and lasted until the summer solstice, constituting a sort of spring semester. After a vacation during the hot months of summer, the autumn session of the Seminar on Classics was held and then Daily Lectures were given until the winter solstice. A winter recess followed before the beginning of the next academic year.

The Ming system was mainly ceremonial in nature; the emperor was not expected to engage in any serious discussions with his lecturers. K'ang-hsi supplemented the seminars with his South Library, an institution less hampered by formalities. Kao Shih-ch'i (1645-1703) and Chang Ying (1638-1708) were selected to be the first permanent members of the new system,[7] and were granted special permission to reside within the Forbidden City (the section of Peking where the emperor lived). Chang Ying's responsibility was to assist the emperor in studying the Chinese classics, a task he had previously performed successfully as an imperial lecturer; the only difference was that now he served in this capacity full time. Kao's appointment was as a copyist, because of his elegant calligraphy.

Kao served K'ang-hsi well, becoming his favorite and most trusted courtier for almost fifteen years. Later (in 1703) K'ang-hsi explained why he had so favored Kao:

> When I began to study [in my childhood], some eunuchs taught me *The Four Books* and writing essays. But it was only after I found Shih-ch'i that I began to master the key to learning. At first I really marveled to see that Shih-ch'i could identify the dates of any poem or essay just by glancing at it. Soon [with his help] I also was able to do so. Although Shih-ch'i had no military merit, yet I treated him lavishly with favors. This is because he attained great merit in enriching my learning.[8]

Curiously, K'ang-hsi made no acknowledgment of his tutor Chang Ying for his assistance in Confucian learning. This might well have been because Kao's forceful, sycophantic personality overshadowed that of Chang Ying.[9] Chang was recognized by his colleagues as a first-rate scholar, unassuming and honest; though close to the fountainhead of power, he was averse to cultivating personal influence. Kao, on the other hand, was clever, scheming, and dishonest. He made the most of his opportunity to be close to the emperor, who was attracted to such a showy character, who displayed style both in manner and in calligraphy.

Kao's contemporaries described how psychologically shrewd he was and how skillful in giving the imperial ego a timely massage. In 1684, for example, shortly after the Rebellion of the Three Feudatories had been put down, the emperor was on his first Southern tour, devised as a public-relations campaign to create the image of monarchy steeped in Confucian learning. In the course of the tour, the emperor and his entourage were visiting the famous Lung-shan Temple, on top of the Chin-shan Mountain, situated in the middle of the Yangtze River. The emperor wished to write a traditional four-character verse as a memento to give to the temple's abbot; but inspiration flagged and K'ang-hsi could not summon up a suitable thought. Among the dignitaries standing by the emperor's side, ready to applaud his "extraordinary literary achievement," was Kao, who was rubbing the ink stick on the ink slab to make ink for the emperor. Inconspicuously, Kao wrote some characters on his palm and held his hand so only the emperor could read them. Like a student cheating on an examination, the emperor quickly glanced at the verse and then wrote it with his vermilion brush: *chiang-t'ien i-lan* ("River and sky in one sweep").[10] The temple later changed its name to Chiang-t'ien Temple, in honor of the verse.

Another anecdote is equally revealing. K'ang-hsi was very proud of his horsemanship, but on a hunting trip one day his horse stumbled and nearly threw him off. This was a great embarrassment to the emperor. The next day Kao showed up at court in a garment spattered with mud. The emperor frostily asked what had happened to him, since wearing such a garment might be construed as lack of reverence for the throne, which could require punishment. How could Kao be so foolish as to make a mistake like this? Kao answered the emperor's query with ease: "Yesterday, when I was riding, the horse threw me off, right into a muddy puddle!" The emperor immediately responded with a hearty laugh and said, "You Southerners are indeed no horsemen. Yesterday I also had a mishap while riding, but I managed not to be thrown off completely!" K'ang-hsi, cheered, forgave Kao for his breach of court etiquette; it was common knowledge that Kao had put on this show deliberately.

Unofficial records also cast doubt on Kao's achievement in Chinese learning. One story says that Kao bribed the emperor's eunuchs lavishly to provide him with information about the emperor's daily schedule of study. With this information, he would quickly duplicate the reading and prepare himself to answer any questions the emperor might raise. The emperor was, of course, always impressed with Kao's extraordinary capacity and facility in Confucian scholarship.

STARTING IN THE early 1680s, K'ang-hsi appointed some of his court ministers, mostly prominent Southern literati, to also serve in the South Library. In 1685 Wang Hung-hsü, vice-president of the Board of Revenue, and in 1688 Hsü Ch'ien-hsüeh, a subchancellor in the Grand Secretariat, were called upon to work in this dual capacity. Such an appointment carried much prestige at court. While holding important posts in the central bureaucracy, the tutors could utilize their physical presence in the inner court to enhance their influence on outer-court politics. It was not surprising that all of them (except Chang Ying, who had no interest in power and dissociated himself from factional alliances in court politics) joined factions to advance their own interests. Kao, Hsü, and Wang formed the so-called Southern Faction, under Hsü's leadership. Its members were almost all Chinese literati, and it opposed the Northern Faction in angry contests for power. The latter faction was led by Mingju, who attracted many adherents from among both Chinese and Manchu officials.[11]

MEANWHILE, AS THE crown prince was coming of age Songgotu began to use his avuncular relationship with Yin-jeng to fight for the power he had lost to the emperor's new confidants. The triangular rivalry soon interfered with K'ang-hsi's efforts to strengthen Yin-jeng's character—K'ang-hsi was just beginning to be uneasy about his son's personality problems. At the same time, the 1680s were witnessing a nadir in court morale, generated by the Northern and Southern Factions' demands for imperial favors. Not all the ministers, however, were willing to become embroiled in the struggle, for K'ang-hsi was blessed by the presence of a small number of loyal ministers who were independent in court politics. Functioning as a sort of "political conscience" in the imperial bureaucracy, they did not hesitate to vent their criticism of irregularities or present blunt remonstrations to the emperor himself. Most of these ministers, as it happens, were Northerners.

By 1686 the heir apparent was twelve and considered by the Chinese to have come of age. His personality problems (the nature of which is not clearly described in our sources, but being spoiled must have been one of them) had apparently become common knowledge in court circles, causing concern among the moralists. They hoped that the boy might profit from being allowed out of the secluded palace circle, and quoting the Ming precedent for the education of an heir apparent, they petitioned that Yin-jeng begin to receive formal education under official tutors in the outer court.

The emperor approved this suggestion and ordered the Board of Rites to consult Ming precedent governing the institution. Meanwhile, he solicited nominations for the tutors to take on this important task. On April 12, 1686, with flowery praise, the emperor appointed the famous Confucianist T'ang Pin to head the tutors, concurrently naming him Chinese president of the Board of Rites:

> When T'ang Pin, governor of Kiangning [capital of Kiangsu], served me as imperial lecturer, his behavior was diligent and careful—this I have known well for a long time. After he was made governor, he was honest and devoted to his duty and inspired his subordinates to the same high standards. He ought to be rewarded with a higher post to honor his stature. Let him be appointed president of the Board of Rites, concurrently to be in charge of the Supervisorate of Imperial Instruction.[12]

On the surface, T'ang's appointment seemed a great honor done to a distinguished scholar. But behind the high praises lay the malice of Mingju and his clique. According to an informed source at the court, the appointment was made after persistent prodding from Mingju, who plotted a subtly disguised scheme of revenge to repay T'ang for failure to show him due respect.

One of Mingju's house servants regularly journeyed to the South to pressure officials into giving money in return for political favors. All the officials dutifully called upon him and yielded to his demands, except T'ang Pin. When the servant arrived at Kiangsu, where T'ang Pin was governor, T'ang did not visit him and offered no present of silver. Instead, T'ang summoned the servant to his office, where he received him attended only by the doorman, a social equal of the servant. Mingju interpreted this as a deliberate affront. Similarly, T'ang also offended Mingju's Chinese henchman, Yü Kuo-chu, a Southerner and a grand secretary, by refusing to offer presents to Yü's representative.[13]

This was the background to Mingju's strong recommendation that T'ang Pin be made the official tutor of the heir apparent. What he told the emperor was: "Mr. T'ang Pin is a scholar renowned for his unrivaled knowledge in Neo-Confucian philosophy. No one is more qualified than he to serve the Heir Apparent in supervising his formal instruction."[14] In making the recommendation Mingju was counting on the inevitability of a clash between pupil and teacher: the heir apparent, spoiled as he was by lack of discipline and the many rivals for his attention, was unlikely to be cooperative with his teacher; T'ang, from Honan and a typical Northerner, was straightforward, blunt, and extremely conscientious. Regardless of which side the emperor supported in the event of such a clash, the beneficiary of the confrontation would, of course, be Mingju.

As expected, T'ang Pin's mission proved to be ill-fated from the start. When he was leaving Kiangsu, the common people, mostly peasants, gathered along the roadside to see him off and to request that he transmit their wish to the emperor that the excessive grain tax be reduced. He was quoted as answering, "I have repeatedly memorialized the Emperor on this matter; my petitions are always rejected by the court deliberations. This time I personally will bring your case to the attention of the throne." Apologizing for his past failure to fulfill their wishes, he added, "I love you people and try to serve you well, but I simply lack the means to alleviate your misery."[15] The next year these words would be distorted by Yü Kuo-chu to make it appear to the emperor that T'ang had defamed the throne. Thus, even before he had left Kiangsu, T'ang Pin had inadvertently provided material that would eventually drive a wedge between him and the emperor.

Upon arriving at the capital, T'ang Pin requested that two scholars join his teaching staff. One was Keng Chieh, also a Northerner from Honan and a reputable Confucian scholar who had studied with T'ang Pin under the prominent early-Ch'ing Confucian Sun Ch'i-feng (1585-1675);[16] he too was blunt, upright, and uncompromising in his principles. The other scholar recommended was a Manchu named Ta-t'a-ha, president of the Board of Civil Appointments. The emperor approved these candidates and ordered that the school for the heir apparent be opened.

Ming precedent called for certain preliminary rituals before the commencement of studies. The first was a visit by the heir apparent to the Feng-hsien tien (Imperial Ancestral Hall within the Forbidden City) to sacrifice to the imperial ancestors. He then went to the Chamber for the Transmission of Heart (Ch'uan-hsin tien) within the Wen-hua Hall to pour libations before the sacred tablet bearing the inscription "The Great Mentor Confucius."[17]

The opening session of studies was largely ceremonial. At dawn the heir apparent paid homage to his father, who held an audience with the entire court at the Hall of Guaranteed Harmony (Pao-ho tien), where the heir apparent saluted K'ang-hsi with three kneelings and nine prostrations. Then he arrived at the Wen-hua Hall, where he had a short session with his Manchu and Chinese tutors on two of the Confucian classics, *Analects* and the *The Book of Documents*. (In addition to Chinese learning, the curriculum was enlarged to include the subject of Manchu tradition, as well as the Manchu and Mongolian languages.) This first session was attended by the entire court and conducted with much pomp. It concluded with a banquet held by the heir apparent to honor his tutors and ministers.[18]

From Peking T'ang Pin wrote to his family about his initial encounter with the heir apparent and his impressions of the prince gleaned during his first two days: "On the twenty-fourth day [of the third month],[19] the Heir Apparent began his formal study in the outer court. We expounded on one chapter from *The Four Books*." Concerning the first daily session, he wrote: "On the twenty-fifth day, I went to the Heir Apparent's palace together with Mr. Kuo [Fen][20] to present lectures. The Heir Apparent was humble and affable. He stepped down the stairway to meet us, and told us that he sincerely admired us. He also stated that he wanted to restore the ancient rite of tutors presenting lectures while sitting rather than kneeling before him." The imperial father's intention to follow the ancient Chinese tradition was obvious. The letter went on: "The Emperor also established the practice that each day the Heir Apparent must try to lecture to us on the same subject that he had learned the previous day. All matters are seriously carried out, unlike practice in the former dynasties, when only formalities were emphasized."

Among other things T'ang Pin was impressed by the heir apparent's achievement in calligraphy: "For eight years, ever since he was six, the Heir Apparent never stopped practicing calligraphy, even for a single day. His style is correct and disciplined. His fine writing is close to the Yü and Liu schools." The letter closed with high praise for the emperor's active participation in the study program: "Every morning before going out to meet court ministers, the Emperor asks the Prince to recite what he learned the previous day. Meanwhile, the Heir Apparent goes to the outer court to study with us. Upon returning to the palace, the Prince immediately goes to the Emperor to repeat what he learned that day. Never has any other emperor in history so diligently sought to educate his Heir Apparent."[21]

Whether T'ang Pin's praise of his pupil and the emperor was an honest reflection of his first impression or merely a formality to show deference to one's sovereign is difficult to judge. But the emperor did involve himself in and seem hopeful about Yin-jeng's education.

By now the heir apparent had done a fair amount of studying of Confucian classics; from age five to nine he had studied the Manchu language, and he had practiced Chinese calligraphy since he was nine. One day shortly after the new program had started, the emperor proudly displayed the heir apparent's workbooks on Chinese calligraphy to his favorite ministers; according to Hsü Ch'ien-hsüeh, these "filled eight trunks, large and small."[22]

Supplementing T'ang Pin's account, Hsü also wrote about the emperor's active role in the program and the daily study schedule:

I have heard that the Emperor educated his children according to strict rules and solemn rites. At dawn, soon after the toll of the imperial clock, His Majesty arrived at the side chamber [of the Ch'ien-ch'ing Palace], where he called in his children one by one to recite the Classics they had just learned. He personally expounded on the Classics to his children before he went out to hold the morning audience with his ministers.

Meanwhile, of course, T'ang Pin and his associates went to the heir apparent for their daily session. This would end before noon. The afternoon hours, also according to Hsü, were reserved for the practice of archery and other activities beneficial to the heir apparent's physical fitness. After the evening lamps were lit, the emperor would hold another session with his princes. "Not a single morning or evening, not for inordinate heat or cold, would the Emperor have ever interrupted this schedule."[23]

The emperor's participation was commendable, although it could also be interpreted as a lack of confidence in the imperial tutors. With doubts already planted in his mind by Yü Kuo-chu, the emperor soon began to question T'ang Pin's motives in selecting certain teaching materials for the heir apparent. One day T'ang Pin lectured on the subject "If the government gathers excessively from the people, the people will disperse," a verse taken from *Mencius*. K'ang-hsi suspected that T'ang was hinting at the possible doom of his own rule, and he asked the heir apparent to press T'ang for clarification by saying, "Since these verses refer to a period in Chinese history when China was divided into many warring states [403-221 B.C.], it is easy to understand why people were driven to disperse [from these unworthy rulers], but how does this apply to people today, since they are living in a unified empire?"

In posing his question, the emperor was apparently rebutting T'ang Pin's statement as irrelevant to the current situation. T'ang, far from revising his interpretation of the quotation, responded by citing the cases of Ch'in (221-207 B.C.) and Sui (A.D. 589-618), two of the shortest dynasties in Chinese history. The founders of the dynasties had each unified the Chinese empire after centuries of civil war, but both dynasties disintegrated shortly after their establishment. T'ang Pin categorically argued, "Under a unified empire, not only do the people disperse, but the calamities that follow become more violent." K'ang-hsi ignored this apparent provocation and did not pursue the question.[24]

A series of incidents followed that thrust T'ang Pin into the middle of factional rivalry. They shattered his dream and optimism about his pupil and brought about his own demise.

In the following year, 1687, a severe drought plagued the nation. Confucian theory held that drought was one of the signs by which Heaven expressed its disapproval of a ruler's performance. A pious ruler should respond by self-examination: evaluating his policies and asking officials to speak up about political evils and maladministration. K'ang-hsi accordingly invited suggestions and criticism from the officialdom. But no high-ranking official was willing to offer criticism, for fear of reprisals. Finally, Tung Han-ch'en, an insignificant member of the Department of Astronomy, broke the silence. He presented a memorial boldly urging the emperor to "pay attention to the education of the Heir Apparent" and "be careful in selecting his chief ministers." Although couched in the polite language of the court, both suggestions clearly amounted to a criticism of K'ang-hsi: the emperor had neglected the now well-known personality problems of the heir apparent and he had condoned reckless acts committed by the Mingju faction in the court. Tung's memorial was subsequently handed down by the emperor to the Council of Ministers (consisting of presidents and vice-presidents of the central bureaucracy) for deliberation.

Not knowing how the council would act, Mingju was alarmed when he learned of the memorial. A Chinese grand secretary, Wang Hsi, a Southerner, comforted him before the meeting: "This memorial," Wang said, "is nothing but childish nonsense. I think [we will just propose to the emperor that Tung be] put to death at once; then the matter will be over and closed!" At the conference, T'ang Pin was the only one adamantly opposed to Wang's proposal. He contended, "Han-ch'en has presented the memorial in response to the Emperor's open request; I find no grounds whatsoever for recommending a death penalty as a reward for his proposal. While high-ranking officials have chosen to seal their mouths, a minor official was not afraid to speak up. I think we high officials ought to reflect upon our own irresponsibility!" He added, "I felt rather ashamed in the face of the example set by Han-ch'en!"

This statement was twisted by the Mingju faction and, together with T'ang Pin's earlier alleged complaints about the excessive tax, was reported to the emperor. K'ang-hsi, furious, demanded an explanation. Since in imperial politics any vigorous argument with the emperor constituted a misdemeanor in itself, T'ang quite wisely chose to defend himself by evasiveness: "Tung Han-ch'en has commented on the matter of educating the Heir Apparent. Since I myself am entrusted with this responsibility and I have repeatedly failed in it with regard to both rituals and proprieties, I feel indeed guilty and at fault for my failures." The emperor reproved him for deliberate ambiguity and order that he explain himself more specifically. T'ang then resorted to a psychological explanation: "Upon receiving Your Majesty's earlier demand for an explanation, I became so panicky and frightened that my answer became disorderly and improper." This answer was as vague as the last. Nevertheless, the emperor pardoned him, after severely rebuking him for his lack of openness.

T'ang Pin's ordeal was by no means over. Mingju and his henchmen continued to harass him by attacking his associates and those who had been recommended by him. Te-ko-le, whom T'ang Pin had highly recommended to the emperor, was the first to fall victim.[25] A Manchu minister, loyal and independent, he too had become concerned about the deplorable political conditions in the court. Earlier that year, K'ang-hsi had called upon him to expound

on the *I Ching* (*Book of Changes*), used in China for divination. On
that occasion, the emperor asked him to cast a lot, according to the
method shown in the book, to determine why Heaven had held up
the rain for so long. Te-ko-le interpreted the lot to mean that
Heaven was angry because "an unprincipled person is wielding
power in the court." Pressed by the emperor, he revealed that person's name: Mingju. Instead of accepting this interpretation, the
emperor denounced Te-ko-le for his unfair reference to Mingju.

And Mingju retaliated. First he started rumors that Te-ko-le had
slandered him under the instigation of T'ang Pin. Then he contended that all officials who had been recommended by T'ang Pin
were ill qualified for their posts, singling out Hsü-yüan-meng as
another conspicuous example. The emperor accordingly ordered
that a special test be given to Te-ko-le and Hsü-yüan-meng, as well
as to ten other officials. The test required them to prove their literary competence by composing a poem. For both Hsü-yüan-meng
and Te-ko-le the results were disastrous. Hsü-yüan-meng was so
nervous that he could not control his thoughts. Te-ko-le was defeated by a malicious ruse: soon after the test started, he received
an imperial order—the nature of which was by no means clear—
blaming him for some sort of misconduct. Instead of composing the
poem, he used much of the time to write a defense. The men's
papers were evaluated by peers; both failed. T'ang Pin was the only
one who stood for their defense. He argued that a minister such as
Te-ko-le ought to be judged by his "moral excellence and outstanding achievements in learning, not by literary skills!"

A month later, T'ang's colleague Ta-t'a-ha, an official Manchu
tutor to the heir apparent, came under attack. He was charged with
having violated protocol while instructing Yin-jeng. The actual
"violation" was probably a clash between teacher and pupil—
perhaps the heir apparent had been offended by a reprimand; perhaps the teacher had shown overt displeasure at his pupil's absent-
mindedness in class; or perhaps the prince had lost his temper with
his teacher and insisted upon punishment. Whatever the cause, the
teacher received his reward for conscientiousness: the emperor
withheld six months of his salary.[26]

Keng Chieh, T'ang Pin's Chinese colleague, did not wait for impeachment; he asked for dismissal, pleading old age. But this request was taken to be grounds for impeachment, and he was accused of being an opportunist. The emperor declined, however, to
punish him, allowing him instead to stay in the court for two more
months and then letting him return to his home in Honan.[27]

T'ang Pin was transferred to another post, and died soon after.
With T'ang's associates discredited, retired, or demoted, the grand

effort of copying the Chinese institution for the education of the heir apparent ended in failure.

What was the significance of the T'ang Pin episode in the development of the father-son relationship? As K'ang-hsi later recalled, these events made him aware of Yin-jeng's personality problems, particularly his lack of affection for his father.[28] In 1689 K'ang-hsi had Yin-jeng's lecturers expound a verse from the *Analects* to their pupil on the importance of "self-respect" and "dignity"; that same year, the *Annotated Classic of Filial Piety*, compiled at the order of K'ang-hsi's father, was published,[29] providing the emperor with instructional material to give his son. But what else did K'ang-hsi do about the situation?

Toward the end of 1687, shortly after T'ang Pin's death, K'ang-hsi's grandmother's poor health suddenly took a turn for the worse: she was dying.[30] K'ang-hsi was greatly troubled. But he was also cognizant of how her dying might provide a lesson for his son.

By now K'ang-hsi had demonstrated a pattern of using hints and exemplary acts to serve as messages to Yin-jeng. He had tried in this way to impress his son with the importance of frugality and simplicity. When, in the early 1680s, he decided to build the Suburban Villa, Ch'ang-ch'un yuan (Garden of Joyful Springtime), on the western outskirts of Peking, he commanded that the main audience hall be constructed without flowery designs and flashy colors. To remind Yin-jeng of the hardships of common people in the countryside, he also ordered that food grains be planted around the Hall of Non-Ease (Wu-i tien), a room in the villa built as Yin-jeng's study.

Now his grandmother's illness provided the emperor with a chance to teach his son the value of filial piety. K'ang-hsi attended Hsiao-chuang day and night. He fasted and prayed for her constantly. When her illness entered the critical stage, he slept on the floor beside her and would get up to check on her whenever she groaned or made any slight complaint. When her illness worsened, K'ang-hsi took an unusual step as a last resort to save his grandmother's life: leading an impressive train of court dignitaries, he marched several miles from the palace to the Altar of Heaven, in the southern suburbs, where he prayed to Heaven to allow him to "lend" a few years of his own allotted life span to his grandmother. In this "memorial" to Heaven, he acknowledged his "infinite indebtedness" to Hsiao-chuang: "Over the past thirty-odd years after the deaths of my parents, I have been personally brought up and educated by my grandmother so that I have become what I am."[31]

When Hsiao-chuang died, on the twenty-fifth day of the twelfth month (January 27, 1688; six days before the Chinese new year), K'ang-hsi showed his extraordinary grief by breaking several well-established Manchu and Chinese traditions. He cut off his queue, eliciting the remonstrance of the Board of Rites, which said that this violated Manchu imperial tradition (cutting one's queue was reserved for one's father or grandfather); he refused to remove his grandmother's body to an outside funeral house before the arrival of the new year (Manchu belief asserted that allowing the dead to remain in the palace would cause the emperor earlier death); and he insisted on observing a twenty-seven-month mourning period, rather than following the Chinese tradition of previous dynasties of observing only twenty-seven days (each month was substituted with a day). Even after her body was transferred to the outside funeral house, three weeks after her death, K'ang-hsi continued to visit his grandmother's casket—as often as three times a day—and insisted on sleeping in a shabby tent erected outside his imperial apartment, the Ch'ien-ch'ing Palace; the normal temperature at this time was usually well below freezing. He contended: "Being the Son of Heaven, I of course cherish my own health. But I, too, have my grandparents and my parents just like everyone else. As sons and grandsons, shouldn't we observe filial piety regardless of our social status?" He then explicitly stated: "We rule the empire with filial piety. This is why I want to exemplify this principle for my ministers and my people—and for my own descendants."[32]

K'ang-hsi seems to have been confident that his example would teach his son the filial duty and devotion that K'ang-hsi had so strongly demonstrated for his grandmother—once his only support in times of great sorrow, now gone.

What were the reactions of the son to the father's message? The meager indication that we can gather tells us that he did not respond favorably.

5
Signs of Conflict

AT the time of the T'ang Pin episode, in 1687, Yin-jeng was thirteen. The crisis of adolescence for him was not the typical one. The usual parent-child conflicts were magnified by the boy's destiny. The question that weighed on the heir was, when would he inherit his father's throne? For his father, the question was, how?

The emperor's attitude toward his son at this juncture can be seen in his increasing tendency to yield power to Yin-jeng's supporter Songgotu—uncle of Yin-jeng's mother and third son of the former regent Soni—at the expense of the Mingju faction. Early in 1688 Mingju and his three chief henchmen—Yü Kuo-chu, Li Chih-fang, and Le-te-hung—were all dismissed under bribery charges from their posts as grand secretaries (leaving only Wang Hsi in the Grand Secretariat). This downfall was brought about by the Southern Faction—mainly Hsü Ch'ien-hsüeh and Kao Shih-ch'i—in collaboration with Songgotu, a marriage of convenience to deal with a common enemy, for nothing else united them. Soon after this, Hsü was promoted to the presidency of the Board of Punishments and Songgotu, who in 1686 had been appointed senior chamberlain of the Imperial Bodyguard, was made chief delegate of the imperial plenipotentiary mission to negotiate with the Russians on border disputes at the northern frontier of Manchuria. (The negotiation resulted in the Treaty of Nerchinsk of 1689.) This was an important post, for the chieftain of the Western Mongols, Galdan, was attacking the loyal Eastern Mongols (Khalkas), who considered themselves vassals of the Manchu regime, and it fell to Songgotu to frustrate a possible alliance between Galdan and the Russians.[1]

That K'ang-hsi continued to entrust Songgotu with important

political assignments was a reflection of his appreciation of Song-gotu's early support during the Oboi regency; but it was also be-cause of Songgotu's intimate relationship with the heir apparent. As K'ang-hsi later testified, he chose to appease Songgotu and Yin-jeng as far as his heart could endure. But Yin-jeng's lack of filial deference was developing into an obstacle to his future accession to the throne: his behavior was straining relations between father and son.

The first serious incident in the conflict between the emperor and the heir apparent occurred in 1690, when Yin-jeng was sixteen and K'ang-hsi was carrying out his most ambitious act of filial piety for his dead grandmother: the solidification of the empire. The fulfill-ment of the goal he had expressed upon his accession to the throne —"the nation to enjoy peace and order"—had yet to be realized, for the vast northern front of his empire was now being threatened by the Western Mongols. K'ang-hsi believed that before he could hand his government to his son, he had first to make good his promise to his grandmother by eliminating what he considered the last enemy that might jeopardize his empire.

The trouble had begun two years earlier, in 1688, when the West-ern Mongols under the khan Galdan suddenly launched an attack on the pro-Ch'ing Khalkas. They plundered the Khalkas and forced them to flee for the frontier of China, where the Khalkas begged the K'ang-hsi Emperor to protect them and accept their allegiance as Ch'ing vassals. In July 1690 K'ang-hsi decided to lead a campaign against Galdan. As K'ang-hsi later related, shortly before he left the capital for the front, his grandmother appeared to him in a dream in which she warned him not to go to battle in person, predicting that something unhappy would befall him if he went.[2]

In spite of his grandmother's warning, K'ang-hsi decided to con-duct the campaign himself. He first visited the dislocated Khalkas and extended sympathy to their chiefs. He paraded his military force to impress the enemy's spies, who were watching his move-ments. After the imperial order was given, the army, fifty-thousand strong, took action. Father P. P. Gerbillon, a Jesuit imperial ad-viser, recorded the magnificent scene in his diary:[3] "All the great lords, officers, and private troops, have a small banderoll of silk, of the colour of their respective standards, fastened behind their casques and to the back of their cuirass: On it is written the name, company, and office of the bearer." And upon blowing the "dis-cordant-sounding trumpet,"

The cavalry of both wings extended in the form of a crescent, as if it were to surround the enemy. The infantry ran directly forward—the first of them with drawn sabres, covered themselves with bucklers. In the middle of the battalion of foot, the artillery moved on, and in the centre came the dragoons, who had alighted: for they march on horse-back, they fight on foot. They advanced thus in good order till they came near the emperor, where they were ordered to halt. After they had given three or four volleys from the cannon and muskets, the cavalry halted; and when they had resumed their ranks, which had been broken a little by such a hasty march, they remained for some time before the pavilion.

Along with impressing the enemy, the display was intended "to convince the Khalkas that the celestial troops had sufficient skill for protecting the most numerous hordes."

Galdan, upon receiving his spies' reports, was not cowed into voluntary submission. Instead, as Gerbillon further recorded, "This unruly chief levied contributions, collected troops, and drew up in a menacing attitude on the frontiers of the steppe. So great was his chagrin at the perfidy of this disturber, that Kang-he [K'ang-hsi] fell seriously ill."

This was Gerbillon's interpretation of K'ang-hsi's sudden illness; the emperor thought differently. He attributed the illness and his failure to defeat the enemy to his rejection of his grandmother's advice. (He perhaps also believed that the subsequent disheartening encounter with his heir apparent was a form of punishment for his lack of filial obedience.)

K'ang-hsi fell ill in early August, and officials urged him to return to Peking for treatment and convalescence.[4] The emperor believed his ailment was so serious that he summoned the Heir Apparent Yin-jeng, who was accompanied by his third son, Yin-chih. The implication was clear: if K'ang-hsi should die, the heir apparent must promptly succeed him on the throne.

On August 28 the two princes arrived on horse-back and went to the imperial lodge to greet the emperor. K'ang-hsi expected at the very least a display of solicitude from his successor, in whom filial piety was deemed a prerequisite of his becoming emperor. Yet to the watchful father, Yin-jeng (and Yin-chih, too) showed no grief or even concern. On the contrary, both in his words and in his countenance he seemed to betray "a secret joy." As the *Veritable Records* further described it, "Seeing that Yin-jeng failed to show the slightest mark of loyalty and love for his imperial father, the Emperor was extremely grieved. He ordered both princes to go away and return to the capital immediately." On this important point the contemporary reports by Father Bouvet substantiated the *Veritable Records* and also revealed the reason for the heir apparent's deportment: he thought that "he would soon succeed his imperial father to the throne"![5]

K'ang-hsi suppressed his anger. His illness lasted until November —prolonged by an intermittent fever—at which time the death in battle of his beloved maternal uncle T'ung Kuo-kang further delayed his recovery. This death provided the emperor with another chance to use the exemplary method to instruct Yin-jeng in filial piety.

After his uncle's body was transferred to the capital, K'ang-hsi insisted that he attend the elaborate funeral, even though his health was so poor that he had to have his ailments painfully treated by cauterization with moxa and his ministers entreated him not to take the risk.[6] And yet, despite this dramatic filial display, K'ang-hsi's message was lost on Yin-jeng. The emperor was also soon to realize that his son's lack of filial behavior was encouraged by the political rivalry raging in court.

IMPERIAL PREROGATIVES were denoted by insignia, honors, and appointments. Would-be usurpers often strove for these trappings as a means of gaining actual power. In 1694 another father-son conflict was caused by the heir apparent's attempt to increase his symbols of power, as prompted by Songgotu. The granduncle had been promoting K'ang-hsi's early abdication in Yin-jeng's favor, with the goal of enhancing his own position in court.

The power balance in court had been shifting over the years. The T'ang Pin episode marked the apex of Mingju's influence; after being dismissed from office for bribery in 1688, he receded from the political scene. By the end of 1689, the Southern Faction leader, Hsü Ch'ien-hsüeh, also suffered a severe setback: he and his associates Wang Hung-hsü and Kao Shih-ch'i were dismissed and ordered to their homes in the South, after being indicted for their alleged corruption.[7] Despite these dismissals, K'ang-hsi's policy toward court factions was conservative. While compelled to remove the factional leaders, he never wanted to root out all their followers (he hoped to "kill one in order to scare away the other hundred," as the Chinese saying goes), so that even after banishment the leaders were able to continue to influence court politics by working through former adherents.

Songgotu had few followers in the civil bureaucracy: his handful of adherents consisted largely of military officials within the Manchu Banner units.[8] Nevertheless, he was now reemerging as the most powerful figure in court and was feared by all. The reason? The heir apparent was firmly on his side. Thus, in promoting the heir apparent's interests Songgotu was strengthening his own position.

The emperor later recalled that Songgotu had begun to support Yin-jeng "ever since Yin-jeng was designated the Heir Apparent." The emperor charged that "He selfishly advocated that yellow [the imperial color] be used for the Heir Apparent in his garments, chariots, and other things relating to the Heir Apparent's preroga-tives. All the protocol and ceremonial matters that he had proposed for the Heir Apparent were practically identical with mine as the Emperor, thus having created the impression that there existed two emperors in one state." The emperor considered Songgotu's pro-posals to be the source of his son's becoming "haughty and reck-less," and he called Songgotu the "greatest sinner" of the Manchu dynasty.[9] The ritual of ancestor worship brought the problem to a head.

In China many filial acts were performed in established rituals. Ancestor worship, for instance, though practiced in various ways by the old Manchus, did not become formalized until the Shun-chih Emperor adopted the Chinese rites. The Pure and Bright Festival (Ch'ing-ming), in the third month of the lunar year, was an impor-tant day for ancestor worship in China. Entire families or even clans would pay homage in their ancestral graveyards, sacrificing and "sweeping clean the graves" to express their devotion to their deceased senior relatives. In the imperial family, a worship cere-mony was also conducted on the day before the festival, at the Feng-hsien Hall—Imperial Ancestral Hall—built in 1657. At the ceremony, it was the emperor's prerogative to worship inside the threshold of the hall; all others stayed outside it.[10]

In 1694, anticipating the forthcoming festival, the emperor or-dered the Board of Rites to suggest the proper procedure for the ceremony now that the heir apparent, having achieved his twen-tieth year (by the Chinese reckoning; nineteenth by Western count), had entered adulthood. This was a sign, in Songgotu's opinion, that the time was right to press for K'ang-hsi's early abdication in favor of Yin-jeng. To have it suggested by the board that the heir apparent be raised to equal status with the emperor at the cere-mony would be a way of testing the emperor's reaction to a pro-posal of Yin-jeng's immediate succession.

When the Board of Rites suggested—at Songgotu's instigation—that the heir apparent's mat for kneelings and prostrations be put inside the Ancestral Hall's threshold, the emperor rejected the idea. The Manchu president of the Board of Rites, Sha-mu-ha, and his associates on the board (who feared Yin-jeng) then requested that the emperor's decision be put on official record—they obviously anticipated the wrath of Songgotu in the rejection of his proposal. The emperor was outraged at being asked to put such a decision in writing, and he ordered that these officials be considered by the

Board of Civil Appointments for "severe punishments." This board advised that Sha-mu-ha be dismissed from his post and handed over to the Board of Punishments for a criminal trial, and that the two Manchu vice-presidents, Hsi-er-ta and To-ch'i, also lose their jobs. (The emperor benevolently reduced the punishments: Sha-mu-ha was merely dismissed, and the vice-presidents were "leniently" forgiven.)[11]

The behavior of the Board of Rites officials indicates the power of Songgotu and the heir apparent. The emperor himself was unwilling to confront these two, so how could court ministers, especially Manchus, dare to oppose their wishes? And yet the officials were answerable as much to the emperor as to his son. Thus, until the emperor changed his policy, the court officials were in a quandary.

If the emperor's policy toward the Songgotu-Yin-jeng faction seemed to be one of appeasement, it was only because K'ang-hsi wished to avoid direct conflict with his son. As was his style, when one of the factions became too powerful, he simply gave more weight to the others. Now with the threat coming from Songgotu, he turned to the Mingju group. Shortly after the Ancestral Hall incident, Fu-lun, Mingju's former henchman, was made president of the Board of Rites, at the same time being allowed to retain his post as governor-general of Szechwan and Shansi. When Mingju's nephew Fu-la-t'a, then governor-general of Chiang-nan and Kiang-si, died three months later, the emperor praised him publicly for having been "peaceful and yet not factional" and for "not being fearful of powerful figures in court." The officials understood who the "powerful figures" were.[12]

In another attempt that year to balance the factions, the emperor enlisted the assistance of his former Chinese advisers: he ordered the three famous Southern literati back to Peking under the pretext of needing them for the compilation of such important works as the *Ming History*. Hsü Ch'ien-hsüeh had died just before receiving the order, so only Wang Hung-hsü and Kao Shih-ch'i responded to the imperial call.[13]

As Songgotu's campaign for K'ang-hsi's abdication persisted, the emperor seemed to be yielding to this pressure. A year later, in 1695, K'ang-hsi formally established a *fei*, legitimate wife, for the heir apparent. This marked a step toward possible abdication, for a consort with the rank of *fei* qualified to become a reigning empress once Yin-jeng was enthroned.[14]

6
Regency

THE father-son conflicts over color of clothing and insignia and the arrangement of the devotional mats in the Ancestral Hall were not trivialities. They were reflections of a serious issue that was developing between the emperor and his heir—succession and its timing. Yin-jeng could assume the throne during his father's lifetime in two ways: by persuading the emperor to abdicate or by forcibly taking the throne. The issue from the father's point of view was not power but filiality, his own and his son's: Had K'ang-hsi fulfilled his promise to his grandmother to bring peace to the empire? Would Yin-jeng be worthy of the position and filial to his father after abdication? K'ang-hsi indeed contemplated abdication and to that possible end decided to make Yin-jeng his regent to test the young man's ability to rule.

The proposition of abdication, advanced primarily by Songgotu,[1] would have been totally unacceptable to K'ang-hsi if he had been as power-centered as that minister. The emperor, however, derived satisfaction from other things, as can be seen from the imperial persons he desired to emulate.

The kind of relationship K'ang-hsi longed to have with his son was epitomized by that which existed between Emperor Kao-tsung (r. 1127-1162), of the Southern Sung dynasty (1127-1280), and his heir, Emperor Hsiao-tsung ("Emperor of Filiality," r. 1163-1189).[2] An examination of that relationship illuminates K'ang-hsi's self-image as the emperor of China as well as his expectations of his heir.

The Sung case contains interesting parallels with the early-Ch'ing court. As with the Ch'ing, the greatest threat to the security of the

Sung dynasty was posed by the northern barbarians, though at the time of Kao-tsung the northern barbarians were of the Jurched tribe, who invaded the Sung and established the alien Chin dynasty in North China and were the ancestors of the Manchus. In 1126-27 the Jurched made a successful raid on the Sung capital, Lo-yang, and captured the Emperor Hui-tsung (r. 1101-1126) and most of his courtiers. A young prince, the ninth son of Hui-tsung, fled across the Yangtze River and established a new capital at Lin-an (modern Hangchow). He was enthroned as Kao-tsung, becoming the first emperor of the Southern Sung dynasty. Unlike his father, who was more interested in the art of painting than the art of ruling, Kao-tsung stabilized Chinese territorial holdings and improved the status of the Sung in relation to the Chin conquerors. He was hailed in official chronicles as the "ruler of restoration" of the Sung. After reigning for thirty-two years, he decided to abdicate in favor of his heir (a nephew he had adopted, having no son of his own). The heir first declined the offer and then only "reluctantly accepted the request when Kao-tsung insisted." Hsiao-tsung continued to treat the abdicated Kao-tsung with great devotion and thus became a paragon of imperial filiality.[3]

K'ang-hsi said in 1708, "I admired Emperor Hsiao-tsung of the Sung, who had set a high example of filiality toward Emperor Kao-tsung and had carefully taken care of his father's well-being and pleased him [after the abdication]; therefore [probably in 1695], I told Yin-jeng: 'I shall abdicate in your favor. I shall then select a good place to live. At that time, I hope to hear good reports about your government; I will just relax and nourish my nature at ease.' "[4]

This is as clear evidence as we can find that K'ang-hsi was actually discussing abdication with his heir apparent. But before relinquishing his government to Yin-jeng, K'ang-hsi needed to discharge his remaining obligation, the definitive suppression of the Western Mongols under the chieftain of the Eleuth tribe, Galdan.

The 1690 campaign had resulted in an uneasy peace with Galdan after his defeat in battle at the hands of Prince Yü—Fu-ch'üan—the emperor's half brother. K'ang-hsi was understandably suspicious of Galdan's sincerity in seeking peace. For guidance he paid visits to the tomb of his grandmother in 1694 and 1696. She then appeared to him in a dream and told him that this time it was all right to go to battle and that he would surely defeat the enemy. Thus K'ang-hsi decided to lead another campaign against Galdan.[5]

The Ch'ing forces marched toward Galdan from three directions. The main force, led by K'ang-hsi, took the Central Route, marching north from Peking toward the Kerlon River, where Galdan was reportedly encamped; the second force, led by Generalissimo Fei-yang-ku (brother of Shun-chih's favorite consort, Donggo), attacked the enemy from Ninghsia, taking the Western Route; and the third force marched toward the enemy from the Amur region, taking the Eastern Route. The Western Route forces were particularly important, as it was K'ang-hsi's strategy to use the Eastern and Central Route forces to chase the enemy westward causing them first to be sandwiched by imperial forces and then annihilated.

Here was an excellent opportunity for K'ang-hsi to test the heir apparent's ability to rule. He made Yin-jeng his regent (*t'ing-li*, "Let [Yin-jeng] carry on the government")[6] in charge of the central administration in Peking. To facilitate their joint rule, changes were made in the transmission of documents and in decision-making procedures. Formerly all documents went to the emperor, wherever he might be. Now all documents originating from the capital would be presented to the heir apparent for decision, important matters first being deliberated by court ministers. Generalissimo Fei-yang-ku would send reports to both the emperor and the heir apparent.[7]

Leading the main offensive, K'ang-hsi commanded a force made up of the best-trained armies in the empire. He ordered his half brothers Princes Fu-ch'üan and Ch'ang-ning, as well as several of his sons, to command major divisions of the army under his direct control. During the campaign K'ang-hsi balanced the Songgotu-heir-apparent faction with the Mingju faction, both on the front and in Peking. On the front, Songgotu, who was senior, and Mingju junior, chamberlain of the Imperial Bodyguard, each took charge of a division of troops while serving as close advisers to the emperor. In the capital, the power of the heir apparent was balanced by the presence of Fu-lun, Manchu president of the Board of Rites, and Maci, Manchu president of the Board of Revenue, both of whom belonged to the Mingju faction.[8]

K'ang-hsi saw his absence from the Dowager Empress Hsiao-hui as another opportunity to display to his son his filial piety. He sent greetings and presents to her and reported on developments at the front.[9] He also conspicuously forwarded greetings to her through the heir apparent; a letter dated KH 35/3/19 (April 20, 1696) reads: "I reverently send my ten thousand greetings to the Dowager Empress. I myself am very well. All your brothers and other princes as well as ministers are fine. How are you, my Heir Apparent?"[10] Yet again, Yin-jeng failed to get the message. He was dilatory in responding to his father, often allowing days to go by without sending even a brief greeting. K'ang-hsi muffled his disappointment, but it is nonetheless evident in his correspondence with his son. For example, in a letter dated KH 35/4/27 (May 27, 1696) K'ang-hsi concludes a discussion of military developments thus:

> I have not received your memorials during these past few days. Nor have I heard any news about the well-being of the Dowager Empress. I am extremely concerned. Yesterday when Sa-pu-su came to deliver memorials, I did not see your greetings memorials to me. This caused me even more concern. I am well. All your brothers are well. How are you, my Heir Apparent?
> Enclosed you will find a memorial addressed to the Dowager Empress. Also you will find a letter that I wrote to Eunuch Ku [Wen-hsing]. This is my special instruction. As for trivial matters, I have already given you my instructions. Today I have nothing new to add.[11]

These letters were obviously written as much to set an example as to communicate.

The campaign was victorious from the start.[12] The enemy fled before any direct encounter, in their panic leaving behind the weak, camels, and supplies. Generalissimo Fei-yang-ku's army on the Western Route had been delayed, and lacking the equipment to pursue the enemy, K'ang-hsi ordered a temporary halt of his troops.

The decision was made on KH 35/5/13 (June 12, 1696). The emperor sent a small crack unit to push Galdan's forces farther west (the unit would first rendezvous with Fei-yang-ku), thus delaying Galdan's return until K'ang-hsi was ready for him. K'ang-hsi planned to resume the campaign early the next spring when he resolved to demolish the enemy. At the same time, he sent a greetings report to the dowager empress, in which he related the propitious signs he had witnessed during the campaign: clear streams had gushed forth in places where no springs had existed; scorched pastures had turned green because of timely rains; and fish were abundant in places where the enemy had found none. It was at about this time that K'ang-hsi wrote Yin-jeng a moving letter, in which he asked that some of Yin-jeng's "old clothes"—"they must be old clothes," he stressed—be sent to him so that he might wear them whenever he was missing his son.[13]

Five days later, on KH 35/5/18 (June 17, 1696),[14] a report arrived that Fei-yang-ku had scored a decisive victory in the battle at Tchao Modo, situated on the upper stream of the To-la River. The imperial forces had annihilated Galdan's remaining troops—a company of some one thousand—all of whom were fierce fighters. The enemy suffered heavy casualties under the combined barrage of archers and artillery, which they were unable to match. Galdan's warrior wife and most of his children were killed. Fewer than a hundred Eleuth retainers escaped capture and fled with Galdan toward Hami, in Chinese Turkestan. At the imperial camp pitched at Chung-t'o-ling (possibly the present Kuei-hua), the emperor ordered a state celebration at which the solemn rite of "presenting the war prisoners to the Emperor" was conducted. K'ang-hsi asked an aged captive, skilled in singing and Chinese, to improvise a song, and the old Eleuth sang a moving ballad expressing the helplessness and frustration of an imperial captive; the emperor laughed at this, and wrote a letter to his heir apparent about the joyous occasion. He also wrote the dowager empress to convey his regret at his long absence and his desire to return to her side.[15]

Everything had gone well. If K'ang-hsi still had misgivings about Yin-jeng's lack of filial devotion, the many intimate memorials written by Yin-jeng in Manchu and K'ang-hsi's responses (the correspondence is preserved in the palace archives and deals with a wide range of problems)[16] reveal that at least K'ang-hsi was satisfied with his son's political ability. Upon his return to Peking, K'ang-hsi was further heartened to hear that the heir apparent's performance as regent had been excellent: Yin-jeng was "praised by the entire court."[17] Whether this favorable report was merely propaganda orchestrated by the heir apparent we have no way of telling. But without a doubt, Yin-jeng's prestige at this time was almost as great as the emperor's.

The experience of the meritorious Chinese general Sun Ssu-k'o, commander in chief of Shansi and Kansu, who had fought under Generalissimo Fei-yang-ku at Tchao Modo, suggests the heir apparent's status. Informed of Sun's approach to the capital on KH 35/8/17 (September 12, 1696), the emperor sent military dignitaries to meet him ten *li* (about three miles) outside Peking; Songgotu and Ma-wu (the emperor's bodyguard) were among them, and they carried tea with which to entertain the general. When Sun reached Peking the next day, he was granted an audience with the emperor. At this occasion, "the Heir Apparent sat on the left side of the Emperor. The eldest son of the Emperor [Yin-shih] and his other brothers sat below the throne. In contrast, all the Manchu princes and court ministers were standing in attendance."

The emperor praised the aging general and asked if Yin-jeng could view the scar of one of his battle wounds. The heir apparent "was greatly amazed at it." Before leaving the capital, the general paid a visit to the heir apparent at his residence, and "The Heir Apparent presented him with a sedan cart drawn by four horses, and said to him: 'My honorable general, since your age is great and your way is far, this sedan, which was given to me for my use by

my imperial father, is now yours.' "[18] Upon the general's departure,
the heir apparent ordered the chamberlain of the Imperial Bodyguard to lead thirty guards from the Upper Three Banners—military divisions under the direct control of the throne—to escort him
ten *li* beyond the city wall. Formerly, imperial officials presented
greetings and bid farewell only to the emperor, but now the heir
apparent was included in these formalities: there was no doubt in
anyone's mind that Yin-jeng might assume the throne at any
moment.

But the political situation at court formed a dark background to
the prospect of abdication. Factional struggles were continuous;
corruption, injustice, and general lawlessness had eroded the moral
fiber of the government. Censorial officials, the "eyes and ears" of
the throne, were muted by "the intimidation of influential court
dignitaries," which, as K'ang-hsi later revealed, clearly pointed to
Songgotu.[19]

In early 1697, a few days before leaving the capital to resume his
military campaign, K'ang-hsi denounced the censors for their irresponsible behavior, dismissing some of them and reinstating others
who had formerly been released for outspokenness. He called upon
these officials to discover any faults committed by "the imperial
children and Manchu princes, as well as high officials at court or in
the provinces. Even I myself," he said, "would want to be reminded
of any mistakes." As may be expected, such an injunction encouraged the anti-Yin-jeng forces to report on the heir apparent's immoral conduct, which, as we will shortly see, was by then well
known. But despite these internal problems, the military campaign
was too urgent for the emperor to be distracted by court rivalries,
and K'ang-hsi soon became intoxicated with the fruit of his military
achievement.

The year 1697 appears to be the pinnacle of K'ang-hsi's happiness. When the Galdan campaign was resumed,[20] the heir apparent
again acted as the emperor's regent. K'ang-hsi requested the company of several of his other sons, including Yin-shih, the eldest, and
the fourth, Yin-chen (the future Yung-cheng Emperor); dignitaries
ordered to accompany the emperor included Songgotu, Mingju, the
emperor's maternal uncle T'ung Kuo-wei, and the grand secretary
I-sang-a, commander of the imperial artillery division. This time
the imperial army proceeded directly to the northwest, where
Galdan, with only about three hundred households of Eleuth followers left, was surrounded by the imperial armies as well as by the
forces of his own nephew Tsewang Araptan, who had deserted
Galdan out of vengeance (Galdan had killed his father and then
married his mother, A-nu).

These formidable forces closed in on Galdan. The Mongol chieftain became extremely dispirited after his son was captured by the imperial army. K'ang-hsi ordered the son transferred to the heir apparent in Peking, where the captive was exhibited to all Manchu princes, court officials, and the common people. Thwarted, Galdan committed suicide. His followers, begging imperial clemency, surrendered.

The emperor, who had considered the subjugation of Galdan his final military obligation, was exuberant. Imperial instructions sent from the front to his trusted chief eunuch, Ku Wen-hsing, expressed his joy. In one letter, dated KH 36/3/22 (April 13, 1697), K'ang-hsi says that everyone is well, making special reference to the nineteen-year-old Yin-chen: "My fourth son even gained some weight"—a Chinese expression meaning "became healthy."[21] In another letter, dated KH 36/4/17 (June 5, 1697), he writes: "I have completed my great task . . . Now Galdan is dead; his followers have all come to show their allegiance. I have completed my great task . . . Through countless hardships, I have indeed achieved this great military merit." And he concludes with the triumphant statement "As for my entire life, one can say it is happy! One can say it is one of perfect success! One can say it is one of ultimate fulfillment!"[22]

A letter dated KH 36/5/22 (June 10, 1697) again expresses his blissful feelings:

When I came out to this northern desert, my heart was as hard as stone; my determination as iron. I had vowed that I would not return until all the brigands were wiped out. Now my purpose is accomplished; my wishes fulfilled. Isn't this the will of Heaven? I am so extremely happy! So extremely joyous! What else can I do except place my hand on my forehead [a Buddhist practice] and thank Heaven by burning incense?[23]

K'ang-hsi's euphoria would soon vanish. His "stone heart" was to be shattered upon his return to Peking, where he discovered how badly he had been mistaken about his son's conduct.

PART III
Denial

7
Bad Omens

K'ANG-HSI returned to Peking in July 1697. After first sacrificing in the Imperial Ancestral Temple to thank his ancestors' spirits for their assistance in the great victory, he left the capital for his summer palace in Jehol, Inner Mongolia, to escape the heat. On that trip, he requested the company of the heir apparent as well as that of five other sons, including Yin-chih (the third) and Yin-chen (the fourth). The imperial party stayed in Jehol for three months. It was probably at this juncture that the emperor was seriously weighing the feasibility and timing of abdication, and that he also discussed the matter with the heir apparent.

On the return journey to the capital, the emperor was informed that some "base characters" "had seduced" the heir apparent, "causing his character to deteriorate drastically." The emperor ordered the immediate execution of several of these "base characters." The incident stirred up the talk at court that the heir apparent was "unfilial" and "evil."[1]

The facts behind this story are vague. The official record merely states that some bond servants serving in the Imperial Household had "frequented the Heir Apparent's residence without permission, therefore, illegally." It also says that some of the "base characters" were personnel from the Imperial Buttery, probably serving men, cupbearers, cooks, or the like; others were "personal attendants" (ha-ha chu-tzu) of a Manchu prince.[2] Since it was perfectly legal for these people to "frequent" the residence of the heir apparent, the charge of "illegal acts" had to refer to some other activity, very likely procuring (introducing "women from outside")[3] for Yin-jeng, perhaps during the trip to Jehol. Whatever the misconduct, it was

obviously serious, for the emperor later revealed that the incident
marked a turning point, that thereafter his love for the heir apparent "began to wane" and that he started to consider him unworthy
of the trust of the Imperial House.[4]

After the incident, K'ang-hsi apparently decided to postpone his
abdication indefinitely. Yin-jeng's ambitious granduncle Songgotu,
however, had grown impatient with K'ang-hsi's procrastination
regarding imperial succession.

Songgotu launched a propaganda campaign to promote the heir
apparent's cause, which used scare tactics: he threatened to kill
anyone who refused to cooperate with him, probably claiming that
K'ang-hsi would soon abdicate in favor of the heir apparent. K'ang-
hsi later charged Songgotu with "having complained constantly"
and "having criticized [K'ang-hsi's] handling of state affairs." The
complaints must have included Songgotu's resentment of K'ang-
hsi's apparent failure to fulfill his intention, revealed to Yin-jeng, to
abdicate in his son's favor.[5]

Since the emperor avoided confronting the power of the heir apparent and Songgotu, officials chose discretion for self-protection.
For this, the emperor frequently denounced the entire court for
their "lack of trustworthiness and reluctance to be frank"; he also
blamed them for only "agreeing on what the Emperor had approved, and disagreeing on what the Emperor has rejected." He exhorted them to follow the examples of the four Chinese officials Li
Kuang-ti, Kuo Hsiu, Chang P'eng-ko (later, however, to be criticized by K'ang-hsi for accommodating Songgotu and Yin-jeng),
and P'eng P'eng, who were renowned for their honesty and conscientiousness: applauding P'eng P'eng's courage in carrying out his
duty as a district magistrate, K'ang-hsi described how P'eng had
"mounted his horse with his long sword upon hearing reports of
bandits, in order to apprehend them personally."[6] The emperor's
praise of these Chinese officials was partly politically motivated, as
the greatest threat to him at this time came from the Manchus,
Songgotu primarily.

The emperor continued to use the technique of teaching by example, and in this he held up worthy Manchus as models, as well as
Chinese. The restoration of the Manchu Hsü-yüan-meng to his
position as tutor, for instance, was in part owing to Hsü's renown
as a filial son. Hsü-yüan-meng had been one of the victims of the
treacherous Mingju in the latter's attempt to sabotage K'ang-hsi's
effort to rehabilitate Yin-jeng, but six years later, in 1693, the emperor reinstated Hsü in the School for Imperial Princes (Shang-shu
fang),[7] a position Hsü would hold for twelve years, until 1715,
when he was made governor of Chekiang.

Another instance of K'ang-hsi's teaching by example involved the special favor he conspicuously bestowed on his fourth son, Yin-chen, in 1700. Toward the end of that year, the emperor assigned Yin-chen the task of drawing up an elaborate list of presents for the dowager empress's sixtieth birthday,[8] an important filial act. K'ang-hsi's selection of his fourth son—rather than any of the three older brothers—to collaborate with him in the project revealed the esteem in which Yin-chen was held.

Yin-chen's virtue contrasted with the faults of his older brothers. The eldest son, Yin-shih, was described by the emperor as "rebellious"; the trait had manifested itself in 1690 when Yin-shih quarreled with his uncle Prince Yü—Fu-ch'üan—the emperor's older half brother. Another time, the emperor feared that Yin-shih would cut off the beard of Ferdinand Verbiest, a Jesuit scientist on the imperial service, who had jokingly said he would not mind Yin-shih's doing so.[9] While it would be superfluous to repeat the unfilial acts of Yin-jeng (the second son), one might wonder why Yin-chih, the third, was not chosen for the birthday assignment, but, as the emperor later stated, Yin-chih was the only one among his children who had doubly erred, by being friendly with Yin-jeng and lacking filiality. Yin-chih had shared Yin-jeng's pleasure at his father's seemingly hopeless illness in 1690, and in 1699, after the death of Min-fei (imperial concubine of the first rank and mother of the emperor's thirteenth son, Yin-hsiang), Yin-chih "shaved his head" before the prescribed hundred-day mourning period was completed, a serious breach of filial conduct. For this offense, the emperor punished him by reducing his princely rank and by ordering all the managers of Yin-chih's household flogged a hundred times for their failure to prevent his son's act.[10]

Yin-chen—the future Yung-cheng Emperor—impressed his father with his trustworthiness, and he meticulously carried out the task of gathering the birthday presents for the dowager empress. The elaborate list included: three Buddha sculptures, a European automatic clock, some pieces of Han dynasty jade, ninety-nine assorted antiques, ninety-nine Sung- and Ming-dynasty paintings, and six horses with double saddles. The culmination was an order to the Imperial Buttery to count ten thousand grains exactly, with which to make a "porridge of jade grains" signifying tribute from "ten thousand nations in the world" to honor the dowager empress.[11]

Meanwhile, the emperor moved unobtrusively to strengthen his grip over the banner forces in Peking, frequently reshuffling military officers during the three years preceding 1700. Although imperial politics in China during this time often seem inscrutable, some of the emperor's moves—as in his rearrangement of the military—revealed purposeful patterns. For instance, because the Song-gotu faction was threatening his rule, K'ang-hsi began to rely more heavily on military officials from other branches of the imperial family (some were related by marriage): most conspicuous was the rising influence of the T'ungs—especially that of the children of T'ung Kuo-kang and T'ung Kuo-wei, two of K'ang-hsi's maternal uncles—and that of the family of the regent Ebilun.

Some of these people to gain power were: Olondai,[12] eldest son of T'ung Kuo-kang—hence a cousin of the emperor—who was made a chamberlain of the Imperial Bodyguard in 1697 and concurrently deliberative minister and lieutenant general; he served in this multiple capacity until 1702. Lungkodo,[13] third son of T'ung Kuo-wei, his aunt (sister of T'ung Kuo-kang) was K'ang-hsi's mother and two of his sisters were married to the emperor, so that he was both a cousin and a brother-in-law of K'ang-hsi's; he was promoted to deputy lieutenant general. And Alingga,[14] fifth son of Ebilun; his older sister was the late Empress Hsiao-chao (a concubine of K'ang-hsi's who had been canonized as empress upon her death); Alingga was made a chamberlain of the Imperial Bodyguard. All three of these men were later found to be hostile to Yin-jeng. But since both Songgotu and his brother Hsin-yü were also senior chamberlains at this time, the heir apparent's faction was by no means unrepresented in the Imperial Bodyguard Division, despite K'ang-hsi's reshuffling of officers.[15]

In the civil bureaucracy as well as the military, changes were being made by the emperor in his attempt to deal with the power threat of Yin-jeng and Songgotu. The emperor's approach was evidenced by the shift in influence from Chinese officials in the central bureaucracy who were friendly to the heir apparent to those who were loyal only to the emperor. The former group was represented by Yin-jeng's close tutor, Hsiung Tz'u-li, the latter by another of his tutors, Li Kuang-ti.

During his younger days, the emperor (now nearly fifty) had shown favoritism toward those Southern literati whose polished essays were written in elegant calligraphy. These literati had detrimentally influenced both court politics and the character of the heir apparent, and Hsiung Tz'u-li was a leading figure among them. The emperor now began to worry about Hsiung's relationship with Yin-jeng.

K'ang-hsi's concern was justified. In addition to being friendly with the heir apparent, Hsiung was very close to Songgotu: as Li Kuang-ti described it, "Whenever the Emperor asked for recommendations for official appointments, Songgotu always nominated Hsiung, and vice versa."[16] Over the past decade of the 1690s, Hsiung had built an impressive power base among the Chinese officials in the civil bureaucracy, and three times successively (and again in 1703) he had been appointed by the emperor—possibly under pressure from Yin-jeng—to the prestigious post of chief examiner of all metropolitan examinations, the topmost of the three civil-service examination levels in the nationwide system.

According to Chinese tradition, the chief examiner of the metropolitan examinations was regarded by all successful candidates as their "honorary mentor"[17]—the passing of the examination was spoken of as a grace bestowed by the "mentor," hence all who passed were expected to show gratitude to him. In fact, during the K'ang-hsi period the examination system was so corrupt that passing was deemed a favor done by the chief examiner, who used the tests to help his friends, and hurt his enemies. This of course led to obligations: favored candidates whom the "mentor" recommended for high government jobs were expected to follow his directions in court politics. For Hsiung the appointment to this post, combined with several other important ones—including grand secretary and the emperor's personal adviser in the South Library—put him in a strategic position. And Songgotu and the heir apparent made good use of their close relationship with Hsiung by building their power base in court through the examination system.

To counteract this bloc, K'ang-hsi turned to the independents and the anti-heir-apparent elements for help. Li Kuang-ti, the most prominent independent, was promoted to governor of Chihli (the province in which Peking is located) in 1698, and after that he often received high praise from the emperor. Wang Hung-hsü, whose opposition to the heir apparent would soon be made clear, was appointed president of the Board of Works in 1699; later he became the emperor's secret informant on court irregularities and Yin-jeng's immorality.[18]

By 1700 the emperor had begun to suspect Songgotu's loyalty as well as Hsiung Tz'u-li's responsible management of the metropolitan examinations. Soon after the metropolitan examination of that year the emperor publicly denounced the unfairness of the results. He said, "Most of the successful candidates at this year's metropolitan examination were children of high officials, whereas candidates with poor family backgrounds were seldom selected. How could you expect people not to complain about this?" He scolded the officials: "Don't you feel ashamed of yourselves in this matter?" He then asked the four aforementioned Chinese provincial officials— Li Kuang-ti; Chang P'eng-ko, director general of River Conservancy; Kuo Hsiu, governor-general of Hu-Kuang; and P'eng P'eng, governor of Kwangsi—to suggest ways to reform the system. On the basis of their responses, new rules were laid down for all three levels of the civil-service examination. One of these rules was that relatives of high officials were to be examined separately, and that they could constitute only ten percent of the total number of successful candidates.[19]

The emperor's increasing distrust of Hsiung Tz'u-li was balanced during the next two years by his growing confidence in and esteem for Li Kuang-ti. This was demonstrated by K'ang-hsi's delegating Li to recruit like-minded officials. In the winter of 1702, for example, while the emperor was in Te-chou during his Southern tour, he asked Li to recommend candidates to staff his South Library and to serve as resident tutors in his children's palaces; among others, Li recommended a noted Southern scholar named Ho Cho, a native of Soochow, in Kiangsu.[20]

Ho Cho had a long record of challenging the Southern Faction.[21] In the 1680s, during the early years of his career, he had been a resident tutor in Hsü Ch'ien-hsüeh's house, and through this association with the leader of the Southern Faction, he acquired a thorough knowledge of Hsü's dishonorable character. After 1685 he competed several times for the provincial *chü-jen* degree (comparable to a Western Master of Arts) in Chiang-nan (this province comprised both Ho's native Kiangsu and Anhwei, which each had a governor). Ho failed repeatedly, not because of a lack of scholarship, but because of his provocation of Hsü Ch'ien-hsüeh, who was the chief examiner. In one essay Ho had included sarcastic comments about the civil-service examination and Hsü's manipulation of it. This, of course, earned him a failing grade. Hsü so hated Ho that he referred to him as "that mad student," and asked the governor in Kiangsu to arrest him, probably in the late 1680s, when Hsü's power in court was at its zenith. Ho had also been a tutor in the house of Weng Shu-yüan, a grand secretary and a member of the Hsü faction. In 1687 when Ho learned that Weng had joined the impeachment drive against the honest T'ang Pin, he sent Weng an open letter asking for severance of their "mentor-student" relationship. Because of this kind of behavior, Ho was compelled to leave home and lead a life of seclusion for many years. It was during this period that he became acquainted with Li Kuang-ti.

Ho Cho's contemporaries described him as "blunt and unrelenting in nature," a person who "often criticized people to their faces." A daring critic of court politics and fiercely polemical in scholarly matters, he was nonetheless respected as an intellect and a writer. Even Fang Pao, one of the most noted essayists of the time— founder of the T'ung-ch'eng School in Chinese literature—admired Ho's literary ability: whenever Fang published an essay, he would ask people how Ho Cho had reacted to it and conceded, "Only I-men [Ho] can point out the real shortcomings in my essay." The two nevertheless constantly disagreed with each other because their personalities conflicted, and other contemporaries criticized Ho for being arrogant about his literary talent.[22]

Despite Ho Cho's arrogance and abrasiveness, the emperor needed such a scholarly official to redress the mistakes he had made in trusting the smooth-talking sycophants among the Southern literati. When the meeting took place between Ho Cho and the emperor, Ho was in his early forties: K'ang-hsi saw a man who was short, had a pock-marked face and long beard, and who wore thick eyeglasses (the emperor would later give Ho Cho a pair made of precious crystal).[23] Ho Cho reported on this meeting in a letter he wrote from Te-chou in the winter of 1702 to his brother Ho Huang:[24] "The Emperor has decided to return to Peking on the twentieth day [of the tenth month], and will resume his Southern tour in the spring, when the weather is warmer. The Heir Apparent has been ill; he is now feeling better and resuming a normal diet. But he can not return with the Emperor, because he is still too weak to ride on horseback."

Ho depicted his physical environment: "Here we had some snow flurries; but it was too light to decorate the earth. I am now borrowing a room from a local resident here. The bedroom is very dark; the outer one is somewhat brighter. I am a passenger here; the Northern wind makes one feel quite shivery." Then he related how Li Kuang-ti had recommended him to the emperor:

My mentor [Li] was kind enough to have presented my name secretly to the Emperor. On the seventeenth day [of the same month] I presented two poems to the Emperor. The Emperor then ordered that after I visit Pao-ting [provincial capital of Chihli], I should then proceed to Peking to assist the Prince [Yin-ssu] in his studies. Since you have loved me so much, I am sure you will want to share with me my joy. My scholarship is shallow; my character is not refined. I am particularly worried that I may bring shame to our family's good name.

After Ho Cho arrived in Peking in late 1702, the emperor appointed him to the staff of literary assistants in the South Library.

The emperor's choice of Ho Cho was not motivated merely by a desire to pay special attention to the education of his children—educating them all so as to keep his options open for the ultimate selection of an heir apparent; he also intended to hold Ho Cho up as a model filial son. The emperor's intention was evident from the way he treated Ho Cho's father during his Southern tour, which he resumed the next spring.[25]

When the imperial retinue arrived at Soochow, Ho's aging father, Ho Tung, appeared with local elders to meet the emperor. Knowing who he was, the emperor asked the senior Ho for his name and ordered him "to wait for an imperial instruction"[26]—probably assuring him that his son would soon receive the emperor's special permission to take the metropolitan examination in Peking. This special permission was designed to show the emperor's respect for the filial Ho Cho, for in giving it K'ang-hsi was defying the regulations of the civil-service examination system. Normally, to qualify for the metropolitan examination a candidate had to obtain the *chü-jen* degree, which Ho Cho had never succeeded in doing. The emperor "granted" Ho Cho the necessary *chü-jen* degree so that he might take the examination for the highest degree, the *chin-shih*. This came as an insult to the chief examiner, Hsiung Tz'u-li, who disliked both Ho Cho and his sponsor, Li Kuang-ti.

K'ang-hsi bestowed honorary *chü-jen* degrees on two other South Library officials, Wang Hao and Chiang T'ing-hsi, who also wanted to try for the *chin-shih*. To the emperor's great embarrassment, the examiners, headed by Hsiung Tz'u-li, were bold enough to fail all three imperial protégés. Though the examination papers were supposedly anonymous, there were hundreds of ways for the examiners to identify and pass the emperor's candidates—but only if they were willing to please K'ang-hsi. One wonders at Hsiung's effrontery.

All successful candidates in the *chin-shih* competition had personally to be examined by the emperor, a ritual known as taking the "palace test" (*tien-shih*), before they could be ranked and assigned official posts. In order to make his candidates eligible to take the palace test, the emperor in an unprecedented move granted all three the required *chin-shih* degree, on the grounds that he personally had the opinion that they were "excellent in learning."[27]

It was clear to all that the emperor in championing his candidates had knowingly slighted both the system and Hsiung Tz'u-li; his motive of commending filial paragons was perhaps not so evident to the court ministers. Ho Cho, however, was convinced of this underlying purpose of the emperor's. In a letter to his brother, he interpreted K'ang-hsi's extraordinary act as designed to "make sure that our father might see in his lifetime that I had finally made it."[28] This was the supreme fulfillment of filial piety.

The case of Wang Hao, one of the three imperial protégés, was similar. In the *Ch'ing-shih* (*Ch'ing History*), Wang Hao's biography was placed under the heading "The Filial and the Righteous." He was said to have cut off a strip of flesh from his thigh so that it could be mixed with herbs into a potion to cure his father, who had been coughing blood. When the emperor took Yin-jeng to Jehol for the summer hunting exercise, he ordered Wang Hao to accompany them and attend Yin-jeng on all fishing and hunting expeditions; he was to carry out his literary assignments near Yin-jeng's tent so that the heir apparent might somehow be inspired by Wang's spiritual influence.[29]

Hsiung Tz'u-li had clearly fallen from imperial favor. He was "released from official duty" on June 27, 1703—four days after the emperor had announced the results of the palace test—because he "had begged the Emperor's permission to retire on account of old age." Granting the request, the emperor kept him in Peking "for continuing consultations," which indicated his fear of allowing Hsiung complete freedom.[30]

Hsiung's resignation was tied to the emperor's handling of the Songgotu faction. Only two days earlier, on June 25, Songgotu's younger brother Hsin-yü had also been dismissed from his posts and deprived of his hereditary title. Two weeks before that, the emperor had publicly blamed Hsiung T'zu-li, together with Wang Hung-hsü, one of the Southern Faction leaders, for errors made in the *Ming History*. On that same day, the emperor promoted Li Kuang-ti to the presidency of the Board of Civil Appointments. The following day, when he exhorted all bannermen to cultivate the habits of filial piety and frugality, the emperor appointed Ming-ju's son K'uei-hsü, then chancellor of the Hanlin Academy, director in charge of the education of the newly selected *shu-chi-shih* (roughly parallel to postdoctoral scholars), among whom were the three imperial protégés, Ho Cho, Wang Hao, and Chiang T'ing-hsi. Ten days later, on July 1, 1703, a crisis forced the emperor to confront Songgotu's conspiracy and order his arrest.[31]

The emperor's climactic action was preceded by a series of incidents that had occurred over several months. The first took place during the Southern tour of the winter of 1702 to inspect the just-completed Yellow River conservation project;[32] because of its constant flooding, the Yellow River was a perennial problem that K'ang-hsi had long vowed to solve. The emperor left the capital on November 4, 1702, with an entourage of trusted grand secretaries and Yin-jeng (now twenty-eight), along with his sons Yin-chen (twenty-four), and Yin-hsiang (sixteen). Although still avoiding any direct disciplining of Yin-jeng, the emperor now actively supervised his son's movements, so that after 1700 K'ang-hsi requested his company on most tours. This new policy was also designed to expose Yin-jeng to local conditions in order to promote the sense of responsibility essential for the emperorship[33]—K'ang-hsi still had hopes for this son.

The imperial train arrived on November 22 at Te-chou, a city in western Shantung along the border of Chihli. The following day, Yin-jeng became suddenly ill with a "bad cold"; the emperor considered the illness "very serious,"[34] and ordered the chamberlains of the Imperial Bodyguard to summon Songgotu from Peking to attend Yin-jeng. K'ang-hsi's thinking was probably that Songgotu could best restrain the bad-humored Yin-jeng, whose violent disposition would be aggravated by illness—as the emperor later recalled, Yin-jeng continually lost his temper during this time and frequently lashed out at his attendants and guards.[35] Another reason for the emperor's action might have been "insurance"—arranging to have Songgotu take full charge ensured that in the event of Yin-jeng's death, Songgotu would have no one else to blame for possible negligence, and this would silence any accusation he might make against the emperor. Always reckless and provocative, Songgotu entered Yin-jeng's temporary lodge in Te-chou by riding his horse "right to the point of the middle gate." This was a breach of court etiquette for which he deserved severe punishment, and the chamberlains brought the matter to the emperor's attention.[36] (It was at this juncture that K'ang-hsi received Ho Cho at the recommendation of Li Kuang-ti.)

The emperor, seeing that the Grand Canal was about to freeze over, soon returned to Peking, leaving Yin-jeng in Te-chou to recuperate. He would resume the tour the following spring. Yin-jeng remained in Te-chou until January 6, 1703.

Two incidents during this period further aroused the emperor's resentment of the Songgotu-Yin-jeng faction. K'ang-hsi received secret reports that some people who publicly "claimed to be from the Imperial Presence" had gone to the provinces of Chihli and Shantung, where the emperor had just visited, "to stir up trouble" —a euphemism in official records for serious misconduct involving extortion or immorality; and no officials dared stop them. The emperor did not name the offenders, but he issued a general order authorizing provincial officials in the future to put such offenders under immediate arrest.[37] Most probably, these offenders were men under the heir apparent, since only he could have been bold enough to order them to identify themselves as being from the "Imperial Presence." The "trouble" most likely included procuring "outside women" for Yin-jeng, as had been done in 1697.

The emperor also discovered, after his return to Peking, that Songgotu's younger brother Hsin-yü had had over thirty of his household servants (*chia-jen*) beaten to death. The law stipulated that "one who has deliberately killed his bond servant shall be punished, but shall be allowed to retain his position." However, as mentioned earlier, the emperor ordered a more severe punishment: Hsin-yü was deprived of his official posts, among them chamberlain, and was stripped of his honorary title, earl of the first rank, which the emperor then conferred on the man's brother Fa-pao.[38]

K'ang-hsi's behavior shortly before resuming the Southern tour in the spring of 1703 reflected his deepening misgivings about the heir apparent. When court ministers petitioned that they be permitted to present gifts to the emperor in celebration of his fiftieth birthday (which was to fall on KH 42/3/18—May 3, 1703), K'ang-hsi flatly rejected the idea, on the grounds that during his trip provincial officials would follow suit, which would give unprincipled members of his entourage a legitimate pretext to extort money from provincials—K'ang-hsi later charged Yin-jeng with having sent his henchmen to do so. Even a japanned screen with the inscription *wan-shou wu-chiang* (long life to His Majesty) was refused; the emperor said he felt unworthy of the praise of his government written on the screen.[39]

The imperial party left Peking on March 3, immediately after the midmonth festival following the Chinese new year. Accompanied again by Yin-jeng, Yin-chen, and Yin-hsiang, the emperor first traveled by land to the T'ao-yuan district, then by water to such Southern cities as Soochow and Hangchow. It was in Soochow that the emperor granted the special audience to Ho Cho's father, and in Hangchow he donated silver to Ts'ai Sheng-yüan, a former imperial lecturer and diarist, to cover the burial expenses of a parent.[40]

The tour was rapid and short. The emperor returned to Peking on April 30, accompanied by his former literary adviser Kao Shih-ch'i.[41] K'ang-hsi invited Kao to his suburban villa, where the two spent long hours in informal conversation, just like friends reminiscing about the good old days. Kao remained in the capital until June 3 before returning to the South. A month after his departure, the emperor ordered Songgotu's arrest. Kao's connection with this imperial decision must be investigated.

When the emperor gave his order, he mentioned that as early as 1700, three years before the arrest, "a household servant" of Songgotu had secretly reported that his master was plotting against the emperor. The emperor then began undercover investigations of Songgotu's coconspirators, and one by one, they were all identified.[42] The body of the Songgotu faction turned out to be only a handful of Manchus. A few of them were military men with the rank of lieutenant general or deputy lieutenant general; others were former ministers of the Boards of Revenue and of Works who had previously been removed from office on criminal charges and had been exiled to the Manchurian frontier, although later they were allowed to return to the capital because of their old age.[43]

The leading intriguers, however, were members of the Songgotu family. The emperor ordered the arrest of Songgotu's sons as well as important figures in his household and placed them in the custody of Songgotu's brothers Hsin-yü and Fa-pao—the Manchu practice at the time was to entrust a criminal to his relatives for imprisonment. The emperor warned that if the brothers were found negligent, the whole clan would be executed.

Among the major Manchu conspirators, the emperor singled out Weng-o-li and T'ung-pao, both deputy lieutenant generals, as "by no means pardonable." The aged former ministers, such as O-k'u-li, were all imprisoned, except for A-mi-ta, who, because of his extremely advanced age, was left free.

A great many Chinese officials were also implicated in the plot; but, as the emperor put it, "if I point out all of them, their entire clans would have to be executed according to law," and since he "did not like killing," he merely warned them to dissociate themselves immediately from Songgotu's faction. The emperor did, however, arrest Chiang Huang, Songgotu's chief Chinese collaborator: many pieces of correspondence between him and Songgotu were discovered after a search of Chiang's house, and the evidence was so overwhelming that it made the charges against Songgotu indefensible. The emperor was tempted to order a search of Songgotu's house as well, but in doing so, he reasoned, "many people will be implicated and the entire court will be in turmoil," so he decided not to pursue it.[44]

The Songgotu conspiracy generated so much interest throughout the empire that it later became the basis for an opera, *Songgotu's Residence Is Searched*. With Songgotu as the arch-villain, the opera's heroes were Shih Shih-lun and Chang P'eng-ko, both having been praised by the emperor as "the most honest officials in the entire nation." Though their role in the Songgotu arrest is in fact uncertain, the opera shows the excitement aroused by this dramatic episode.[45]

Songgotu died in confinement shortly thereafter. The record is vague as to why the emperor waited three years to quash the plot, and who actually reported the conspiracy. Whereas in the official record the emperor identified the accuser as "a household servant of Songgotu," a contemporary observer named Kao Shih-ch'i.[46]

If it was Kao Shih-ch'i, the secret was well kept, and the heir apparent was obviously not aware of Kao's hostility to Songgotu. At the end of Kao's visit, Yin-jeng showed him unusual deference and cordiality, which suggests a special relationship that Yin-jeng wanted to maintain.[47] The prince summoned Kao to his palace and talked to him kindly; he offered him many parting presents: a poem he had composed, a four-character plaque reading "Everlasting Springtime in the Southern Terrace," a felt cap, and two silk robes with the imperial-dragon motif—one of which was inlaid with diamonds and other precious stones. Yin-jeng also ordered his bodyguard, Ssu-ko, and his trusted eunuch, Chou Chin-ch'ao, to escort Kao to T'ung-chou, and he gave Kao his own donkey to ride. Even after Kao left Peking, Yin-jeng asked some servants to hurry after him to proffer additional gifts: four snuff bottles and a can of snuff.

The emperor did not forget Kao once he had returned to the South. Possibly suspecting collusion between Kao and the heir apparent, he authorized Sung Lao, governor of Kiangsu, to report on Kao in "secret palace memorials," a means of confidential communication K'ang-hsi had developed in the early 1690s in order to learn more about local conditions throughout the empire. Li Hsü, the Soochow textile commissioner, was another secret agent instructed to spy on Kao.[48]

Shortly after his return to the South—when the summer heat was unbearable—Kao died. Some said that he was poisoned by Mingju because Mingju wanted to avenge his betrayal by Kao in 1688.[49] Such a sensational interpretation of the death reflects the intensity of contemporary hatred for this man who had been a corrupting influence on the emperor and on court morality.

Knowledge of the Songgotu conspiracy must have convinced the emperor of the danger that a similar attempt might be made again by supporters of the heir apparent. He felt "uneasy day and night, not knowing whether I would be poisoned today or killed tomorrow."[50] Naturally, he began to lean more and more on the loyal independents at court and to think about the inevitable confrontation he was approaching with the heir apparent.

It is still not clear whether at this time K'ang-hsi believed Yin-jeng knew any details of the Songgotu plot; but he was persuaded that it was unwise to leave Yin-jeng alone in Peking. When he went on a western tour later that year, he again took the heir apparent with him. Leaving Peking on November 19, 1703, the imperial party visited T'ai-yuan, provincial capital of Shansi, and Sian, provincial capital of Shensi; both cities were in strategic locations, where heavy military forces—banners as well as the Green Standard (Chinese forces)—were stationed. The trip took sixty-eight days.[51]

Accompanying the emperor besides Yin-jeng were his third son, Yin-chih, and his thirteenth son, Yin-hsiang. Also in the party were trusted officials such as the grand secretary Maci; Li Kuang-ti, president of the Board of Civil Appointments; and Ch'a Sheng, the emperor's favorite literary secretary in the South Library, whose calligraphy K'ang-hsi particularly admired.

The governor of Shansi, Gali, was the heir apparent's man, corrupt and cruel. K'ang-hsi had intended to visit Shansi in order to learn about the hardship of the people; what Gali did to the citizens both before and during the trip only aggravated their problems. Li Kuang-ti noted in his diary that before the arrival of the imperial party, Gali had ordered the populace to await the emperor on the roadside all night—and the temperature was below freezing; Li asked the people why they had endured this, and they said, "We have been forced to come by official warrants; we did not dare to refuse to comply."

Gali was bold enough to tell Li Kuang-ti and his colleagues how much his elaborate preparations had cost: "I spent 180,000 taels of silver just for the temporary palaces; and now I need at least 150,000 additional taels to be used for presents and gifts."[52] He could not have failed to remember how the emperor had sternly warned governors not to exact money from the local people for imperial visits or for presents to members of his party; "courts-martial" were threatened for any violators of the decree.[53] Gali's quotation of these figures mocked the emperor's claims that his tours were entirely financed by the Imperial Household. This governor's audacity in defying the emperor suggested one thing: he had a powerful backer, who was probably no less a personage than the heir apparent.

Li further revealed in his diary how Gali had supplied the imperial party—who else, if not the heir apparent himself?—with Southerners for sexual pleasures. On the temporary palaces Gali set up for the imperial visit, Li wrote: "At every stop of the imperial party, a temporary palace was built. Pleasure boys and courtesans mingled with the service personnel in it. Every other year, famous experts were hired from the South to be their trainers."[54]

Yin-jeng was the one possible figure behind Gali's outrageous behavior—later the emperor was to charge only Yin-jeng with illicit sexual acts committed during the western tour; he never accused the two other sons who had accompanied him, Yin-chih and Yin-hsiang. But still the emperor did not speak out in public against his own son.

8
The Lure of
the South

K'ANG-HSI made six Southern tours in his lifetime. He made the first in 1684, the second in
1689. During the ensuing decade, he was preoccupied with the
Galdan campaigns and was unable to make his third tour until
1699. The last four tours (not counting the unfinished one in 1702)
were made within eight years: 1699, 1703, 1705, and 1707.[1]

The emperor's stated reasons for these tours, such as to "inspect
river-conservation works" in the Yellow River region or "to learn
firsthand about local conditions and customs," were not his only
motives in visiting the South. Doubts about the political stability of
the area and about the loyalty of the Southern literati prompted
him to keep in close touch with the region. In addition, the fascina-
tion the South held for him played a role in K'ang-hsi's involvement
with that part of his empire.

Contemporary records of the 1705 tour provide us with an excellent opportunity to examine the behavior of the emperor and the
heir apparent within the social milieu of the South; the cultural influence of the South on the Manchu conquerors; and the political
reasons for K'ang-hsi's increasingly frequent tours at the turn of the
eighteenth century.

The political stability of the South had long been a concern of the
emperor's. The region had harbored anti-Manchu sentiment since
the founding of the Ch'ing regime, as Yangchow, Hangchow, and
others cities near T'ai Lake were the sites of the worst atrocities
committed by Manchu horsemen. The Ssu-ming Mountains, southeast of Hangchow and not far from the port of Ningpo, were also a
trouble spot, because of the large-scale banditry carried on there.
Since the South was on the sea, the early Ch'ing emperors—K'ang-

hsi and his father, Shun-chih—were alert to possible alliances between Southern dissenters and foreign enemies. In 1700, for example, K'ang-hsi learned from some Ningpo copper merchants that
there were disturbances in Japan which might indicate military
movements for an invasion of China; alarmed at this news, the
emperor asked the textile commissioners from Soochow, Hangchow, and Kiangning (Nanking), who were all imperial bond servants, to send Imperial Household spies to Japan to assess the danger. (The agents returned with their reports in 1702.)[2]

But the most ominous threat from the South was the persistent
rumor of the existence there of a certain Chu San T'ai-tzu, meaning
"the third Heir Apparent of the Ming royal house," a son of the last
emperor of the defunct Ming dynasty.[3] Given the inadequacy of
K'ang-hsi's own crown prince, it is understandable that the emperor was worried about this possible pretender to the throne.

Meanwhile, the Songgotu plot had caused K'ang-hsi to suspect
Yin-jeng's collusion with the Southern literati, and he accordingly
ordered agents to spy on such men as Kao Shih-ch'i and, later,
Hsiung Tz'u-li. (Hsiung, after resigning as grand secretary in 1703
and being detained by K'ang-hsi in Peking, was then allowed to retire to Nanking, where the secret agent Ts'ao Yin continued to report on his daily movements.)[4]

Confucian ideology held that the lack of virtue at the center of
the empire would inevitably evoke Heaven's response on the peri-
phery—unrest and calamities, man-made or natural—as a warning
that it would withdraw its Mandate. The combination of conspiracy
at court, anti-Manchu sentiment in the South, and the rumor of a
Ming pretender posed a serious threat to the security of the K'ang-
hsi regime.

Not surprisingly, the emperor, as he revealed later, wanted to
take Yin-jeng along on his Southern tours so that the heir apparent
might become "acquainted with local customs and the people's
hardship";[5] K'ang-hsi believed his successor had a duty to know the
real empire, with all its problems. It was a final attempt to mold
Yin-jeng's sense of responsibility, an attempt, in fact, to change his
personal behavior. But the emperor's preparations for the tour suggest that he had serious misgivings.

The 1705 tour was preceded by secret correspondence between
the emperor and Ts'ao Yin, in Nanking. On August 29, 1704, Ts'ao
Yin had sent a palace memorial, in which, after greeting the emperor and thanking him for his appointment as salt censor for the
Liang-Huai region (which covered Yangchow, Nanking, and Soochow), he then requested an audience with K'ang-hsi. The emperor
wrote in response: "I am very well. You don't need to come here.

Next spring I intend to have a tour of the South, although I have not really decided on the matter." Then the emperor, having perceived that Ts'ao Yin wanted to report something confidential, continued: "In case you have matters difficult to handle or you feel perplexed about them, you may ask me for instruction by sending me a secret memorial." The emperor closed with an apprehensive warning about the breach of confidentiality: "But you should never allow anyone else to write the secret memorials for you. For if there should be any divulging, the consequences might be very grave. Be careful! Be careful! Be careful! Be careful!"[6]

The tone of this imperial note suggests that K'ang-hsi's intention of touring the South was not just for the inspection of river dikes. Rather, he was more motivated by political concerns. The impact on the South of his forthcoming tour was much on his mind; among other things, he promised courts-martial for anyone who dared to bribe members of his retinue.[7]

The imperial entourage left Peking on March 3, 1705, and returned to the emperor's Suburban Villa, outside Peking, on June 18.[8] A diary written by an anonymous member of the imperial retinue describes the interaction of the emperor and his son during this trip.[9]

Most important, the heir apparent made himself visible: despite tensions between father and son, both seemed intent on projecting an air of harmony. When audiences were being granted to local officials, Yin-jeng sat next to his father to accept their greetings. He asked their names, even trying at times to be informal with some of his father's favorite local dignitaries. When Captain P'an Ch'ao-en appeared to greet the emperor, the heir apparent struck up a dialogue with him, saying, "What kind of official are you?" P'an answered, "I am a naval captain, taking charge of river control. I received this post last time [during the 1703 tour] as a favor bestowed upon me by Your Excellency, the Heir Apparent!" After the audience, the emperor ordered that P'an be promoted to brigade general, because "His Majesty was struck by P'an's impressive physique!" P'an "bumped his head against the ground to kowtow in gratitude for the imperial favor."[10]

The emperor was generous in his favors to military officials, which probably reflected his preoccupation with local unrest. An example of this is his cordiality to the Chinese commander in chief, Chang Yün-i, son of Chang Yung, a famous general with impressive military records in the emperor's campaigns against the Three Feudatories and the Western Mongols.[11] Upon seeing the commander in chief, the emperor said, "You look ill and skinny!" "Yes," Chang said, "I have been ill. I have used all the medicine

Your Majesty granted me before, and did not dare to request more." The emperor replied, "You are different from the others! Any time you want medicine, just ask for it!" Then he turned to Yin-jeng and said, "You remember this. As soon as we return to our temporary palace, we will send medicine to the commander in chief." Yin-jeng remembered, or his father remembered without prompting, for after their return K'ang-hsi sent his eunuch Liang Chiu-kung with quinine for Chang. He also sent gifts: an ink slab, robes and hats worn by the emperor himself, and a horse K'ang-hsi had ridden—all signifying rare intimacy between the emperor and a military official. Chang Yün-i was rewarded the most lavishly of all the officials encountered on the tour.

The heir apparent later sent a special message to the commander in chief, hinting that he might not have allowed the emperor to give Chang the ink slab: "That particular ink slab was made according to my personal specifications and offered to the Emperor as my personal present. I have just learned that the ink slab has been given you as a gift, but I am very happy. This is because you, my commander in chief, are an intelligent and careful person, who must know its value. Had it been someone else, I would not have consented to its being given away!"[12] The heir apparent, realizing the value of a loyal and competent commander in chief, was making an effort to woo him.

This audience was held in Soochow. Later the emperor took the time to visit Sungkiang, where Chang's headquarters were located, and stayed there for six days. This gesture, along with the imperial gifts, reflected both admiration and the emperor's concern with the importance of the unswerving loyalty of a key military commander.

Another feature of the tour was the extravagant offering of gifts and money by officials to the emperor and the heir apparent, even though the emperor had warned local officials not to do this. On April 7, when K'ang-hsi arrived at Chin-shan Temple, just south of the Yangtze River, one hundred tables laden with delicacies were prepared for the imperial party, and presents were offered to the emperor, including various antiques, curios, rare books, T'ang- and Sung-dynasty paintings, foreign lacquer-ware cups, jade cups, and a parrot carved in white jade.[13]

On such an occasion, despite his orders to the contrary, K'ang- hsi's custom was to accept a few rare books, or a brush stand or similar calligraphic article, and return everything else. But this pattern was not followed when presents were offered to both the emperor and the heir apparent. In these cases, the anonymous diarist did not indicate that the emperor returned anything, implying that he was compelled to keep the presents in order to go along with the heir apparent. For example, on the same day as the Chin-shan

Temple visit, salt merchants from Yangchow presented a hundred antique items, sixty for the emperor and forty for his son, and all were accepted. In addition, the heir apparent received antiques and other items from the attending officials.[14] On May 5, Asan, governor-general of Chiang-nan, presented a large variety of gifts to the emperor, the heir apparent, and even the imperial concubines and other palace women. Included were 160 bolts each of silk and satin; thirty antique pieces, and thirty Szechwan horses—the heir apparent received twenty antique items, and for the women there were also pomanders, powder puffs, fragrant pillows, and perfume. The diarist made a special note: "All these items were accepted."[15]

In return, Yin-jeng, apparently cultivating his image as a good prince, was deferential to family members of meritorious officials, and sometimes he made them gifts of his own literary pieces, to be displayed in their houses.[16]

As extravagant as the gifts, the entertainment provided in the South delighted both emperor and heir apparent. The excellent Southern food and opera particularly appealed to them. On June 26, again in Soochow, the emperor was so pleased by a banquet given by the commander in chief Chang Yün-i that he instructed the Imperial Banqueting Court to invite the local cooks to the imperial boats to give lessons to the members of the Imperial Buttery.[17]

The emperor's interest in Southern theater went back a long way. Beginning in the 1680s, Southern operas were enjoyed in the palace. In 1693 the Soochow textile commissioner Li Hsü—one of K'ang-hsi's secret agents—pleased the emperor by informing him that he had "discovered a few young girls, whom I hope to present to Your Majesty for your enjoyment after I have properly trained them." The emperor responded by dispatching a special voice instructor, most probably a Southerner who was training the imperial troupers in Peking, to Soochow to help teach Li's new troupe. Thus, opera performances on the Southern tours had a well-established tradition.

The arrangements for the imperial banquets and theatrical productions were handled largely by the local salt merchants, who were beholden to the emperor for the salt monopoly. The "head merchant," Ch'eng Wei-kao, was conspicuously mentioned in the diary.[18]

It is not surprising that the emperor and his party made extended stays in Soochow both on the way south and on their return to Peking; on the 1705 tour a total of fifteen days were spent in Soochow.[19]

K'ang-hsi probably never anticipated the consequences of his enjoyment of the beguiling Southern culture, especially in Soochow. But he was soon to realize that this pleasure was both costly to the local people and detrimental to his son's character, as well as the morality of the imperial court.

The expense of the Southern entertainment was great. Li Hsü, for example, spent tens of thousands of taels just for the costumes for one play. Other expenditures, such as for the orchestra, sets, and other equipment, must have been equally large. The drawing of funds from the government treasury to meet these costs was one of the main reasons for the empty coffers at all levels of government in the South.[20]

The banquets were similarly extravagant, and the frequency of these galas was such that a tour became almost a pure pleasure jaunt. On March 30 during the 1705 tour, the imperial group entered the province of Chiang-nan, and within three weeks the emperor enjoyed no fewer than fourteen banquet-operas staged by officials or prominent local gentry. The diarist recorded some glimpses of these occasions:

> On April 2 [at Yangchow] eleven plays were performed in the imperial traveling lodge. They were performed by six actors or actresses selected from the troupe of the Ch'eng family, members of the local gentry. The Emperor was greatly pleased by the superb performances.
>
> The salt merchants of Yangchow had prepared a garden villa to serve as the Emperor's temporary palace. On April 5 Ts'ao Yin, the salt censor, begged the Emperor to lodge in it, along with the Heir Apparent, the thirteenth son of the Emperor [Yin-hsiang], and the female members of the imperial family. Operas were performed; banquets given.
>
> Tso Pi-fan, prefect of Yangchow, known for his superb official performance, was granted an exceptional promotion to the post of director of the palace stud.
>
> At about 10 p.m. dragon lanterns with five colors shone as brightly as daylight.[21]

In addition, while the imperial party was sailing to Soochow, operas were staged along the Yangtze River. Upon their arrival at Soochow—where the party stayed in the house of Li Hsü—K'ang-hsi, Yin-jeng, and Yin-hsiang each demonstrated their archery, after which the emperor granted an audience to local officials. Then the banquets and operas started again.[22]

Sometimes the emperor selected the opera to be performed; to commemorate his fifty-second birthday (April 11, 1705), for example, he ordered that the story *Happiness of Peace* (*T'ai-p'ing lo*) be enacted. His love of Chinese theater was so strong that when rain prevented a performance, female singers were summoned to perform for the imperial party.[23]

The diary does not mention the titles of the operas that were staged, but a Soochow gazetteer records that the emperor's current favorite, in which Li Hsü had painstakingly drilled his troupe, was taken from the story *Romance of the Palace of Eternal Life (Ch'ang-sheng tien ch'uan-ch'i)*. This story was the source of more than fifty episodes, and one can safely assume that at least some of these episodes were performed for the imperial party during the 1705 tour.[24]

The play is a historical tragedy with a theme tailored to the emperor's pedagogical approach to the heir apparent (who was by now infamous for his extravagance and indulgence in sensual pleasures, according to later comments by K'ang-hsi). The hero of the play is the Emperor Ming Huang (A.D. 685-762), of the T'ang dynasty. Upon ascending the throne in 712, he consolidated his rule by crushing a contender—his aunt. Striving to check court tendencies toward extravagance and debauchery, he set an example for his subjects as a monarch of great austerity, and his reign saw one of the peaks of prosperity in the entire history of imperial China. A patron of literature and himself a celebrated poet, Ming Huang extolled Confucian morality by publishing an edition of the *Classic of Filial Piety;* fond of music, he is credited as the founder of Chinese theater.

In 734 Ming Huang's character suddenly began to deteriorate after he fell madly in love with the renowned concubine Yang Kuei-fei. "From this time forth," Ming Huang held "no more audiences in the hours of early morn"—as Po Chü-i vividly depicted her influence on the emperor in his famous poem "The Song of Everlasting Regret." Serious neglect of his administration, owing to indulgence in sensual pleasures under the tutelage of his beloved "subverter of empires," eventually caused Heaven to withdraw the Mandate from Ming Huang. An insurrection broke out and the monarch had to flee the rebels to Szechwan. Yang Kuei-fei was murdered by his own soldiers, and Ming Huang abdicated in favor of his son.[25]

K'ang-hsi brought another historical example of deterioration to Yin-jeng's attention. This was the story of Sui Yang-ti (personal name: Yang Kuang), a famous emperor of the Sui dynasty (A.D. 589-618).

Sui Yang-ti made frequent visits to Yangchow, where he was overwhelmed by the exotic Southern culture: wine, women, and sensual luxuries. He was murdered and buried in Yangchow, where his tomb became a reminder to imperial rulers of the corrupting influences of the Southern way of life. This tragedy was obviously on K'ang-hsi's mind when he visited that city.

On April 6, the second day that he was entertained in the fabu-

lous garden villa prepared by the Yangchow salt merchants, K'ang-
hsi composed a poem, accompanied by a brief prefatory note. First
the note:

> Every time I visit the South, I am fascinated by the elegance of its
> scenery and the beauty of its rivers. Though your sovereign, I possess
> the same desire to enjoy the charms of mountains and rivers. I would
> not want to linger here too long, however, lest I should bring inconve-
> niences to the people. This is why I am afraid that staying here even one
> more day may evoke criticism in the future and thus distort the truth.
>
> The temporary palace at the Chu-i Creek was established by salt mer-
> chants and the local people to show their gratitude. Although this in-
> volved no local officials, the costs amounted to several thousand taels. I
> remember reading the story about Emperor Wen, of the Han [r. 179-155
> B.C.], who was praised by later generations for his regrets about spend-
> ing one hundred taels for a pavilion [?]. How much more should I feel
> regretful for having had you spend ten times more for only three days of
> my stay. I have thus composed the following poem as a self-warning. I
> also want to post these verses on the wall of the villa in order to show
> my feeling to the people of Yangchow.

The poem reads:

> Once again, I am dwelling in the Tower Creek and beholding
>   the quintessence of things;
> But it is shabby cottages surrounded by hemp and mulberry
>   trees that I see first.
> While gentle breezes waft everywhere in the city of Yangchow
> Timely rains fall on every house in the Chekiang and Kiangsu
>   region.
> A ruler, following the Way, levels the giant mountains for the
>   nation—I take him as my mirror.
> Sui Yang-ti indulged himself in watching rare Yangchow
>   flowers—I pity him with a long sigh.
> Oh, that my heart might be filled with the knowledge of
>   Classics and histories, so as to bring peace to the nation;
> Oh, that I would not let it be driven to follow my lusts and my
>   craving for extravagance.[26]

K'ang-hsi's reference to Sui Yang-ti's deterioration after his ex-
posure to Southern culture is poignant because, despite more than a
thousand years between the two rulers, the schism between China's
North and South still existed. And the lure of Southern ease and
elegance still exerted a powerful attraction. K'ang-hsi felt the pull
and, more serious, Yin-jeng seemed to have been ensnared by the
South, much as Sui Yang-ti had been.

Given Yin-jeng's behavior on the western tour of 1703—when he had ordered his henchman Gali to hire Southern "trainers" to coach those "pleasure boys" and "courtesans" (undoubtedly also from the South)—one would certainly expect him to repeat this performance while in the exciting South. Our anonymous diarist of the 1705 tour reported two visits to temples made by the imperial family; these occasions are fully described.[27] But whenever the diarist mentioned Yin-jeng's visits to temples, only a terse sentence—"The Heir Apparent paid a visit to such-and-such a temple"—is provided. The omission of details in these entries arouses suspicion about the nature of Yin-jeng's visits to temples, since temples were the sites of amorous adventures.

According to a Soochow custom encouraged by some "licentious monks," local women swarmed to temples to engage in religious worship at night; these women "were topless, with candles kindled on their shoulders," a practice known as "burning the fleshly candlestick." Day in and day out, they "mingled with men" in the temples "to repay the debts" to their dead mothers.[28] The Soochow monks were found to "have invited prostitutes" to their temples. Wealthy and powerful, the men "drank wine, ate meat, loved gambling and engaging in illicit sex." They were accused of having "secured women through kidnapping or other fraudulent means and storing them in their temples for personal pleasures." Often nuns—who were not all religious, having entered convents for economic reasons—dressed themselves in flashy male garments, without shaving their heads, to entice men and women alike, so that "they were no different from prostitutes."[29]

Gaily decorated boats, moored along the Yangtze and its many tributaries, provided yet another way for the heir apparent to pass his nights. On these boats Southern literati—who were fond of composing "erotic verses"—held drinking parties, where "wine, music, and courtesans"[30] were in abundance.

These are conjectures about Yin-jeng's activities, but they are later (1708) reinforced by K'ang-hsi's confessions, in which he accused Yin-jeng of leaving the temporary palaces and the imperial boats during his tours: "When I toured Shensi, Chiang-nan, and Chekiang, I either stayed in temporary palaces or lived on boats. Never did I stray to outside places for illegitimate reasons; never did I cause disturbances to the people. But, alas! Yin-jeng and his men behaved recklessly, perversely, and evilly. They almost exhausted all possible depravity."[31]

Yin-jeng's "straying to outside places" pointed to amorous adventures, and the emperor said, "It would be a great embarrassment for me to use words to describe it!"[32] But, shortly after the above charge was made, the emperor described Yin-jeng's offense much more specifically—to the extent that the style of official language would allow: "I never allowed women from outside to frequent my palace; nor did I ever allow fair-looking boys to serve me at my side. I have thus kept my body absolutely clean, without blemish . . . Now the Heir Apparent had done all these!"[33]

Supporting K'ang-hsi's statements, the Korean envoys at Peking twice reported to their king on the heir apparent's immoral behavior. A report from 1708 says, "The common people all spread the words, saying [the heir apparent] is disloyal and unfilial; he secretly gathered women from outside."[34] And a 1712 report says, "The Heir Apparent did not change his old habit of getting intoxicated by wine and women; and he dispatched personal agents to affluent places all over the thirteen provinces in order to extort money and to gather beautiful women by force."[35] Since Yin-jeng's amorous behavior was characterized here as an "old habit" and the emperor was too embarrassed to use words to describe it, it is possible to deduce what happened in 1705.

Yin-jeng's interference in local politics during the tour was well documented. One incident concerned the victimization of an honest and loyal Chinese official, an independent belonging to the Li Kuang-ti group, named Ch'en P'eng-nien. In preparation for the emperor's tour, the governor-general of Chiang-nan, Asan—as much the heir apparent's man as was Gali in Shansi—proposed to add a surcharge to the tax in his provinces. Ch'en P'eng-nien, prefect of Soochow under Asan's direct jurisdiction, was adamantly opposed to this idea, and protested that the emperor had expressly forbidden such a practice. Ch'en was probably unaware of the fact that Asan's proposal was intended to please not the emperor but the heir apparent. Though Asan dropped the proposal, he was offended by the stubborn prefect and sought to ruin Ch'en.

When the emperor's party made a stop at Lung-t'an, a city in Ch'en's prefecture not far from Kiangning (Nanking), K'ang-hsi was enraged to discover "earthworms and other loathsome things" in his bed—put there by Asan's men. The heir apparent said this was Ch'en's fault and pressed the emperor to put him to death. K'ang-hsi was intelligent enough to guess what had happened, but he was reluctant to oppose Yin-jeng. It was said that he first asked the opinion of Chang Ying, a retired grand secretary and longtime tutor of the heir apparent, who commended Ch'en's moral integrity. When Yin-jeng insisted and the emperor seemed to yield to his pressure, Ts'ao Yin intervened at the risk of his life: he "bumped his head against the ground unceasingly," kowtowing to the emperor and pleading forgiveness for Ch'en P'eng-nien. Only then did

K'ang-hsi spare Ch'en's life. A year later, Asan again attacked Ch'en, accusing him of "disrespect" for imperial instructions and requesting his immediate execution. The emperor, striking a compromise, released Ch'en from his post and ordered him to serve as an editor of imperial compilations in Peking.[36]

At the same time in Peking, an even more shocking miscarriage of justice was taking place that could be traced to Yin-jeng. This was the trial of Ch'en Ju-pi, director of selections on the Board of Civil Appointments, who had crossed members of Yin-jeng's faction by his refusal to make certain appointments that they desired. Ch'en's trial at the top level of the Chinese judicial system—the Court of the Three Judiciaries—was a travesty. The heads of each of the three components of the court were united by loyalty to Yin-jeng: Shu-lu, of the Censorate; Wang Shan, of the Board of Punishments; and Lao Chih-pien, of the court of Judicature and Revision. Fortunately, through the reports of his informant Wang Hung-hsü, K'ang-hsi learned the full details of the torture, twisted testimony, and outright buying of the judges. He was therefore able to clear Ch'en Ju-pi and dismiss a number of important officials involved in the case. Again, although Yin-jeng's involvement was never directly mentioned, only the heir apparent could have had the power to intimidate so many senior bureaucrats and to make Wang Hung-hsü beg the emperor himself to be cautious.[37]

THE SPYING AND counterspying between the emperor and the heir apparent during the 1707 trip to the South—the last of K'ang-hsi's six grand tours of the region—exacerbated the father-son tension. With new insights into Yin-jeng's immorality, K'ang-hsi's policy of tolerance toward his son faced a stern test: continuation of such a policy might cost him the Mandate of Heaven, that most essential element of Confucian political philosophy. Fear of losing the Mandate was closely connected in the emperor's mind with the supreme value of filial piety, for the greatest act of unfilialness would be to lose the empire that he had inherited from his father and which he had strengthened with the indispensable assistance of his grandmother. But the Heir Apparent Yin-jeng was also an inheritance K'ang-hsi had received from his grandmother. Here, then, lay K'ang-hsi's dilemma.

There were clear indications that K'ang-hsi's heart was troubled the year before the 1707 tour, when he began to read Heaven's bad omens. In early 1706 K'ang-hsi was distressed by a drought, and expressed his apprehension at this sign in a secret correspondence with Li Hsü: "Furthermore, I have something to remind you earnestly. Whenever you run into those stupid fools from the capital

telling you to do this or that, you must not listen to them at all
times. This idea of mine is very important. Don't you be negligent
about it."[38] One wonders why the emperor was so indirect in handling those "stupid fools." He could simply have ordered Li Hsü to
arrest them. Why was he so fearful of confronting the power behind these people?

Shortly after this secret communication to Li Hsü, more worri-
some signs appeared. Rice prices in Soochow took a big jump, a
severe earthquake shook the imperial palaces in Peking, and there
were indications of a possible revolt in Taiwan, which might swell
into an invasion of the mainland.[39]

K'ang-hsi's responses to these omens remained indirect or at best
preventative. It was in late 1706 that he ordered Hsiung Tz'u-li—
whom he had detained in Peking following his resignation—to
return to his native Nanking, in the South; no explanation was
given for the action. Ts'ao Yin then kept a close watch on Hsiung,
for K'ang-hsi strongly suspected him.[40]

The emperor maintained his surveillance of Yin-jeng. In early
1706 he took Yin-jeng with him on a tour of the vicinity of the capital; then they traveled to the Jehol summer palace during the hot
months, and, upon returning to Peking, the two went to the Tombs
of Filiality, where the emperor sacrificed to his father and grandmother.[41] In imperial politics such an apparently pious function
could not be interpreted merely as a routine exercise in filiality, for
in K'ang-hsi's case it often meant that he had a problem and wished
to consult his grandmother's spirit. The question this time was
whether he ought to accept the suggestion that he make another
tour of the South.

The tour was not at all justified, but the heir apparent's faction
pushed for it, since Yin-jeng wanted to return to the sensual South.
When Asan, governor-general of Chiang-nan and Kiangsi, and a
strong supporter of the heir apparent, first memorialized that
K'ang-hsi must go south to investigate the Liu Huai-t'ao project for
flood control, K'ang-hsi rejected the petition on the grounds that
his presence was not necessary; it was significant that he added in
his refusal that he "had caused nuisances" to the local people in his
previous Southern tours. Despite the repeated efforts of the entire
bureaucracy to urge him to accept Asan's suggestion, K'ang-hsi refused to make a quick decision on the matter. Meanwhile, on December 24, 1706, Asan was transferred from the South to Peking to
fill the newly vacated post of the Manchu president of the Board of
Punishments, a post controlled by Yin-jeng's henchmen.[42]

After long reflection, K'ang-hsi finally decided to make the trip
south, but only after he had protected himself with the cloak of

filial piety. He referred the matter to the Dowager Empress Hsiao-hui for "instruction." Very likely under the prodding of the heir apparent, the dowager empress advised K'ang-hsi to accept the suggestion to make the tour, for, she argued, "I think the project is a weighty matter; this is why the court petitioned you in one accord. It would be very beneficial to the locality as well as the local people if you could make a visit to give your personal instructions." K'ang-hsi announced to the court on January 30, 1707, that he would travel south, "in obedience to the instruction of my August Mother."[43]

The visit turned out to be nothing but a farce. It took the emperor a month to get to the site of the project—through the frozen Grand Canal, in which the thick ice had to be broken up by hand—but it took him only one day to discover that he had been deceived by his officials. The project was found to be utterly unworkable: it did not follow the plans previously presented to him; people's houses and fields as well as their ancestral graveyards would have to be destroyed; and the plans called for the nearly impossible task of cutting through high mountains.[44]

Only an official who had apparently lost his senses would ever have dared to deceive the emperor in this manner. The emperor's word was law and he could order the execution of such an offender. But instead of dealing with the real author of the fraudulent scheme, K'ang-hsi rebuked the director-general, Chang P'eng-ko, and all the local officials involved in the project. Only after he returned to the capital did he order the dismissal of Asan from his post as president of the Board of Punishments, when he had acquired reliable information that "Asan alone insisted on the workability of the project, ignoring the strong objections from Chang P'eng-ko and other high provincial officials."[45]

In the meantime, once he had arrived at the flood-control project, K'ang-hsi decided to travel farther south. During the rest of the tour the emperor received more reports about his son's behavior while traveling with his father. Yin-jeng's frenzied hunting for "pretty girls" and "fair-looking boys" explained why he had urged his imperial father to make another Southern tour, even if it required setting up a fake river project.

On April 18, the second day after the imperial party had arrived at Soochow, K'ang-hsi passed a note to Wang Hung-hsü by the hand of his trusted chief eunuch, Li Yü.[46] The note contained a secret order to Wang to begin a personal investigation of the illicit traffic in young girls and boys. K'ang-hsi judged the matter so sensitive that he warned Wang: "You must write your report secretly with your own hand. You must not let anyone else know of your

report. If it should be known by others, you will run into problems."[47]

Wang's reports contained startling revelations of vices and crimes
committed by personnel either from or closely associated with the
Imperial Household and the Imperial Bodyguard. These people
were indeed trafficking in girls and boys, resorting to any number
of outrageous methods. Local officials in charge of maintaining law
and order openly assisted them in their crime; they issued "warrants" and used the threat of force to make parents sell their children to buyers. These officials claimed authority "from the Imperial presence." Local influential salt merchants and copper brokers who traded with Japan—as contractors of the Imperial Household, these people represented its economic interests—participated
in this illicit operation. "Too many people and too many parties"
were involved in the enterprise, as Wang reported to the emperor.[48]

The operation was partly a side effect of K'ang-hsi's patronage of
Southern culture, specifically, his love of Southern opera, known
as the *k'un-ch'ü* (opera of the K'un-shan style). By now, thanks to
K'ang-hsi, *k'un-ch'ü* had become a great vogue in Peking. Manchu
princely families, fascinated by Southern culture, strove to keep up
with wealthy Chinese scholar-officials and renowned art patrons.
The previously mentioned *Romance of the Palace of Eternal Life*,
completed as an opera in the late 1680s by the Southerner Hung
Sheng, was a must for festivals and family gatherings—birthdays,
weddings, and the like—in the capital city. Similarly, local officials
considered it essential when entertaining the emperor on his Southern tours.[49]

The social status of actors and actresses was very low in imperial
China; they were discriminated against and, together with courtesans, were classified as "mean people." Their children were barred
from taking the civil-service examinations. It was legal for wealthy
people to buy youngsters from poor families, provided that the
bargain was conducted with the consent of the youngsters' parents.
The children were to be made concubines (if girls) or bond servants,
or to be trained as entertainers in privately owned theatrical
troupes. It was an established duty, for example, of Li Hsü, imperial bond servant and textile commissioner at Soochow, to purchase children in the South for K'ang-hsi's personal troupe of
actors.[50]

But the human trade in the South had ballooned into a scandal
that damaged the image of the throne. Since illicit buyers all claimed
"the Imperial presence" as the authority to support their actions,
every sign pointed to the Heir Apparent Yin-jeng as the power
behind the operation. The sexual perversions with both "outside"

women and fair boys that K'ang-hsi in 1708 accused "Yin-jeng and his private agents" of committing applied to this present tour as much as to the previous ones.

The secret reports from Wang Hung-hsü corroborated the emperor's charges, providing detailed descriptions of the criminal operation. It is understandable from these reports why K'ang-hsi was fearful that he might lose the Mandate to rule the Chinese empire.

The buying of children indeed involved "too many people": customs personnel, palace guards, even the director of the Department of the Privy Purse—all members of the Imperial Household or the Imperial Bodyguard—were implicated. Also included were dismissed officials who wished to regain posts by making voluntary contributions to the government. The heir apparent's involvement was compounded by the participation of his confidant Ling-p'u, husband of his wet nurse, who had just been appointed minister of the Imperial Household, with special jurisdiction over the Department of the Privy Purse. K'ang-hsi later confessed that he had named Ling-p'u to this post as a means of appeasing Yin-jeng, for with Ling-p'u holding the purse strings, Yin-jeng could obtain funds any time he wanted them for his extravagant uses. Now even the director of that department was hunting for youngsters, along with the others.[51]

Wang's investigation zeroed in on the activities of a certain conspicuous figure, Fan P'u. A sketch of Fan's background will illuminate the nature of the so-called benevolent despotism under K'ang-hsi, as well as the shadowy role of the heir apparent in the human trade.[52]

Fan was a native of Hui-chou prefecture in Anhwei province. From this prefecture there had risen many powerful salt merchants and copper traders. Both the Fan and Ch'eng families, including Fan's close relative, surnamed Ch'eng, in Soochow—were among their powerful numbers. Being the capitalists of the time, these merchants were influential in the imperial bureaucracy as well as locally in the South: not only were their annual profits guaranteed by their salt monopoly, but they were also able to make great profits by using their money to manipulate the price of copper coins. Throughout the first half of the Ch'ing regime, these merchants repaid the emperor for his favors by contributing annually to the government coffers in huge amounts. A single salt merchant would donate in one stroke millions of silver taels, especially when an emperor needed money to finance a military campaign. This income, along with that from the selling of public offices, constituted a major revenue source for the government.[53]

The Department of the Privy Purse of the Imperial Household was empowered to contract with these merchants for rights to the salt monopoly and licenses as the government's brokers in procuring copper—they were referred to as "merchants of the Imperial Household"[54] in contemporary government documents. It is easy to see why the merchants were generous in entertaining the imperial party during the tours; it also explains why they participated in the illicit human traffic in collaboration with officials from the Imperial Household. This was another means of repaying the Imperial Household for favors received.

As a member of this merchant class, Fan P'u may be described as a "bureaucratic capitalist." Formerly a subprefect, he now was trying to secure the post of circuit intendant; in exchange for having his name put on the priority waiting list for that post, he had donated to the government a number of horses for military use. Widely connected with officials in the capital, he was related by marriage to Ch'a Sheng, the emperor's literary secretary in the South Library and one of the most influential of the courtiers.[55]

In procuring youngsters Fan had the support of the heir apparent's local henchmen. The newly appointed judicial commissioner of the Kiangsu province as well as the assistant prefect charged with grain-tax collections were local law-and-order officials who worked for Yin-jeng. The assistant prefect, Chiang Hung-hsü, issued warrants—at Fan's request—ordering parents to sell their youngsters simply because they happened to have a pretty girl or boy. The judicial commissioner, Ma I-tzu, formerly circuit grain intendant of the prefectures of Soochow and Sungkiang, received his new appointment "by a special Imperial order" on April 28, after K'ang-hsi had made an on-the-spot decision to promote the incumbent judicial commissioner, Chang Po-hsing, to the governorship of another province. Chang, from the Northern province of Honan, was known as "one of the most honest officials in the empire"; Ma I-tzu was a favorite of the heir apparent. It is highly likely that Chang's promotion was a ploy used by the heir apparent to put his own man, Ma, into the supreme position of law and order in Kiangsu. As the Board of Punishments in the capital was controlled by the heir apparent's henchmen, so the judicial and police departments in the South were dominated by his loyal adherents.[56]

Knowing this background, we can see why Fan P'u was so bold as to claim authorization from "the number-one man in the Imperial presence" to conduct his illicit trade, and why he dared to "parade prostitutes" through the streets of Soochow while holding "an Imperial arrow" (a symbol of imperial authority) in his hand, even when the emperor was in the vicinity of that city.

Naturally, Fan P'u became K'ang-hsi's prime target for investigation. He is ours too—for his connection with the heir apparent. Wang's reports supplied the details. On May 15, four weeks after Wang had received the secret edict, he submitted his first report to K'ang-hsi when the imperial party was returning from Hangchow to Soochow, passing by Shih-men. Mingling with local officials ostensibly to greet the emperor at Shih-men, Wang slipped the report to the eunuch Li Yü. After thanking K'ang-hsi for the secret commission and for his thoughtfulness, Wang wrote:[57] "Ever since I was entrusted by Your Majesty with my secret mission, all my memorials have been written by my own hand. No one has had the opportunity to see them. Since this matter involves too many people and too many parties, how much more I feel that I must be doubly cautious. I have been following this principle at all times reverently and tremblingly."

He first mentioned two less conspicuous buyers: "A secretary from the Soochow Customs House purchased a girl surnamed Sheng from K'un-shan [where the *k'un-ch'ü* opera originated], another girl surnamed Wu from T'ai-ts'ang, and still another surnamed Tsou from Kuang-hsing. The dismissed supervising censor, Ch'en Shih-an, is now buying boys and girls in order to use them for regaining his post through certain channels." It is worthwhile noting that K'un-shan was the native home of "the three Hsü brothers": Hsü Ch'ien-hsüeh, one time leader of the Southern Faction, and his two brothers, Yüan-wen and Ping-i, who each had served in K'ang-hsi's court as grand secretary and vice-president of the Board of Civil Appointments. And T'ai-ts'ang was the home of Wang Shan, then president of the Board of Punishments, a loyal supporter of the heir apparent. These prominent Southerners had exerted a corrupting influence on the K'ang-hsi bureaucracy, and now human merchandise from the same region, purchased by office-hunting brokers, contributed to the erosion of the moral fiber of the Manchu regime—Fan P'u's notorious behavior in this operation suggested how far the erosion had progressed. Wang Hung-hsü's report continued:

Fan p'u, formerly subprefect of Chih-p'ing prefecture, is now hoping to be named to the post of circuit intendant and has donated horses to the government for this purpose. A native of Hui-chou, he has established wide connections with officials in the capital, being their liaison man for illicit activities.

The other day he was granted an Imperial arrow after he had presented flowers [to Your Majesty?]. He then led prostitutes walking through the street, holding the Imperial arrow in his hand.

Fan P'u also bought, by force of threat, the young son of Chao Lang-yü for five hundred taels. But the boy was not an actor. Fan made the boy's parents consent to the sale simply because a certain licentiate, by the name of Yen Liu, had recommended the boy to him. He ordered Chiang Hung-hsü, the assistant prefect charged with grain-tax collection, to issue a warrant forcing the boy's parents to consent to the deal.

The authority behind Fan P'u's actions seemed to be "people serving in the Imperial presence":

It may be added that whenever Fan P'u forced people to sell their boys and girls, he always claimed authorization from personnel serving in the Imperial presence. No one knew the whereabouts of the boys and girls after they were taken away. Whenever the parents refused to sell their children, Fan P'u simply ordered Chiang Hung-hsü to issue a warrant demanding their compliance with the sale.

As in any illicit business, these buyers had code names for their merchandise, and even a native such as Wang Hung-hsü said he was ignorant of the connotations of these terms. "The merchandise listed on the official warrant was termed 'little hand' (*hsiao-shou*) or 'jade chrysalis' (*yü-yung*). I was told that 'little hand' refers to a boy, and 'jade chrysalis' a girl—I myself honestly don't know the origins of these terms." Wang perhaps did not know the meanings of these names, or maybe he pretended ignorance for the sake of propriety. "Little hand" was a local euphemism for male prostitute, and presumably "jade chrysalis" was a female prostitute.[58]

The report went on to describe the activities of others who were close to the "Imperial presence": imperial bodyguards and personnel connected with the Imperial Household:

Wu-ko,[59] the imperial bodyguard, bought a woman at the price of 450 taels; another at 140 taels; and also a maid at 70 taels. The last transaction was negotiated through a woman go-between. Another bodyguard, Mai-tzu [K'ang-hsi inserted an interlinear note beside his name], is running around hunting for suitable people to buy. Te-ch'eng-ko, director of the department of the Privy Purse of the Imperial Household (*kuang-shan k'u*), has also bought some women. I heard that he concealed the women in a boat [used by some members of the imperial party].

But these were not the only buyers. "In addition, many other buyers were running around everywhere. Some bought people for themselves, some bought people as presents for important officials to curry favor. The buyers invariably used pseudonyms; and all transactions were fraudulently arranged. Parents who sold their children could only go to the broker's house to collect the silver: they did not know who the real buyers were."

In closing his report, Wang urged K'ang-hsi to try his best to understand it, and begged him to keep the confidentiality of their correspondence by returning the report to Wang "in a securely sealed envelope."

K'ang-hsi's notation at the end of the report revealed nothing of his feelings: he just wrote, *"chih-tao liao,"* which amounts to "noted" or, at most, "I have understood." The interlinear insertion beside the name Mai-tzu, however, tells us more about K'ang-hsi. It reads: *"wu tz'u ming jen,"* meaning, "no one I know of by this name."

The significance of this insertion is twofold. First, although the emperor did not recognize the name Mai-tzu, it seems quite probable that he was the same Mai Kung ("Mr. Mai") who—along with Wu-ko, "a guard officer at the Ch'ien-ch'ing Gate"—had accepted money from Wu Ts'un-li, onetime governor of Kiangsu (1716-1723) and a notoriously corrupt Southern official (as given in a secret report in the palace archives).[60] The other significant point about the emperor's insertion is that, since K'ang-hsi singled out only Mai-tzu as a person he did not know, he must have recognized the other buyers. Had Te-ch'eng-ko not been the real director of the Privy Purse, for instance, K'ang-hsi would have noted beside his name something like "no such director by this name"; furthermore, Wu-ko was the guard officer he frequently assigned to errands dealing with missionaries. One wonders why the emperor did not take action against these lawless officials from his own private bureaucracy.

K'ang-hsi kept the report for ten days, until he had arrived at Yangchow on his return trip to Peking. He and the heir apparent were again entertained by the salt merchants in that fabulous garden villa situated on the Creek of the Precious Pagoda (Pao-t'a wan). There were undoubtedly numerous luxurious amusements arranged by the hosts—banquets and operas, of course, but also one might well have been able to find quite a few "little hands" and "jade chrysalises" in some quarters of the temporary palaces or in the imperial boats moored along the creek. One thing was certain: K'ang-hsi took advantage of the flurry of activity in the villa to slip the first report back to his agent on May 25, through the same eunuch, Li Yü.[61]

K'ang-hsi arrived at the capital on June 21 and then proceeded to his suburban villa. Wang did not present further reports, "for fear of arousing suspicion." The emperor left Peking for his summer retreat at Jehol on July 5, to stay there until November 13. On July 15 Wang sent his second report to K'ang-hsi by enclosing it in some correspondence on literary matters from the South Library.[62] This report treated two types of local buyers—merchants and a high-ranking provincial:

> I have gathered information on this matter. A copper merchant sur-named Yen bought three persons: One was surnamed Wu, native of T'ai-chou, seventeen *sui* [about sixteen years old]; a certain girl, Chang San-niang, eighteen *sui*, skilled in musical instruments; a person named Wang, seventeen *sui*, daughter of a money exchanger whose store is located in front of the magistrate's office of Wu-hsien district.
>
> Also, Huang Ming, financial commissioner [of Chekiang] at Hang-chow [whose function was comparable to that of a deputy governor], bought three youngsters, one of whom was the daughter of Lu Nan-lin, a rice-store owner; the other two names I was unable to identify.
>
> Also, salt merchants with the responsibility of salt shipments (*shang-kang*)[63] from Yangchow swarmed to Soochow to buy people.

Wang then added, "all the above buyers bought people publicly and lawfully without using fraudulent means." Again, Fan P'u was unique in the human trade:

> Fan P'u was the only person who claimed to have authorization from important personages . . . I have reported to Your Majesty last time how he had bought Chao Lang-yü's young son against the parents' will. Later I heard that the boy's mother went to Hu-ch'iu [situated outside the city of Soochow, where there was a temporary palace] and at-tempted to make a direct appeal to Your Majesty. The prefect Chia P'u mistook her for someone who attempted to redress her complaint against local officials, and ordered the runners to take her away for temporary custody. Her direct appeal thus failed.
>
> Fan P'u also bought by force of threat a girl surnamed Liu, daughter of a sesame-oil-store owner, and a prostitute, also by threat. In addi-tion, he bought eight youngsters, all of thirteen to fourteen *sui*, who were sent to an unknown place.

The heir apparent's role in the operation becomes quite clear when we learn that Wang was "frightened" after his clandestine mission was made known to Fan P'u—only five days after the sub-mission of his first report—by the "number-one man before the throne," who warned Fan that someone had said "bad things" about him:

> Only two days after Your Majesty had arrived at Hu-ch'iu, returning north, Fan P'u spoke with his relative surnamed Ch'eng [possibly a salt

merchant] and said, "Since some Chinese minister had said bad things about me [to the emperor], I think I am not going to see the Emperor off." Ch'eng said, "Has any eunuch passed on this message to you?" Fan P'u said, "It was not a eunuch, but the number-one man before the throne [K'ang-hsi's interlinear notation beside this sentence: "Who is this number-one man?"] who passed on this message to me." And so forth.

One doubts K'ang-hsi's sincerity in his interlinear query, for there was only one "number-one man" at court—the heir apparent. (It would indeed have been difficult for him to decide who was the number-four man "before the throne," or even the number-two man "before the throne," since at this time K'ang-hsi had not yet selected an alternate candidate for the throne; the audience arrangements show that all his other children sat below the throne in front of him, with only Yin-jeng sitting on his right-hand side.)

Wang had another basis for his alarm: "Fan P'u was related to Ch'a Sheng by marriage, being the father-in-law of one of Ch'a Sheng's second son's children. In the past Ch'a Sheng has established many contacts with imperial bodyguards, and all sorts of people serving in the residences of Manchu princes. This is why I know someone has indeed passed on a message to Fan P'u." Wang warned the emperor: "Here I must make it very clear to Your Majesty in advance: Fan P'u is a person full of fantastic tricks.[64] With the assistance of Ch'a Sheng, well known as a big mouth [gossip] and busybody constantly looking for trouble, I will certainly be the target of their subtle attacks."

When Wang went on to urge the emperor to heighten his own vigilance of "someone" who was spying on him, Wang all but named the heir apparent:

I would earnestly like to present a few additional words. I know Your Majesty has handled matters with extreme caution and with extreme secrecy; no other emperor from time immemorial has been able to surpass Your Majesty in these respects. But I am afraid the situation has changed in recent days. Someone has been spying on Your Majesty's daily movements and repose. I beg that Your Majesty will be secretly on guard, never lightly divulging Your Majesty's secret to others. I am sure Your Majesty will gain a thorough knowledge in this matter if Your Majesty will try to comprehend the situation every time certain things happen.

Though a modern reader may accuse Wang of lacking directness, for a minister of the emperor he had gone as far as was permissible in making his point clear. Believing that he had in fact written too frankly, Wang felt the need of an apology: "I have said the above out of my naked loyalty. I apologize for my bluntness and would like to beg Your Majesty's pardon and tolerance."

Nevertheless, he was sufficiently frightened to entreat the emperor quite bluntly: "I humbly request that Your Majesty will comment on this secret memorial promptly and return it to me secretly. I further hope that Your Majesty will personally instruct the chief eunuch to deliver it to my hand in person, in order to avoid the misfortune that anyone should open the envelope and see it." He even suggested how K'ang-hsi should seal his envelope: "Also, please add another paper wrapper outside the envelope and seal it securely. In order to conceal my name, please write only the following phrase, *Nan-shu-fang shou* [meaning, "To the South Library"], as your addressee, and write *chin-feng* [meaning, "securely sealed"] on the seams.[65] I have herewith reverently presented this secret memorial." This time K'ang-hsi only wrote one character in response at the end of the memorial: "*shih*" ("right").

Wang persevered in investigating the Fan P'u affair even after he had learned that his mission was known to Fan P'u himself. He wrote his third report from Peking after receiving information from his own agents working in the South. Only the first half of this memorial deals with the mysterious Fan P'u (the second half deals with deteriorating local conditions). Wang wrote: "Your humble minister reverently and secretly memorializes . . . When I first heard what Fan P'u had told his relative, I felt extraordinarily frightened. Immediately I asked someone [close to Ch'eng] to ask him who the number-one man was: Was he a close imperial bodyguard or someone even higher up? Ch'eng replied: 'This I don't dare talk about.' Hence I was unable to identify this person."[66]

Wang used an agent to try to discover the mystery person's identity, believing that K'ang-hsi, too, wanted this information. He described his second attempt to get Ch'eng to speak: "While in Yangchow, I sent someone again to go back to Soochow to pay a personal visit to Ch'eng. Yesterday I received a family letter that says that Ch'eng said, 'Do you think that this person is an ordinary person? I don't dare mention his name no matter what!,' and so forth."

As far as K'ang-hsi was concerned, the pretense had to go on. At the end of Wang's memorial he responded: "Concerning this person Fan P'u, no one else knows of this matter. If there is someone who has divulged the matter to outsiders, it must have been Ma-wu, my bodyguard. As to the number-one man, I haven't the faintest idea who he is!"

Now that K'ang-hsi had the facts on his son's conduct, he must have begun to comprehend the extent of Yin-jeng's moral aberration and the role that Southern pleasures had played in this deterioration. Yet the only public response was no more than an imperial decree, issued toward the end of 1707, promising "severe punishments to anyone who should dare to engage in human trafficking through kidnapping."[67] Only after a year did he confess, in vague terms, his knowledge of Yin-jeng's involvement in such crimes—after Heaven had demonstrated further displeasure at his government through graver omens.

9
A Pretender

IN the fall of 1707, sometime before early November while still at the Jehol summer palace, the emperor told Yin-jeng that he "felt the imminence of an incident."[1] Although we cannot penetrate the nature of K'ang-hsi's premonition, we do know that what he had learned from his secret agent during his last Southern tour caused in him considerable apprehension. In addition, Heaven's increasingly threatening omens in the South certainly intensified his anxiety.

Banditry in the South was spreading. Wang Hung-hsü's report relates that while the imperial party was still in Hu-ch'iu, a suburb of Soochow, a large gang of robbers firing cannons swarmed into the city and took all the silver reserves in the provincial treasury. The robbers possessed "illegitimate orders" from the "vice-president of the Board of War," which represented the anti-Ch'ing forces in the area. This amounted to a serious insurrection, even though the governor of Kiangsu glossed over the incident with a vague statement to K'ang-hsi about an "ordinary banditry" case[2] (the governor did not want to incriminate himself by revealing Heaven's anger, as evidenced by such an insurrection, at his maladministration).

The deepening local unrest was aggravated by the insensitivity of provincial bureaucrats. In Chekiang the financial commissioner Huang Ming, apparently a protégé of the heir apparent, proposed a three-percent increase in the surtax to make up the province's deficits, which had resulted from his improper use of provincial funds to entertain the imperial party and to purchase young girls and boys to offer as presents during the last tour. His proposal evoked a strong protest in the provincial capital, Hangchow.[3]

106

Alerted by Wang's report, K'ang-hsi nervously watched for other bad omens. His secret correspondence with his bond servants Li Hsü and Ts'ao Yin betrayed his frame of mind. He wrote to Li Hsü: "Soon after I returned from the South, I heard of many cases of banditry. I don't know what the local officials were doing! Recently I also learned that the weather is very dry in Kiangsu and Chekiang. I am afraid that banditry will increase accordingly."[4] To Ts'ao Yin he wrote: "The South is suffering a severe drought; my heart is extremely troubled. I heard that banditry cases were numerous."[5]

Later in the year he wrote to Li Hsü, with the traffic in children clearly in mind: "The harvest is bad this year. By all means, you must avoid buying any more people for me. You must detach yourself from getting involved in local affairs. I heard a rumor that some local officials were levying surtaxes without my authorization. Is this true?"[6] K'ang-hsi's worries were well founded. Soon after his return from the South, he received further reports from various sources on local unrest in the region. The revolt of the monk I-nien presented the uneasy emperor with his first major shock.

On November 19 it was reported that a Buddhist monk named I-nien "had issued forged official papers and deluded the people into following him." He also "had made people swear oaths of blood brotherhood before starting the revolt"; his followers "wore red turbans and displayed the imperial flag of the Ming dynasty"; and the certificates of official appointments passed out by I-nien bore a seal stamped, "The T'ien-te Reign of the Great Ming Dynasty." Some of the rebels were arrested—I-nien escaped.[7]

Official reports to the throne played down this incident as another case of "ordinary banditry." They attributed the death of an army major to an injury incurred in falling from his horse, when actually the officer was killed in combat with rebel forces one-thousand strong.[8] Such concealment of the seriousness of local unrest made it extremely difficult for the emperor to obtain reliable information, and when a situation as complex as the I-nien revolt was brought to his attention, it increased his anxiety.

Why were Buddhist monks involved in local insurrections in the South? From the beginning of the Manchu conquest of China, many Chinese intellectuals loyal to the Ming dynasty had retired to temples. In retreating from the world they declared their detachment from the current regime; they also were able to hide their identities behind religious aliases. I-nien was just such a "monk."

K'ang-hsi took extraordinary measures to subdue the I-nien effort. He dispatched an imperial commission, headed by Mu-tan,

Manchu president of the Board of Revenues, to try those of I-nien's followers who had already been arrested; he specifically instructed Mu-tan to issue a general announcement to all Buddhist monks in the South urging them to cooperate with the government in flushing out I-nien, and sternly warning them that anyone who dared offer refuge to the rebel monk would be severely punished.[9]

The emperor was concerned about the far-reaching effects of the I-nien revolt. When Li Hsü reported the same case from Soochow, the emperor wrote in response, "I have known of this case for a long time already. But I heard that in Chekiang there were also rebels in the Ssu-ming mountain range. Make a very secret investigation on this matter and report back to me." To Liang Nai, then governor-general of Chekiang and Fukien, the emperor wrote, "Recently I heard that there have been numerous bandits in the Ssu-ming Mountains. What are the local officials doing these days? Investigate and report!" On another occasion, he instructed Liang Nai: "All the remaining bandits must be searched out without fail!"[10]

The emperor was concerned about the interpretation the common people of the South would assign to the I-nien case. In response to a report from Li Hsü on the Ssu-ming Mountains bandits he asked Li, "Are all the bandits cleared out yet? Make further investigations. How are the common people taking this matter?" The I-nien case was in fact so serious that it became a subject of interest abroad as well as within China. In Japan it was known that I-nien's portrait was distributed by the police to all provinces, like FBI "Wanted" lists. (I-nien was eventually captured and the following year, 1708, executed by being slowly sliced.)[11]

While the nationwide search for I-nien continued, K'ang-hsi was fully occupied with another even more threatening revolt, this one allegedly directed by Chu San T'ai-tzu, meaning "the third Heir Apparent of the Ming royal house." The Chinese pretender had come to K'ang-hsi's attention as early as 1705, but he was implicated only after the arrest in early spring, 1708, of two leaders of another popular revolt, which had originated in Shao-hsing, in Chekiang. Chang Nien-i (an alias; his real name was Chang Chun-yü), who was arrested with his brother Chang Nien-erh (real name: Chang Chun-hsi), confessed to the court that they regarded Chu San T'ai-tzu as their emperor.[12]

Chu San T'ai-tzu's name was Chu Tz'u-huan; he actually stood fourth in rank among his brothers. The true Ming heir was the second eldest brother of the last Ming emperor, Ch'ung-cheng (r. 1627-1643). This brother had been executed in 1655 by K'ang-hsi's father, Shun-chih, on the trumped-up charge that he had "falsely pretended" to be the heir apparent of the Ming house. With the death of this heir, the name Chu San T'ai-tzu was invoked by Ming loyalists to legitimize their insurrections.

The first revolt in the name of Chu San T'ai-tzu during K'ang-hsi's reign had occurred in 1673, coinciding with the outbreak of the eight-year Rebellion of the Three Feudatories. Though similar uprisings took place sporadically thereafter, they were easily quelled, without causing K'ang-hsi much anxiety. But now that the emperor's own heir apparent was showing every sign of unworthiness, the reappearance of the Ming pretender must have heightened K'ang-hsi's fear that he had indeed transgressed Heaven's Mandate.

In fact, Chu Tz'u-huan probably never took any direct part in the attempted subversion of the Ch'ing regime. When the Manchu conquerors had entered Peking, in 1644, he was only a nine-year-old boy. Leading a fugitive life since that time, he had first fled to Honan, where he was taken in by a Ming loyalist and set about farming. Later he moved south and became a Buddhist monk, possibly as a cover. A man who was impressed by Chu's literary talents offered him his daughter in marriage. Chu also acquired a concubine and sired six sons and three daughters.

In 1705 Chu went to Ningpo, where he became acquainted with a local scholar by the name of Chang Yüeh-huai (also known as Chang Hsüeh-lien), and he assumed an alias, Chang Lao Hsien-sheng, meaning Old Gentleman Chang. In 1706 he was identified and charged with the crime of engaging in "weird things" and "mustering troops." During August of that year, three of his sons and one grandson were arrested and imprisoned; all six women in his family (two wives, three daughters, and one daughter-in-law) hanged themselves. Chu fled to Shantung, where he took another alias, Wang Shih-yüan, and was known as Wang Lao Hsien-sheng, Old Gentleman Wang. In early 1708 the captured rebel leader Chang Nien-i revealed Chu's whereabouts, causing his eventual arrest in Shantung. At the age of seventy-five, Chu Tz'u-huan, in chains, was transferred to Peking for trial by the Board of Punishments.[13]

Initially, the board did not find Chu guilty of any subversive act.[14] K'ang-hsi, too, adopted a fair stance toward the Chu case. Earlier, when K'ang-hsi had sent his imperial commissioner Mu-tan to Chekiang to conduct the preliminary trial, he had instructed Mu-tan: "Chu San is a descendant of the Ming Imperial house. He is now seventy-five. He and his sons have been wandering about looking for tutorial work, seeking food and shelter."[15]

After Chu was transferred to Peking, K'ang-hsi ordered Ming eunuchs to verify his identity. They did not name him as the actual

Ming prince, because, on the one hand, they literally could not detect the face of the nine-year-old boy in the visage of a seventy-five-year-old man; and on the other hand, remembering the 1655 case, in which all who recognized the Ming heir apparent were killed, they dared not identify him.

Though the board was unable to convict Chu on hard evidence, it came up with an arbitrary verdict, stating, "There is no evidence to prove that Chu San engaged in a conspiracy of rebellion; nevertheless, it is possible that he had harbored such an intention."[16]

This tenuous argument brought Chu the sentence of death through slow slicing into a thousand pieces. The Board of Punishments was controlled by the heir apparent's faction, and the board's recommendation of the death sentence probably originated with Yin-jeng.[17] We can see that the heir apparent desired the elimination of the Chinese pretender to the throne, and K'ang-hsi's willingness to victimize an innocent person was perhaps owing to the need to alleviate his anxiety about any lingering mandate of the Ming house.

In late July, shortly before the harsh decision was handed down K'ang-hsi received a secret memorial from Ts'ao Yin about the ground caving in at the Nanking tomb of the Ming emperor Hung-wu. Ts'ao Yin reported the event to K'ang-hsi because he feared that the unusual occurrence might become a source of rumors that would "distort the truth and trouble Your Majesty's heart."[18] The emperor was indeed concerned, for the local people might interpret the event in two ways: either that the mandate of the defunct Ming was truly lost, or that Heaven was displeased with K'ang-hsi himself. The latter was plausible in K'ang-hsi's mind because he had repeatedly paid visits to the tomb while on his Southern tours—even having his autograph inscribed on a stone slab displayed within the tomb grounds—so that perhaps Heaven was showing contempt for his pious gesture toward the founder of the Ming dynasty. Small wonder that he responded nervously to Ts'ao: "It was right that you reported this to me. Make further inquiries. Is there any other gossip? Let me know in a secret memorial."[19]

Though K'ang-hsi sentenced Chu Tz'u-huan to death before receiving Ts'ao's next report, he ordered Chu's execution only after that report had arrived, bringing favorable news: "Rumors flying in Yangchow and Chekiang were roughly the same [as I heard in Nanking]. Some said that the cave-in was caused by illegal excavations for the site's treasures, since the tomb was not carefully guarded; some said the cave-in was a sign from Heaven indicating that the Ming mandate has eternally gone. In addition, there are all sorts of rumors fabricated by inconsequential people."[20]

Ts'ao was actually concealing negative talk in the vague phrase "all sorts of rumors." Foreign diplomats, such as the Korean envoys, presented quite a different picture of the rumors, which were detrimental to K'ang-hsi's prestige. Even after the emperor had put Chu to death, favorable rumors about the Chu forces were still rife in the South. One was "The military forces of Chu San T'ai-tzu are superior to the government forces"; another said, "Court ministers proposed that 700,000 troops (400,000 for Chiang-nan and 300,000 for Chekiang) be sent to quell the rebels in the South."[21]

Both the I-nien and Chu San T'ai-tzu cases were known in Japan through Japanese intelligence sources (Chinese merchants engaging in the copper trade between Ningpo and Nagasaki). Two entries under the year 1709 in the Japanese record read:[22]

[1] A Zen monk by the name of I-nien, who had mustered bandits in the Ta-lan mountain at Ningpo, was arrested last spring in Soochow prefecture and executed, together with forty-odd followers, during the eleventh month [December 13, 1707-January 11, 1708] last year. [2] Also, the third Heir Apparent of the Ch'ung-cheng Emperor of the great Ming Dynasty, by the name of Old Gentleman Wu [sic], who had lived in Shangtung hiding his identity, was accused of attempting conspiracy to rebel. He was arrested at Shangtung and executed in Peking.

The two incidents made an impact on the heir apparent, according to K'ang-hsi's later recollection. After their occurrence, Yin-jeng said to the emperor, referring to K'ang-hsi's premonition at Jehol, "My Imperial Father, your prediction is now fulfilled." The emperor's reply sounds both sarcastic and prophetic: "I am afraid there is something else yet to come." In retrospect K'ang-hsi wrote, "Saying this, I did not know what was to happen next."[23]

10
Dismissal

THE climax of the father-son tragedy occurred in 1708, during the emperor's autumn hunt at Mulan, his hunting ground 100 miles north of Jehol, part of the annual Jehol retreat.[1] For K'ang-hsi, the retreat was not a period of "sweet repose and rest," but rather a working vacation that stretched from early summer to late fall. Jehol, situated in Inner Mongolia, is close to both the Manchus' homeland, in the east, and their allies the Khalka Mongols, in the north. The rugged mountain terrain at Mulan was ideally suited for hunting exercises, which combined the joy of the chase with the training of troops to maintain the high standard of the Manchu fighting tradition.

On September 2, 1708, K'ang-hsi left Jehol for the hunt with an entourage of thirty thousand: selected members of the central administration; bodyguards and soldiers from the Eight Banners, including riflemen and falconers; Chinese literati from the staff of the South Library; and even an approximation of a foreign press corps in the persons of European missionaries such as Father Ripa, who recorded the news and provided close-up views of the emperor's life with his family in a secluded environment.

Members of the imperial family accompanying the emperor always included the imperial consorts, escorted by a host of ladies-in-waiting, amahs, eunuchs, and various imperial sons and their wives and children; this time, K'ang-hsi particularly desired the presence of his sons Yin-jeng (now thirty-five) and Yin-chieh (age seven).[2] Yin-chieh had been born to the famed imperial concubine Lady Wang, officially known as Mi-fei. The emperor's relationship with this young son—as well as his mother—makes up part of the prelude to the climax of the conflict between K'ang-hsi and his heir apparent.

At this time of his life—he was now fifty-four—K'ang-hsi was drawn to Chinese rather than Manchu women, and of these Chinese women, Lady Wang was clearly the favorite. K'ang-hsi's changing preference, as seen in the relationships he had with the more than twenty concubines in his harem, is significant, for it was of great interest to his children, especially the heir apparent.[3]

Yin-jeng knew of the behavior of his grandfather Shun-chih, who had removed his first legitimate empress and disdained the second (Hsiao-hui, now the dowager empress) because of his infatuation with his favorite concubine, Donggo; most important, Shun-chih had intended to establish Donggo's son as his heir had the boy not died in infancy. K'ang-hsi's new affection for the Chinese concubine and her young child seemed to parallel the situation of Shun-chih, so that Yin-jeng very likely wondered whether he was going to be rejected as the heir apparent.

Since the status of an imperial consort could determine her sons' qualifications for the heirship, K'ang-hsi had been very cautious in granting any concubine the rank of empress. Hsiao-ch'eng, Yin-jeng's mother, was the only woman K'ang-hsi had both loved and made empress. After her death he would establish two more empresses: Hsiao-chao, daughter of the regent Ebilun, in 1677, and Hsiao-i, daughter of T'ung Kuo-wei and K'ang-hsi's cousin on his mother's side, in 1689. In both cases, K'ang-hsi did them this honor more out of pity than love: both women were barren—thus no son would be born to threaten Yin-jeng's position as heir apparent—and both were gravely ill (Hsiao-chao died seven months after becoming empress; Hsiao-i died the day after her appointment).

Cautious in his assignment of status, K'ang-hsi was generous with his emotions. Even while the beloved Empress Hsiao-ch'eng was still alive, he frequently "visited" his concubines: Ho-fei bore him two sons, the first of whom died in infancy and the second, Yin-shih, survived as his eldest son; Jung-fei was the mother of Yin-chih (his third son), as well as four sons who died and a daughter.

If the number of children (male in particular) suggests anything about the emperor's preferences, then between the deaths of the empresses Hsiao-chao and Hsiao-i, from 1678 to 1689, K'ang-hsi's favorite concubine was Te-fei, mother of Yin-chen (the fourth imperial son and future Yung-cheng Emperor). She bore K'ang-hsi more children than any other consort during this period: three sons and three daughters; her son Yin-tso died at the age of six, and Yin-t'i (K'ang-hsi's fourteenth son) was later to become an active candidate for the heirship during the last few years of the emperor's life.

Second in imperial favor was I-fei, mother of Yin-t'ang, the ninth imperial son and another contender for the throne; I-fei also bore

K'ang-hsi's sons Yin-ch'i (his fifth) and Yin-tz'u (his eleventh who died in 1696). Next in favor were two concubines who each had a son and a daughter. Wen-hsi, sister of the Empress Hsiao-chao, was apparently very much liked by K'ang-hsi, for he granted her the title *huang-kuei fei*—imperial concubine of the first rank, a status second only to that of empress—two years before she bore him a son (Yin-o, his tenth); with other concubines, elevation to a higher rank was an imperial honor awarded only after the birth of male children. The other woman, Min-fei, was the mother of Yin-hsiang (K'ang-hsi's thirteenth son) and two daughters; as early as 1702 Yin-hsiang was considered a strong candidate to replace Yin-jeng as heir apparent (recorded in Ho Cho's letters to his brother)[4] and he later became the famous Prince I, under the Yung-cheng Emperor. Both Wen-hsi and Min-fei died young, in 1694 and 1699.

The three other preferred concubines, each of whom bore K'ang-hsi a son, were Ch'eng-fei, mother of Yin-yu (the seventh imperial son); Liang-fei, mother of the most aggressive aspirant to the heirship, Yin-ssu (the eighth son); and Ting-fei, mother of Yin-t'ao (the twelfth son) and sister of the future very powerful general commandant of the Gendarmerie of the Capital City, Tohoci (in Chinese: T'o-ho-ch'i). (Another woman, T'ung-pin, bore K'ang-hsi two sons and one daughter, but both boys died in childhood.)

These were K'ang-hsi's favorite consorts, who were primarily Manchu, up to the year 1689; by then the emperor was thirty-five and the majority of his sons had been born—fourteen out of the twenty-four that survived him. All the brothers who later contended for the succession came from this group of princes.

It was from 1690 to 1708 that K'ang-hsi showed a growing preference for Chinese ladies over their Manchu counterparts—out of the thirteen imperial concubines who gave birth to any child during this time, ten bore Chinese surnames. The most striking Chinese woman was Mi-fei (Lady Wang), who had been admitted to the palace as a very young lady-in-waiting in the late 1680s. She is described in a 1709 Jesuit account as "that famous Chinese woman whom the Emperor loves passionately."[5] The only information about her family is that her father was a onetime district magistrate, and probably a Chinese bannerman. She bore the emperor three sons, Yin-wu (his fifteenth) in 1693, Yin-lu (the sixteenth) in 1695, and Yin-chieh (the eighteenth) in 1701.

Lady Wang must have been a beautiful woman, for K'ang-hsi was willing to ignore court etiquette and allow his Jesuit artists to paint a portrait of her. (When K'ang-hsi entertained his former tutor Kao Shih-ch'i at his suburban villa in 1703, he discussed the "miraculous vividness" of the Jesuits' artwork. On that occasion, he showed Kao two portraits of his "favored concubines," saying, "This one is a Chinese" and "This one is a Manchu." He explained to Kao, "Since you are an elderly person and have served me in the palace for many years, I think it would not matter if I showed you these portraits of my ladies." According to Kao, the two pictures were so alive they seemed to leap from the surface of the scroll, on which K'ang-hsi had requested that the Jesuits paint.)[6]

That the Jesuits called Lady Wang "that famous Chinese woman" must have been owing to their unusual opportunity to observe her beauty while painting her portrait. But her fame was no doubt based as much on other qualities, for K'ang-hsi was known to pay the highest attention to "virtues," "talents," and "skills." She most likely was well-versed in Confucian classics and literature, wrote poems with elegant calligraphy, and sang and danced well.

Another Chinese lady, Hsiang-pin, from the Ch'en family, was also very much in K'ang-hsi's heart. She, however, could not match Lady Wang's record in producing healthy, attractive sons. Her first boy died in infancy, and the surviving son, Yin-wei (K'ang-hsi's twentieth), was mentally retarded. In contrast to these children, Lady Wang's son Yin-chieh was appealing and one of K'ang-hsi's favorites.

While K'ang-hsi's special affection for Lady Wang and her son perhaps evoked particular jealousy and hatred in the heir apparent, the emperor's delight in all the many concubines and palace ladies probably caused general confusion and resentment toward his father in Yin-jeng. Unaware that the emperor's association with women was carried on within the legitimate framework of the imperial marriage system and that "women from outside" were shunned, Yin-jeng might well have wondered, "Why can you, but not I?" As Father Ripa witnessed in Jehol in 1711, the emperor was always accompanied by his ladies wherever he went: "With his ladies on foot around him, he is carried about the grounds by eunuchs, in an open chair; with them he sails in little boats, fishing in the canals and the lakes; with them he eats." While employed in reading and writing, he was always surrounded by women who "remained sitting upon cushions, as silent as novices." Even "when the Emperor's presence was required in the outer court palace on some business . . . he always came in a boat with some concubines, and with a train of other boats loaded with ladies."

When Father Ripa saw the emperor in the gardens, "He was always carried in a sedan chair, surrounded by a crowd of concubines, all walking and smiling." Sometimes the atmosphere could be quite jolly, as when he teased his ladies. He would sit "upon a high seat, in the form of a throne, with a number of eunuchs standing around him; and, watching [for] a favorable moment, he suddenly threw among his ladies, [who were] grouped before him on carpets of felt, artificial snakes, toads, and other loathsome animals, in order to enjoy the pleasure of seeing them scamper away with their crippled feet"[7]—these women were, obviously, Chinese, for Manchu women were forbidden to bind their feet.

Despite such pleasures, the emperor's life at Jehol was not all ladies and leisure. If K'ang-hsi's infatuation with Lady Wang suggests how deeply he had become a captive of the Chinese, the annual hunt at Mulan testifies to his determination to maintain the equestrian superiority of the Manchus.[8] It was against this backdrop that the father-son tragedy reached its climax.

The huge imperial party left the Jehol summer palace for the hunt, arriving first at Yung-an pai-ang-a, one of the parks at Mulan. It was here that the young prince Yin-chieh was stricken, on September 26, with an acute illness, possibly a severe cold (the boy's health must have been good before the departure, or else he would not have been taken along on such a fatiguing expedition).[9] Leaving the child in the care of nurses, the emperor proceeded onward; upon receiving word that Yin-chieh's condition was worse and that he might die, K'ang-hsi hurried back to the boy. The emperor then took his son and his entourage back to Jehol, sacrificing the hunt to give the child a chance to live.

On the return trip to Jehol, the emperor's anxiety was aggravated by disheartening news about his other sons. Some of them had taken to having Manchu ministers and even princes beaten. K'ang-hsi denounced this behavior as cruel, and also called it a "usurping" of his imperial prerogative. He promised that thereafter those who were assaulted could challenge the beater for an explanation; if that was unsatisfactory, they could appeal to the emperor directly. Though the emperor later named both Yin-shih and Yin-ssu as the sons who had had their retainers thrashed, neither was found to be so outrageous as to have ordered the whipping of a prince. The perpetrator of that crime was, of course, Yin-jeng.[10]

Meanwhile, by October 11 Yin-chieh's health had further declined as complications set in, possibly pneumonia. Knowing the emperor's fondness for the child, the ministers worried that the boy's death might impair his own health. Yin-jeng's reaction to the situation was delight at the prospect of the death of a potential competitor for the throne; his gladness recalled his response to the emperor's illness in 1690. Once again, the emperor was deeply hurt by Yin-jeng's behavior; he rebuked him for "absolutely lacking brotherly love" and castigated him for "having the evil intent to see the deaths of all my other children." Irritated by his father's scolding, Yin-jeng lost his temper and quarreled heatedly with him.[11]

Four days later, on October 15, the emperor told his ministers that he could not afford to allow worry over his child's illness to injure his own health. This seemingly strange shift in mood was owing to K'ang-hsi's sense of filial and political responsibilities: he had to stay strong for the sake of the dowager empress and the officialdom, as well as the people of his empire. Leaving his dying son in Jehol, he set out again for Mulan. He lodged at Pu-erh ha-su-t'ai, a hunting ground north of Yung-an pai-ang-a.[12]

Suspicious of Yin-jeng, K'ang-hsi asked his eldest son, Yin-shih, who was a competent fighter, to stay by the emperor's side at all times to protect him. K'ang-hsi's suspicions were increased by the news that every night Yin-jeng was peeking into his tent through a ripped seam, and that during the day Yin-jeng spied on his every movement. The emperor later recalled his fear: "I simply could not predict whether I would be poisoned today or assassinated tomorrow . . . I was troubled day and night at the height of my vigilance." He claimed that the reason behind his son's behavior was that Yin-jeng wanted to avenge the death of Songgoto, who had been killed for helping him carry out the attempted usurpation.[13]

In the middle of the night of October 16, the emperor was awakened by someone approaching him in the dark. He jumped up from his mattress, and a terrible turmoil ensued. Alarms were sounded; chamberlains, bodyguards, and horsemen rushed to the emperor's side. But the intruder escaped, together with his associates. The emperor felt sure of the intruder's identity, for he had observed his movements and heard names shouted. Moreover, the arrangement of the imperial camp precluded the possibility of an outside invader, which lent substance to his opinion that the offender was Yin-jeng.[14]

Security at the camp was tight; it was almost impossible for an outsider to break into the center of the camp, where the imperial tent was pitched. Prince Chao-lien in the eighteenth century described the setup:

> The Emperor's tent was erected at the very center of the campground. It was enclosed first by wooden walls painted yellow. The main entrance of the wooden enclosure was covered with a yellow canopy. There was still another enclosure surrounding the wooden one, made of nets. This net enclosure had three gates: the southern entrance was protected by Imperial Guards of the Plain White Banners, the eastern entrance by Guards of the Plain Yellow Banners. Each guard consisted of two brigades. The eastern entrance and the western entrance were con-

nected with the entrance to the Imperial tent, where the chamberlains and personal detachment of the Imperial bodyguards were stationed. Captains-general with their subordinate officers and soldiers were in charge of security at night around the net enclosure's entrances. Outside the net enclosure there were the military officials from the various divisions of the Eight Banners, each living in their own tents. Furthermore, the Emperor's tent was flanked by four Eastern Banners and four Western Banners, at a distance of a hundred paces from each Imperial tent.[15]

Though Chao-lien made no reference to the location of the emperor's family members, they were within that yellow enclosure with the emperor. So the heir apparent was nearby.[16]

The next day, K'ang-hsi received word of Yin-chieh's death.[17] This was the final blow. Summoning all his sons, ministers, bodyguards, and other civil and military officials, he then ordered Yin-jeng to kneel in front of the throne. Bitterly the fifty-four-year-old emperor poured out all his complaints against the heir apparent. Some of the charges included:[18]

The emperor had "tried his best to tolerate Yin-jeng's evil conduct for more than twenty years," alluding to the T'ang Pin incident of 1687; he "had hoped that Yin-jeng would eventually repent and change his behavior . . . This is why," he explained, "I have covered up and tolerated his evil deeds until today."

Yin-jeng had usurped imperial prerogatives in having Manchu princes beaten: "Since I believe that the state should have only one ruler, how could Yin-jeng willfully thrash Manchu princes, court ministers, and other officials? For example, Na-erh-su, prince of the blood of the third degree, and P'u-ch'i, also a prince of the blood, have all been beaten under his orders. In addition, few officials, ranging from Manchu ministers to soldiers, have been able to escape his cruel treatment." K'ang-hsi said that Yin-jeng had assaulted these princes and ministers because they were not willing to adhere to the heir apparent's faction. Prince Hai-shan, for one, was known to be a member of the Yin-ssu faction. (Hai-shan was Yin-jeng's first cousin, son of the emperor's younger half brother Ch'ang-ning.)

K'ang-hsi went on to say that although he was aware of all this, he hesitated to ask the Manchus for information about Yin-jeng, resorting to Chinese ministers (such as Wang Hung-hsü), because "If any Manchu official should dare to mention his evil conduct, [Yin-jeng] at once would treat him as an enemy and retaliated with whipping and flogging. This is why I never tried to ask Manchu officials about his action."[19] (Yin-jeng had the feudal power to thus treat the Manchus; he could not punish Chinese officials in this way.)

Yin-jeng's extravagance had led him to plunder, through extortion, national and provincial treasuries; and yet the emperor had tried to satisfy his son's appetite for money: "Whereas I am very thrifty and frugal, Yin-jeng is extremely extravagant. Since I knew he was prodigal, I appointed his nurse's husband, Ling-p'u, to be the chief minister of the Imperial Household in order to facilitate his access to money. Who ever could have expected that Ling-p'u was even more corrupt and covetous and that he was hated by all the bond servants in the Imperial Household?"

In court politics, Yin-jeng "was fond of intervening . . . Either minimizing this person's case or magnifying another's, his favoritism was beyond computation. And I knew all about it."

Yin-jeng had indulged in sexual perversions, both on his western tour and the tours of the South; he and his retainers had done "all sorts of things, exhausting all possible means," which, as we have noted, the emperor felt were too embarrassing to specify.

The heir apparent had jeopardized the emperor's good relations with the Khalka Mongols: "Yin-jeng also sent his men to intercept tribute bearers from Mongolia. They willfully stole horses the Mongols had brought as presents to the Emperor, and the Mongols were resentful and complained about it."

And, last and most serious, Yin-jeng had lacked filial piety since he was born—that is, starting from when his birth caused the death of his mother, K'ang-hsi's beloved Empress Hsiao-ch'eng: "Furthermore, Yin-jeng caused his mother's death at birth, being incompatible with the horoscope of his mother. This, according to the ancients, was regarded as an act of unfiliality."[20]

In conclusion, "Since Yin-jeng must want to see the disintegration of my state and want to kill all my people, how can I make such a person the emperor? What would become of the empire I have inherited from my ancestors?" With that, K'ang-hsi announced his decision to depose Yin-jeng as the heir apparent. He then collapsed on the ground, weeping violently.

The emperor added that he would personally report his decision to Heaven as well as to his ancestors at the ancestral hall in Peking. Meanwhile, seven of Songgotu's sons were to be executed and several Manchus banished to Manchuria, because of their presumed complicity with Yin-jeng. Then K'ang-hsi ordered Yin-jeng's arrest.[21]

As a protective measure, the emperor challenged all the assembled Manchu princes, ministers, and soldiers to "speak out as to

whether the charges I have laid against Yin-jeng are true or false."
They all sobbed and bumped their heads against the ground, saying, "Your Majesty's insight is both sacred and enlightened; all that
you have said about the Heir Apparent is true—every bit of it!"[22]

K'ang-hsi ordered Yin-jeng put in chains and imprisoned. As
Father P. d'Entrecolles wrote, "It was a very sad scene to see the
one who just previously walked almost like the Emperor loaded
with iron. His children, his main officers, all were enveloped in his
disgrace."[23]

But the emperor suffered even more than Yin-jeng. For six days
he was so distressed that he could not sleep. Never again, he later
confessed, was he able to regain his original health.[24]

Yin-jeng was committed to the custody of his brother Yin-shih
during the trip back to Peking. Upon the party's arrival, the emperor ordered a felt tent erected within the palaces next to the
Palace Stud, in which to imprison Yin-jeng. But, instead of Yin-
shih, Yin-chen (the fourth imperial son) was appointed Yin-jeng's
supervisor.[25] This switch of assignment marked the beginning of
K'ang-hsi's doubt about Yin-shih's loyalty to his father.

PART IV

Hesitation

11
The Yin-ssu Faction

IN 1708 Yin-ssu, K'ang-hsi's eighth son, emerged as the leading candidate for heir apparent. In court circles he had successfully projected the image of "a virtuous and wise prince."[1] Three of his brothers—Yin-t'ang (the ninth son), Yin-t'i (the fourteenth), and, to a lesser degree, Yin-shih (the eldest)—supported him in his ambitious cause.

The Yin-ssu movement can be traced back at least to the attempted coup of 1703: when K'ang-hsi ordered Songgotu's execution, signifying his intense displeasure with the Heir Apparent Yin-jeng, the hopes of other aspirants to the throne were raised. Of the allied brothers, Yin-shih, then thirty, was never very strongly committed to Yin-ssu, partly because of his own emotional instability and partly because of his interest in assuming the throne himself. Yin-t'i, then only fifteen, was too young to play an important role in the faction. But Yin-t'ang, twenty, worked closely with his twenty-two-year-old brother, Yin-ssu, in the effort to place him on the throne.

The background of Yin-ssu's mother, Liang-fei, was a major hindrance to his being considered as a candidate for the heirship. She was the daughter of an imperial bond servant in the *Sin jeku* of the Imperial Household; her father's highest post was that of an overseer in that department. Up to 1708, she had remained an imperial concubine of low rank.[2] Perhaps conscious of this flaw in his heritage, Yin-ssu assiduously tried to improve his qualifications, even through fraudulent means. He was good at public relations and the use of influential people to improve his chances with his imperial father.

In contrast to his mother's rank in the Manchu feudal hierarchy,

123

the social status of Yin-ssu's wife was high and therefore an asset to the would-be emperor. Her mother was the daughter of the re- nowned Yolo, Prince An.[3] (The princedom had been inherited by Yolo's eldest son, Ma-erh-hun, who became known as Prince An the Younger after the death of his father, in 1689. Ma-erh-hun and his two younger brothers, Ching-hsi and Wu-erh-chan, figured prominently in court affairs and supported Yin-ssu in his struggle with Yin-jeng for the throne). However, except for her social stand- ing, Yin-ssu's wife did not in fact represent an advantage to her hus- band. She was a domineering woman, whom Yin-ssu greatly feared; she, not he, made all the decisions in their marriage. Fur- thermore, she was barren (and out of jealousy she forbade Yin-ssu to take a concubine—a normal practice among imperial princes— for which "cruelty" K'ang-hsi was later to scold her, saying that her cruel character came from her grandfather Yolo).[4] Yin-ssu's lack of offspring certainly discouraged K'ang-hsi from considering him for the heirship, for this would cause yet another succession crisis in the next generation.

Because of these various problems, Yin-ssu's position previous to the emperor's action against Songgotu had not been viewed as strong. Rather, court speculation focused on the emperor's thir- teenth son, Yin-hsiang, then eighteen years old. A letter Ho Cho sent to his brother documents the situation:

> Mr. Yang Kuo-wei has been assigned to assist the thirteenth prince in studying . . . Yesterday, when some newly appointed *shu-chi-shih* [post- doctoral students] were selected by the Emperor to become resident tutors in the various residences of the imperial children. His Majesty made special reference to Mr. Yang, saying that, in poetry as well as in essays, he is superior to all. Since the thirteenth prince is dearly loved by the Emperor, what will become of him, no one can even guess at this time.[5]

The last sentence implied, as much as could be done without risking charges of treason, that the emperor so loved his thirteenth son that he had assigned the most reputable scholar as resident tutor to pre- pare him to be a possible replacement for Yin-jeng as the heir ap- parent.

But in spite of these drawbacks, Yin-ssu waged an active cam- paign for the throne, particularly after Songgotu's execution sparked new hope. He took two approaches. The first was directed at the emperor: Yin-ssu hoped to impress his father with his talent and personality. The second was aimed at Yin-jeng: he planned to have him murdered by assassins.

Knowing their father's strong interest in Chinese learning, an imperial child who aspired to be emperor naturally strove to appear a paragon of erudition and cultural refinement. In creating this image the resident tutors were instrumental. Politically, the tutors could also act as intermediators between the princes' palaces and the imperial bureaucracy: they served as lobbyists in court for their pupil's cause.

After Ho Cho was appointed Yin-ssu's resident tutor—in 1703—the prince began to use him to demonstrate to his father his enthusiasm for Chinese learning and admiration for Southern intellectuals. Ho, a native of Soochow, was well connected with eminent Southern scholars; he was also valuable to Yin-ssu because of his connection with the increasingly influential minister from Fukien, Li Kuang-ti, who had first recommended Ho for the South Library staff. In addition, Ho served concurrently in the Imperial Printing Establishment, so that he was doubly useful to Yin-ssu in having two means of access to the emperor.

Ho quickly became involved in Yin-ssu's campaign for the succession. Meanwhile, Ch'in Chih-sheng, also known as Ch'in Tao-jan,[6] had been assigned to tutor Yin-ssu's brother and supporter, Yin-t'ang. The tutors' intimate relationships with these two princes was eventually to cause the scholars much misfortune.

Yin-ssu first sent Ho Cho's younger brother to the South to purchase rare Chinese books. "Chinese literati in the South" were thus impressed by Yin-ssu's interest in learning and praised him for "being indeed a fine prince." This tactic was intended to establish a reputation that would gain Yin-ssu the support of Southern literati in court, who would then relay their impression to the emperor.

But the emperor was not satisfied with Yin-ssu's scholarly achievement: his penmanship—an indication in China of intellectual excellence—was so bad that K'ang-hsi instructed him to improve it by writing ten sheets of Chinese characters every day. Unwilling to endure such torture, Yin-ssu asked other people to do his homework.[7]

Early in 1704, when Ho Cho was in the South to mourn the death of his father, Yin-ssu sent him a letter of condolence. He first greeted "Mr. Ho" and Ho's younger brother, and then informed him that "Your daughter, Mr. Ho, is extremely well here in my house." The letter concluded with some friendly advice: "Take care of yourself, do not be overly sorrowful, so that you may repay your gratitude to the Emperor in the future. This is my earnest advice!" Yin-ssu might well have intended the phrase "Emperor in the future" to refer to the future emperor as much as to his father. (K'ang-hsi interpreted it in the latter way when the letter fell into his hands in 1715, during the search of Ho Cho's house, after the tutor's arrest.)[8]

Through Ho Cho, Yin-ssu established friendly relations with other prominent Southern literati who were respected by Chinese scholar-officials, as well as by the emperor. One of the literati was P'an Lei, of Kiangsu,[9] a first-rate essayist who had studied under the early-Ch'ing Confucian giant, Ku Yen-wu.

P'an Lei had achieved national fame in 1679 when he passed the special examination given by K'ang-hsi for "Great Confucianists of Broad Knowledge"—he was the youngest on the list of successful candidates. The examination was part of K'ang-hsi's campaign to win Chinese support during his battle against the Three Feudatories; it was designed to honor Chinese scholars who had distinguished themselves in the late Ming and early Ch'ing regimes. P'an was subsequently appointed to a post in the Hanlin Academy and was made one of the compilers of the imperially sponsored *Ming History*. Forced to retire in 1684, most probably because of outspokenness that had offended Songgotu, P'an was reappointed to his post by K'ang-hsi during the 1703 Southern tour, at the time that the emperor decided to have Songgotu executed. After 1703 P'an's influence with Southern literati as well as with the emperor was a valuable resource for Yin-ssu to exploit.

The prince's friendly relationship with P'an at this time is demonstrated in Yin-ssu's correspondence with Ho Cho. Sometime between 1704 and 1708, Ho Cho had asked Yin-ssu to do P'an a favor —perhaps find an official post for P'an's son—and Yin-ssu responded in an amiable letter, in which he first repeated his greetings to the Ho brothers and told Ho how "very well" his daughter was in his house, and then said, "Concerning the matter that you asked me to attend to for P'an Lei, I have personally instructed the general-in-chief of that locality to manage it for me. I told the general earnestly that he must not fail my expectations. I think this matter must have been taken care of by now. The fourteenth day of the third month."[10]

In addition to attempting to establish an intellectual reputation through the Chinese scholars, Yin-ssu used influential family members to improve his image with the emperor. Fu-ch'üan played a leading role in this strategy. A half brother of K'ang-hsi, he was antipathetic to Yin-jeng, who had cursed him with venomous insults. But he loved Yin-ssu, more than any of his other nephews. After Fu-ch'üan had retired from court service, he enjoyed a tranquil life at home, where he entertained many literary celebrities in his garden—this intercourse undoubtedly benefited the cause of the favorite nephew.[11]

Before Fu-ch'üan's death, in 1703, K'ang-hsi had paid him several visits—an extraordinary act of respect on the part of the emperor. On his deathbed Fu-ch'üan revealed the illicit activities originating in the Imperial Household, especially those perpetrated by personnel in the Department of the Privy Purse; this probably served to prove Yin-jeng's immorality to K'ang-hsi—Manchu ministers had persisted in concealing it from the emperor. Fu-ch'üan then praised Yin-ssu for his "talents and moral integrity" and recommended him to be K'ang-hsi's heir apparent. This speech followed the practice of a dying minister demonstrating his loyalty by presenting his last advice to the throne—even at the risk of offending the emperor. K'ang-hsi had profound affection and high respect for his elder brother, and these final words must have made an impact on him at a time when Yin-jeng showed no signs of improving and Songgotu was pushing his plan to seize power. It was after his visits to the dying brother that K'ang-hsi ordered the arrest of Songgotu. Because of these conversations, it seems likely that K'ang-hsi considered Yin-ssu as an alternative candidate for Yin-jeng's position.

Much of our information about Yin-ssu comes from the deposition of Ch'in Tao-jan, the Southern scholar who had been appointed Yin-t'ang's resident tutor. Ch'in described the coordinated effort of the triumvirate, Yin-ssu, Yin-t'ang, and Yin-t'i: "[They] had conspired in one accord to bring about the downfall of the Heir Apparent through treacherous means. They made every effort to please old Prince Yü and asked him to recommend Yin-ssu to the Emperor. Therefore, even while seriously ill, Prince Yü strongly recommended Yin-ssu to the Emperor for his talent and virtue [when the Emperor was paying a personal visit to his dying elder brother]."[12]

In a statement of 1708, K'ang-hsi confirmed that the deathbed conversation had taken place. Prince Yü had indeed recommended Yin-ssu and said that "Yin-ssu is a good-natured and unassuming person." The emperor then recalled: "court ministers had also commended Yin-ssu for his being a virtuous and wise prince"—some of these court ministers no doubt were among those literary celebrities Prince Yü had received in his garden.[13]

Yin-t'ang remained the strongest supporter of the Yin-ssu cause. He joined the faction not so much to gain power as to protect his wealth and way of life. Not only "fat and clumsy," as Yin-chen described him, Yin-t'ang was also a man chiefly interested in "wine and women" and all the "good things of life," according to Ho T'u, his onetime literary adviser.[14] At least twice Yin-t'ang had sent his trusted eunuch Ho Yü-chu to Soochow and Yangchow to buy "boys and girls from families with good backgrounds," (that is, not from entertainers' families). As Mingju's son-in-law, Yin-t'ang was connected with Mingju's former household bond servant An San (also known as An Shang-jen), who had become the most wealthy man in the South through the salt monopoly; some of the girls bought for Yin-t'ang were purchased by An San's son An Feng (alias An Erh) to be presented to the prince that "they might be trained as actresses." In fact, a variety of devious methods were used to acquire these pretty girls for Yin-t'ang's sexual enjoyment. Whenever a girl's parents were unwilling to sell her, Ho Yü-chu disguised himself as a bridegroom and claimed to be the son of An San. After he had "married"—though a eunuch—the girl, he transferred her to his master's chamber in Peking.[15]

To his own supporters, Yin-t'ang had tried to convey the impression that he had voluntarily declined the heirship, even though a miraculous sign at the time of his birth seemed to indicate that he would be the next emperor. "A sun," he was fond of saying, "entered the bosom of my mother. She also dreamed of the Dipper descending upon her." But privately he confessed that he had no chance of being selected, because of his father's dislike of him.[16] He was practical in choosing a friendly brother to support as future emperor, who would guarantee the continuation of both his power and his pleasures.

Yin-t'ang, too, worked to get support from the Southern literati. Like Yin-ssu, he appreciated the value of his Chinese resident tutor, Ch'in Tao-jan, albeit not in his appointed role as tutor. Rather, Yin-t'ang made Ch'in his household and financial manager (in violation of an imperial order that said such a position could be held only by a household bond servant, not by a government official). Ch'in also functioned as Yin-t'ang's public-relations man, frequently stating that "Yin-t'ang's face manifests an imperial air."[17]

Possibly through Ch'in Tao-jan, Yin-t'ang became acquainted with other Southern literati. In 1704 he first patronized the Southern scholar Ho T'u, in granting him a ten-room house as a gift; ten years later, he contributed money to the government in exchange for a military post for Ho T'u, and he financed Ho T'u's travel to the front.[18]

Yin-t'ang was the richest prince among all his brothers, and later Yin-ssu relied heavily on his financial backing. Much of Yin-t'ang's fortune was gathered through illicit means. The several clerical posts in the Board of Revenue were "reserved" as his own sphere of influence and patronage, thus facilitating his illegitimate manipulations through that board. According to Wang Hung-hsü's secret reports, Yin-t'ang was a leading sponsor of the contraband ginseng trade between Manchuria and China proper; this trade provided a major source of Yin-t'ang's wealth (ginseng was believed to help ensure long life). Added to this income, after the death of his brother-in-law K'uei-hsü, son of Mingju, Yin-t'ang inherited most of the vast Mingju family fortune (because K'uei-hsü had no male offspring).[19]

Yin-t'ang also resorted to blackmail and extortion to increase his fortune. Such activities he entrusted to his close eunuchs, notably Yü-chu-erh and Ho Yü-chu. At one time they blackmailed Yung-fu, Mingju's grandson, who had married Yin-t'ang's daughter, to the tune of 300,000 taels. In another case, Yin-t'ang proposed to "adopt" the wife of Yung-shou (Yung-shou was probably Yung-fu's brother), for which privilege—the chance to become related to him, the emperor's son—he asked Yung-shou for 80,000 taels. Six thousand taels was extorted from Ch'en Ju-pi, the director of selections of the Board of Civil Appointments, who was victimized in the Court of the Three Judiciaries. Similar sums were extracted from many others.[20]

The conspiratorial activities of the Yin-ssu faction resembled both traditional court intrigues among power holders and the clandestine behavior of folk rebels outside the power structure. The cohesive force within the Yin-ssu group was not so much brotherly love as the espousal of *i-ch'i*, the "spirit of unswerving loyalty and faithfulness" towards friends, especially as demonstrated by blood-oath brothers among folk heroes. *I-ch'i* represented horizontal loyalty—loyalty even unto death—among friends: stressing mutual commitment, it conflicted directly with the vertical relationships between children and parents or between subjects and the emperor (filial piety and loyalty towards the throne). Many of the elements of folk religions—popular Taoism and Buddhism—are based on the heroic *i-ch'i* theme.

Such a stated commitment within the Yin-ssu group reveals how deeply the Manchu ruling elite had been absorbed into Chinese culture. The folk heroes in the Chinese novel *Shui-hu chuan* (*All Men Are Brothers*, or *Heroes of the Water Margin*) had been loved by the Manchus even before the Manchu conquest. The story had been translated into the Manchu language in the 1630s, along with *San-kuo yen-i* (*Romance of the Three Kingdoms*); much of the strategy described in the latter novel had been employed by the Manchus to defeat the Ming forces.[21]

Claiming this folk ideology, and in spite of their apparently single-minded interest in power, the members of the Yin-ssu faction considered themselves righteous "rebels" against the oppressive Heir Apparent Yin-jeng. Legally, they were Yin-jeng's subjects, but since they were cruelly treated by him, the rebel principle of *i-ch'i*—

"carrying out the Way on behalf of Heaven"—overrode their sense of loyalty to Yin-jeng, as well as to their imperial father.

K'ang-hsi was aware of the dangerous influence of such a rebel ideology. In 1708 he scolded Yin-t'ang and Yin-t'i: "Are you two betting your hope on Yin-ssu's becoming the Heir Apparent so that once he is enthroned you may be made Princes of the Blood of the First Degree?" He then alluded to the heroes in the *Shui-hu chuan:* "You guys want to show that you are men of *i-ch'i* and you are real heroes; but I think your *i-ch'i* belongs only to that valued by [the bandits] of the Water Margin at Liang Mountain!"[22]

This was in fact a good characterization of the behavior of the Yin-ssu faction. On the one hand, they engaged in clandestine activities as though they were righteous dissenters (Yin-ssu and Yin-t'ang—whose palaces were separated only by a wall—continually held strategy conferences);[23] on the other hand, they employed the bribery of imperial eunuchs to spy on their father.

Yin-ssu was profoundly interested in consulting *i-jen*—people considered to have extraordinary or supernatural gifts—among the Taoist and Buddhist monks. He sent men out to search for famous astrologers, physiognomists, kung-fu practitioners, and people who had been visited by miraculous signs, and invited them to his palace to offer secret advice. On Yin-ssu's behalf, Yin-t'ang then paid them consultation fees, sometimes one hundred or two hundred taels.

A famous physiognomist called Chang Ming-te had been hired by some Manchu officials and princes to tell their fortunes (feelings of uncertainty were widespread within the court), by interpreting the structure of their faces. Yin-ssu heard of this and invited Chang to his palace. Chang told him that his willingness to accept the invitation was motivated by a sense of righteousness, because he thought the heir apparent was incurably wicked. He predicted that Yin-ssu was destined to achieve "a position of the highest honor," meaning the throne.

In his meetings with Yin-ssu and other Manchu officials, Chang Ming-te proposed a plot to have Yin-jeng assassinated. He volunteered to carry out the conspiracy if he could have their cooperation.[24] Chang's offer is understandable, for "to kill the cruel and bring peace to the good" is considered a noble mission given by Heaven to the popular heroes in Chinese lore. Yin-ssu, impressed by Chang's enthusiasm and excited by the rosy promise, went to Yin-t'ang and Yin-t'i and related Chang's plot to them in order to see whether they would support such a venture. The brothers were not prepared to go that far, and, according to their deposition given later, after their arrests, they "chased him away" in order not to get involved in so drastic a measure. None of the brothers did report Chang's conspiracy to their imperial father.[25]

It was Yin-shih, who had never seemed a strong supporter of Yin-ssu, who reported Chang's conspiracy to the emperor.[26] He also told the emperor that Chang had been trying to recruit some *fei-tse* ("flying bandits"), Chinese equivalents of Robin Hood, sixteen of whom were famous at the time. Yin-shih revealed that Chang believed that if Yin-ssu could win more than half of the New Manchus,[27] Yin-ssu's chances of succeeding in the assassination would be great. (New Manchus, several hundred of whom served as bodyguards of the emperor, were warriors of extraordinary ability and valor, prized by both K'ang-hsi and his ancestors. The emperor referred to them as "people from the eastern provinces," because they were aborigines of the border area between Manchuria and Korea, along the Yalu River. They had maintained tributory relationships with Nurhaci and were "treated like treasures" once some of the tribesmen decided to become direct retainers of the Manchu founders, although they became part of the Manchu military establishment only in 1671, when their chieftain requested K'ang-hsi's permission to move inside the border near Ningguta. From then on they were called New Manchus.)

K'ang-hsi feared that the assassination plan would be extended to include himself,[28] and he recruited more bodyguards for his protection. Although badly troubled by the situation, he did nothing else about it, so great was his confusion.

While the emperor was fretting, the Mulan hunting-trip incident made the assassination plot superfluous: Yin-jeng was now safely out of the picture. But would the emperor choose Yin-ssu as his new heir?

12
Reversals

"THE sky suddenly darkened" (he later recalled) the day K'ang-hsi ordered the imprisonment of the heir apparent; and on October 28, 1708, a day before his arrival in the capital, a whirlwind arose in front of the imperial carriage.[1] These and other strange events caused the emperor to question his decision to depose the heir apparent.

As the sky changed its color, K'ang-hsi's feelings began to change too (he immediately ordered that dishes served at the imperial table be given also to the deposed heir). He sternly warned his other sons: "If anyone among you conspires to the post of Heir Apparent, I shall consider him a traitor; I will punish him by law."[2]

The Yin-ssu faction committed its first major blunder out of misjudgment of the emperor's intentions. Seeing that the emperor had taken a resolute stand against Yin-jeng, they assumed that K'ang-hsi would go as far as having Yin-jeng completely eliminated. On the day of Yin-jeng's imprisonment, Yin-shih, who had been charged with the supervision of the heir's confinement, went to K'ang-hsi and said, "Yin-jeng's behavior has been so mean and shameful that he has completely lost everyone's respect. The physiognomist Chang Ming-te predicted that Yin-ssu would receive the highest honor. If you, my imperial father, wish to get rid of Yin-jeng, it can be done without using your own hand."[3] Shortly thereafter, Yin-shih told the emperor that he would not mind becoming Yin-ssu's assistant, if that brother could be made heir apparent.[4] The emperor was startled by Yin-shih's remarks, and to insure Yin-jeng's safety he committed him to the custody of imperial guards—even though still under the nominal supervision of Yin-shih—while he was being transferred from Jehol to Peking.

While on the road, K'ang-hsi began to inundate his court with descriptions of Yin-jeng's strange behavior. On October 24 he said:

I have observed Yin-jeng's behavior recently. He is greatly different from a normal person. Sleeping soundly all day, not until midnight does he want to eat. Ten mugfuls of drink would not make him drunk. When faced with religious tablets, he was frightened and was unable to worship properly. Whenever there is thunder and lightning, he becomes fearful, disquieted, and confused. Speaking in a disorderly manner, he is absolutely abnormal, as if having gone mad, as if having been possessed by evil spirits.[5]

And on October 28, a day before he entered Peking, the emperor suggested that the evil spirits had originated in the imperial palace: "As to the Chi-fang Palace, where Yin-jeng's ladies-in-waiting reside, it is a place very dark, gloomy, and unclean. People living there often become sick or die. Yin-jeng has frequently visited that place, and has unconsciously been possessed by evil spirits. From this it is clear that everything he has done has been caused by devilish beings. This is surely a strange matter."[6]

On the same day, when the wind swirled in front of K'ang-hsi's carriage, he interpreted it as a protest from the spirit world about the unfair treatment received by the heir apparent. Upon his return to Peking the next day, the emperor reported more evidence to support this interpretation: "Yin-jeng now has been possessed. His original nature has been darkened. He suddenly rises and sits down; he sees ghosts often. Owing to a mysterious uneasiness, he frequently changes his sleeping place. After eating seven or eight bowls of rice, he feels hungry still; after twenty or even thirty big cups of wine, he does not get drunk. When he was interrogated, he told about many more horrible happenings."[7]

Fatherly compassion toward Yin-jeng had been revived. At the capital, after Yin-jeng was confined in the special jail next to the Palace Stud, the emperor assigned Yin-chen, as well as trusted eunuchs and imperial bodyguards, to assist Yin-shih in his supervision of Yin-jeng: this was to guard against any menacing of the heir apparent by Yin-shih.[8]

K'ang-hsi was not at this point prepared to go so far as to rescind his decision to depose the heir apparent. To conclude the procedure of deposition, K'ang-hsi, as the Son of Heaven, wanted to address a memorial to that power. Before announcing this, he asked Yin-shih and his brothers to take the memorial to Yin-jeng to read. Yin-jeng responded sarcastically, "Since my Heir Apparentship was granted me by our imperial father, if he wants to take it back, let him just do it; I would rather that he omit this step of reporting his decision to Heaven." K'ang-hsi was displeased at this answer, saying to Yin-shih and his brothers, "He is talking quite confusedly. An Emperor receives his Mandate from Heaven; how can it be possible that he doesn't report to Heaven on such a weighty matter?" Then he instructed, "Hereafter, whatever he says, I don't want to hear!"

Informed of the emperor's reaction, Yin-jeng told Yin-shih and his brothers, "I admit that all the charges our imperial father laid against me are true—every one of them. I would like you to convey just one thing to our imperial father: I never had the intention of killing him." Yin-shih dismissed the request coldly, saying, "Our imperial father has instructed us not to transmit any report; who dares to go against his will?" But Yin-t'ang, perhaps fearing punishment for negligence, said to Yin-chen, "This is a matter of great consequence. It seems that we ought to transmit this report to the Emperor." Yin-chen agreed. Yin-shih remained unsympathetic, but after Yin-chen threatened to go alone to the emperor he agreed to the transmission of Yin-jeng's message.

The emperor's heart was indeed softened. He asked his children to tell Yin-jeng: "You have been imprisoned under chains because you have gone mad." And he ordered that "the chains around Yin-jeng's neck be unlocked, only leaving the rest [on his feet and hands] intact." According to Yin-t'ang's interpretation, this was when the emperor began to consider reinstating Yin-jeng as heir apparent.[9] But how was K'ang-hsi to handle Yin-jeng's madness?

K'ang-hsi had first discussed the possibility of spiritual influences at a meeting with Li Kuang-ti, grand secretary and imperial tutor, soon after his return to Peking. Li recorded the conversation:

I said: "Concerning the night alarm at the hunting camp, I wonder if Your Majesty has indeed got the correct name of their leader? I venture to ask whether Your Majesty might have been mistaken about it."

(A long silence followed.)

The Emperor said: "In this whole matter, I am afraid we have been tricked by ghosts. Otherwise, how could he have behaved as if he had been out of his mind?"
I said: "Even I, who am only a minister under Your Majesty, have never been annoyed by ghosts. How much less could they dare to touch an Emperor?"
The Emperor said: "Then is there any cure for it?"

Li gave a frank, typically neo-Confucian diagnosis of Yin-jeng's personality problem:

It is a common law in human nature. When one has obtained honor and glory, he becomes arrogant. When one has acquired ease and comfort, he indulges in reckless acts. When one has been always arrogant and reckless, his mind becomes progressively darkened day by day. At first, he will just want to enjoy an easy life; gradually he begins to hate righteous people. Just a single criticism will make him feel as if there were a thousand thorns pricking against his back. He becomes panicked, perplexed, and topsy-turvy. When this darkness of mind grows to its extremity, he will behave as if he were possessed.

"In reviewing his entire life," the emperor responded, "this is exactly the case." And he asked again, "But is there any cure for this?" Li answered:

The best method of cultivating one's heart is to curtail one's desires. If you can keep him away from the theater and women [literally, "sound and color"] that stimulated his lust, while helping him to concentrate his will and practice quietness, then his spirit will become pure and clear and unpossessed. More and more, normal spirit will be generated from within, which in turn will gradually bring the luster of the original heart to shine forth.

The emperor nodded many times as he listened to Li's common-sense approach to mental disturbance.[10]

Meanwhile, events had led to the arrest of Yin-ssu on November 11. After Yin-jeng's confidant Ling-p'u had been dismissed from the ministerial position of the Imperial Household, the emperor had appointed Yin-ssu acting minister of that organ, with the special assignment of investigating the corruption charges against Ling-p'u. Now the emperor accused Yin-ssu of glossing over Ling-p'u's corruption so that Ling-p'u might shift his loyalty to him. Furthermore, K'ang-hsi charged Yin-ssu with having conspired both to have Yin-jeng assassinated and to become the new heir apparent through Yin-shih's recommendation. K'ang-hsi therefore ordered Yin-ssu's arrest and imprisonment while rebuking him in front of his other children.[11]

Yin-ssu of course had his defenders. After he was locked in chains, Yin-t'ang and Yin-t'i conferred and decided to intervene. Yin-t'i first spoke up for Yin-ssu, saying, "Our eighth brother is innocent; we would like to guarantee him." Yin-t'ang also supported Yin-t'i's argument. Enraged by this, the emperor drew his sword and lunged at Yin-t'i. Yin-t'i's good-natured brother Yin-ch'i (the fifth son) leaped behind the emperor and held his arms. All the other brothers kowtowed before their father and begged him to pardon Yin-t'i. K'ang-hsi struck Yin-t'ang's face so hard that it swelled. Yin-t'i was punished by being flogged twenty strokes.[12]

On November 12 the emperor first paid a visit to the dowager empress to inquire about her well-being; then he publicly informed the court that he had decided what to do about the heir apparent-ship, but he did not specify what he had decided. On the following day, Yin-ssu was deprived of his title of *pei-le*, prince of the third degree, and degraded to the status of imperial clansman without rank. The physiognomist who had conspired with Yin-ssu to have Yin-jeng assassinated was executed by slow slicing, with all those who had been involved in the conspiracy forced to watch.[13]

Yin-jeng's sympathizers began to take an offensive stance against the Yin-ssu cause. Yin-jeng's friendly brother, Yin-chih, reported to the emperor that Yin-shih for some time had been using Mongolian lamas to cast spells against Yin-jeng. On November 25 the emperor ordered the arrest of Yin-shih's bodyguards, Se-leng and Ya-t'u, and specified that they be interrogated. The investigation substan-tiated the accusation. On November 26 effigies and other articles used by the lamas for their black magic were discovered in ten places within Yin-shih's courtyard. The emperor said that these articles had caused Yin-jeng's insanity. Five days later, he ordered Yin-shih's permanent confinement.[14]

The emperor was increasingly of the opinion that Yin-jeng was possessed. When he learned that Yin-jeng had suddenly recovered his senses on the day the magic devices had been discovered, this reinforced his conviction (or obsession), and he commented:

> On that day the deposed Heir Apparent suddenly became hysterically mad, behaving in all sorts of strange ways. At one point he wanted to kill himself. Fortunately, palace attendants brought him under control and guarded him by forming a circle around him. After a few moments, he suddenly came to himself again, and with surprise asked his eunuchs: "What have I just done in the last few moments?" I have hitherto be-lieved I knew the truth about his past evil conduct. But now I have no doubt that all of that was caused by evil spirits.[15]

On December 4, during the annual hunt at Nan-yuan (the pre-serve in the southern suburb of Peking), the emperor fell seriously ill (his condition remained critical until the end of the year; not until March 2, 1709, did he regain his health, with the help of a Jesuit physician),[16] and he saw this illness as punishment for his unfair treatment of his sons Yin-jeng and Yin-ssu. K'ang-hsi imme-diately called in Yin-ssu, and then Yin-jeng, to his presence, and talked with them briefly; then he sent them back to their respective places of confinement. Then, before the chamberlains and grand secretaries, he said that since deposing Yin-jeng he had shed tears every day. Now, after seeing Yin-jeng, his fatherly sentiments were satisfied. He promised never to mention the past again.[17]

K'ang-hsi's punishment of Yin-shih was severe. On December 12 he sentenced Yin-shih to solitary confinement for life and removed his princely title and banner retainers, which he divided between Yin-t'i and Hung-wang, son of Yin-ssu. Yin-shih was first imprisoned in his own home, then in the spring of 1709 he was transferred to a small house, so as to be separated from members of his household before the emperor left Peking for his Jehol summer palace. The emperor appointed a special team of civil and military officials in addition to the usual capital police to guard this new jail and to prevent his supporters from rescuing him. Yin-shih was kept in jail until his death, in 1734, because the emperor asserted that he was absolutely insane.[18]

Why was K'ang-hsi's punishment of Yin-shih so harsh in contrast to his leniency with Yin-ssu and his other sons? Because Yin-shih was the only one who had posed a serious military threat to the power of the emperor. In addition to his own retainers, Yin-shih recruited a band of professional ruffians and used them to assassinate his enemies (Yin-shih locked his doors securely at night, and his bodyguard K'ua-se boarded up his bedroom windows; assassinations and counter-assassinations were no mere fantasy among these princely rivals and their retainers).[19] After Yin-jeng was arrested, in October 1708, Yin-shih was said to have transferred troops under the commander in chief in Tientsin to Ku-pei Pass, through which ran the route between the capital region and Jehol; his loyal troops were scattered "all over the nation,"[20] as the emperor put it in early 1709.

The most serious threat represented by Yin-shih came from his supporters among the banners stationed in Peking.[21] In addition to Manchuria and the frontier regions, the Eight Banners were distributed strategically throughout the empire, with a significant number of them in the capital and the adjacent region; the frontier troops were called Banner Garrisons, and troops in and about Peking were the Metropolitan Banners. The Upper Three Banners were under the control of the emperor and his children, once they came into their titles; the remaining Lower Five Banners were controlled by imperial clansmen and other princely houses.

During the latter part of K'ang-hsi's reign, feudal loyalty within the banner system remained strong; members of the Lower Five Banners were regarded as the personal "slaves" of their feudal lords, to whom they often were more loyal than to the emperor (and the lords' loyalty to the emperor was not total, owing to animosities that dated from the time of Nurhaci). Yin-shih, however, controlled not only his own bannermen from the Upper Three Banners and his *pao-i* companies, but also a company from the Bordered Blue Banners, one of the Lower Five. Moreover, he had gained the support of influential court ministers and imperial palace guards, as well as the allegiance of many of the younger soldiers among the Lower Five Banners. The potential danger was very obvious to the emperor. Thus he wanted, in dealing harshly with Yin-shih, to make it clear to the entire court that Yin-shih had been ruled out as a candidate for heir apparent.

With both Yin-shih and Yin-ssu falling into oblivion, Yin-jeng once again was the star emerging from behind the cloud of the emperor's displeasure. After the December 4 audience, K'ang-hsi, full of fatherly love, again summoned Yin-jeng, in order to ascertain his mental condition. Meanwhile, Lao Chih-pien, senior Chinese vice censor-general and a leading supporter of Yin-jeng, openly memorialized that Yin-jeng be reinstated. In response to this proposal the emperor on December 19 denounced Lao and declared he would not yet make a decision on Yin-jeng, "since Yin-jeng still betrays signs of madness."[22] He ordered Lao dismissed from his high office and flogged forty times before the court.

On December 25, believing his days to be numbered, K'ang-hsi told his ministers: "Although I have been resting comfortably recently, I feel my strength is fading away. It is hard to predict one's life, yet I don't have anyone to whom to entrust [the government]." He therefore instructed the ministers to nominate candidates for the vacant heir apparentship. The emperor assured his advisers that, except for his eldest son, Yin-shih, "Whosoever among my children is recommended by my ministers, I will accept the nomination."[23]

A short while later that day, when the recommendation was submitted following a court conference, the emperor was shocked to find that the nominee was Yin-ssu. Sorely displeased, he asked the ministers to reconsider their recommendation, saying that Yin-ssu was not qualified to be heir apparent for two important reasons: he had just been convicted of crimes and imprisoned, and his mother's background was inferior.

Ironically, K'ang-hsi now felt that Yin-ssu and Yin-shih each posed more of a threat to the solidarity of the Manchu ruling elite than did Yin-jeng. He thus asked his court ministers about the viability of reestablishing Yin-jeng, the lesser evil. K'ang-hsi had in fact earlier tested the sentiment toward this idea among the Manchu dignitaries before the full court nominated Yin-ssu. A Jesuit wrote from Peking: "The Emperor asked the dignitaries of the empire several times if he had not the power to give freedom back to his son whose innocence had just been highly acknowledged? Most of the lords answered him, somewhat coldly, that he was the master, and that accordingly he could order whatever he wanted to."

The Jesuit's letter reveals that K'ang-hsi's request for a nomination from his court ministers had actually been induced by some Manchu dignitaries who "expected to see the Emperor's death come soon" and thought "it was high time for him to set the Empire's tranquility in order by naming a successor." In submitting the unanimous nomination of Yin-ssu they hoped to pressure the emperor into a decision: "they proposed his eighth son, for whom they showed great esteem; this amounted to excluding the Heir Apparent . . . They no doubt feared that having contributed to Yin-jeng's deposition by their counsels [to the emperor], the former would be bound to avenge himself once reestablished."[24] Nevertheless, one of Yin-ssu's supporters, Alingga (son of the former regent Ebilun and K'ang-hsi's brother-in-law), declared that he would rather kill himself than see Yin-jeng reestablished.[25]

At this critical moment, K'ang-hsi was clearly looking for some signals from the court—despite its nomination of Yin-ssu—that would tell him that he had been wrong to depose his beloved son and that the charges against Yin-jeng had been fabrications. Failing to receive any such statement from his ministers, K'ang-hsi declared that he had been sent otherworldly signals: both his dead grandmother and his dead empress (Yin-jeng's mother) had appeared in recent dreams. While the empress spoke to him in clear words, saying that her son "had been unfairly dealt with," the grandmother's reaction was unusual: "The Great Dowager Empress's countenance had a most unhappy look. She just sat there far from me—quite unlike her appearance in former dreams."[26] He interpreted the grandmother's attitude to mean that she disapproved of his deposition of the heir apparent—the fruit of the marriage she had arranged and the heir she had nominated.

The next day, December 26, K'ang-hsi again summoned his ministers and informed them that he had been deeply troubled ever since Yin-jeng's deposition; he also asserted that the dowager empress agreed with him and felt it a very regrettable matter. The following day, convinced that evil spells could affect the human mind and will, and that Yin-jeng now was exorcised, K'ang-hsi ordered his son's release and, in front of his court, asked Yin-jeng if he had anything to say. The erstwhile heir apparent replied:

My Imperial Father's instruction is both extremely sacred and enlightening. All the occurrences were caused by my own lack of goodness; this is why others wanted to betray me and kill me. If under such circumstances I still hate people and harbor vengeful feelings, rather than changing my evil conduct, Heaven would not tolerate me. Now I have no other wishes. If you court ministers still hope to install me as the Heir Apparent, this I will by no means want to accept!

The emperor responded to Yin-jeng's rhetoric with an exhortation to live peacefully with his brothers and seek their advice constantly, and to "cleanse his heart and change his conduct by reading more of the neo-Confucian books on human nature and self-cultivation."[27]

Would K'ang-hsi, then, reinstate Yin-jeng? If so, why?

HAVING REGAINED his good health, on March 2, 1709, the emperor summoned the court ministers to a special audience to discover the prime movers behind Yin-ssu's nomination for heir apparent. He was told that they were Maci, a Manchu grand secretary, and T'ung Kuo-wei, K'ang-hsi's maternal uncle.[28] The emperor was further told that although he had earlier forbidden these two to participate in the nomination—because they had previously told K'ang-hsi that "Yin-jeng is absolutely not releasable"[29] and that they favored Yin-ssu's candidacy—they had appeared in court to discuss the Yin-ssu recommendation. Insisting to the grand secretaries that "public opinion favored Yin-ssu as the candidate," T'ung Kuo-wei also had given court ministers the impression that "originally" (meaning probably after Songgotu's abortive plot) the emperor too had leaned toward Yin-ssu as the heir apparent and that T'ung had urged the emperor to sustain his "original intention." The court ministers thus had approved the nomination as their "unanimous recommendation," although the leading independent, Li Kuang-ti, had kept silent—a Chinese way of abstaining—during the conference.

Upon hearing all this, the emperor was furious. He publicly rebuked T'ung for violating the imperial decree and promoting Yin-ssu's interests. A heated exchange between the emperor and the imperial uncle ensued, and at one point T'ung challenged the emperor to kill him for the righteous role he had played; the emperor refused to do so on account of their family relationship. K'ang-hsi's reaction to Maci was quite merciless: for arguing with the emperor, Maci was flogged in front of the court.[30]

The emperor's refusal to accept the court's recommendation was not entirely irrational, for there was the real danger of usurpation of imperial power by ambitious court ministers and the emperor's relatives, especially those from the influential T'ung family. T'ung Kuo-wei, for instance, was not only the brother of K'ang-hsi's mother, he was also twice K'ang-hsi's father-in-law (one of his daughters was the late Empress Hsiao-i). Before retiring, T'ung had occupied high posts in court as chamberlain of the Imperial Body-guard and deliberative minister in the *I-cheng-ch'u* (Council of Deliberative Princes and Ministers). Other significant T'ung family members were T'ung's son Lungkodo, his nephew Olondai, and his grandson Sunggayan, an imperial son-in-law.[31] These men had ori-ginally backed Yin-shih, but shifted their support to Yin-ssu after Yin-shih was imprisoned and eliminated from the succession con-test.[32]

It is easier to appreciate the emperor's misgivings about the T'ungs if one understands the extent of their influence in the Divi-sion of the Imperial Bodyguard, as well as the importance of this institution. The division was composed chiefly of outstanding young men selected from the Upper Three Banners. Its duty was to escort the Emperor, perform various offices in the interior of the Palace, and guard the security of the Emperor's person.[33] Imperial Bodyguards at the Ch'ien-ch'ing Gate maintained the security of the emperor's living quarters immediately inside the gate; they also transmitted memorials to the throne (through eunuchs) and de-livered imperial instructions to the bureaucracy. Most of the high-ranking Manchu ministers, provincial governors-general, and com-manders of the banner forces were promoted to their positions in the central bureaucracy after successful service in the Division of the Imperial Bodyguard, which illustrates the prestige of this divi-sion.

The Imperial Bodyguard was commanded by six chamberlains holding the highest ministerial rank, 1A, who were assisted by six senior assistant chamberlains with the rank of 1B, as well as by an indefinite number of junior assistant chamberlains with the rank 2B.

Of the six chamberlains, four promoted the interests of Yin-ssu. Pa-hun-te,[34] who was probably chief chamberlain, was the first Manchu minister to second the motion in favor of Yin-ssu's nomi-nation. T'ung Kuo-wei's nephew Olondai was another chamberlain who supported Yin-ssu. On April 7, 1709, the emperor denounced Olondai and other T'ungs: "Olondai, Lungkodo, and Sunggayan are all good friends of my eldest son—a fact known to everyone. Now you three wish to establish my eighth son as the heir appar-ent. Where do you want ιo put me, the Heir Apparent, and all my other children?"[35]

The emperor had other reasons for disliking Olondai. Olondai had behaved recklessly toward K'ang-hsi and at times even showed contempt for the throne.[36] Irritated by the emperor's rejection of the recommendation of Yin-ssu, Olondai refused to kneel before the emperor. When K'ang-hsi was seriously ill, unlike all the other court ministers who had called upon him to show concern and extend greetings, Olondai played archery games with a group of imperial bodyguards at the Ch'ien-ch'ing Gate, immediately outside the emperor's living quarters. He was once caught urinating in the palace yard, within the Ch'ien-ch'ing Gate, an offense punishable by death. Because of their family connections, however, the emperor had chosen to pardon Olondai on all occasions.

Two other Imperial Bodyguard chamberlains who adhered to the Yin-ssu faction were Alingga and O-fei. While little information is available about O-fei, Alingga's role in the struggle is well documented.[37] His family was related to the emperor in many ways and his influence was derived from generations of connections with the imperial house. His grandmother was a *mei* (sister or cousin) of Nurhaci; his father, Ebilun, had been loyal to the late Shun-chih Emperor at the time of Prince Dorgon's threat to imperial power, and had been one of the four regents during K'ang-hsi's minority; one of his sisters had married K'ang-hsi, and in 1677 was made K'ang-hsi's empress Hsiao-chao. As previously noted, Ebilun had hoped to see this daughter of his established as first empress in 1665, and after being disappointed he had sided with Oboi against Soni, father of Songgotu. This animosity toward the family of Yin-jeng's supporter Songgotu led Alingga to back Yin-ssu in the struggle for the heir apparentship.

The other two chamberlains in the Division of the Imperial Bodyguard, Po-erh-pen and Shang Chih-lung, were evidently neutral on the subject of succession.[38]

Among the lower-echelon officials in the Imperial Bodyguard, the most prominent was Lungkodo, T'ung Kuo-wei's third son.[39] Since his father's sister was the emperor's mother and two of his sisters were married to the emperor, he was both a cousin and a brother-in-law of K'ang-hsi's. At the time of the unanimous recommendation of Yin-ssu, Lungkodo was a senior bodyguard of the first rank (3A), a position just below that of assistant chamberlain. Later, in 1711, when Yin-jeng's henchman Tohoci was removed from the post of general commandant of the Gendarmerie of the Capital City, Lungkodo was appointed to that position, which he filled until the emperor's death in 1722.

The strength of the T'ungs in the Imperial Bodyguard was matched by the influence of the Manchu ministers who supported Yin-ssu in the central bureaucracy. The most important civil official in favor of Yin-ssu was K'uei-hsü, second son of Mingju.[40] After serving in the Imperial Bodyguard, K'uei-hsü was made chancellor of the Hanlin Academy for fourteen years (1703-1717). Since all Chinese officials normally had to go through the academy before their appointment to the bureaucracy, K'uei-hsü during his long tenure as chancellor was able to establish a broad power base in the officialdom. K'uei-hsü utilized his political influence and the immense wealth he had inherited from his father to campaign for Yin-ssu's imperial cause. He and others "spread slander about the Heir Apparent Yin-jeng, stressing his unworthiness, and tried to stop his reestablishment after his deposition."[41]

While K'uei-hsü worked for Yin-ssu in the Hanlin Academy, Maci represented Yin-ssu's strength in the Grand Secretariat and the central administration.[42] Maci was not related to the emperor, but he had unique qualifications among K'ang-hsi's courtiers. Of the Fucha clan and a member of the Manchu Bordered Yellow Banner, he achieved increasingly important positions. First serving on the Board of Works in 1669, he then was supervisor of local customs houses, governor, imperial commissioner, censor-general, deliberative minister, and in 1699 chief grand secretary, the top of the bureaucratic ladder. This was the post Maci held at the time of Yin-ssu's nomination. An able administrator, he was also good at diplomacy with the Mongols and the Russians. The emperor had granted him as retainers the members of one of China's two Russian banner companies (composed of the descendants of a father and son who had deserted from Russia in 1648). Maci's standing in court was paramount: once, for example, he received no punishment for cursing in front of the emperor, one of the emperor's most trusted Chinese officials, Chang P'eng-ko: "You, no good stuff, deserve only to be killed!"[43]

Among the Chinese ministers who followed Maci were Wang Hung-hsü, now president of the Board of Revenue, and Li Chen-yü, president of the Board of Rites. In Wang's capacity as the emperor's secret informant, he had contributed much to K'ang-hsi's knowledge of Yin-jeng's evil conduct, and it was Wang, together with Alingga, Olondai, and K'uei-hsü, who "had secretly communicated with court ministers" and made the motion to nominate Yin-ssu for heir apparent.[44]

The grand secretary Li Kuang-ti was the only high official who had consistently maintained a neutral position on the question of the heir apparent. Being an independent, he was disliked by both the Yin-jeng and Yin-ssu factions, and to protect himself from retaliation he had kept silent when Yin-ssu was nominated at the court conference.[45]

In addition to the support Yin-ssu received from ambitious court ministers and imperial relatives on his mother's and consorts' sides, he also had backing among the imperial clansmen (relatives on his father's side, descendants of Nurhaci). At the time of his nomination, the imperial clansmen numbered less than a thousand, so that their loyalty was something the emperor could not afford to lose. The part played by Sunu in the Yin-ssu faction is a case in point.[46]

Sunu was descended from Nurhaci through Nurhaci's son Cuyen. When K'ang-hsi denounced Sunu's involvement in the Yin-ssu cause, he traced Sunu's ill intentions back to earliest times: "Yin-ssu . . . has Sunu as his clique member. For generations, the Sunu family has been disloyal. His great grandfather Cuyen was executed by Emperor T'ai-tsu [Nurhaci] after he had committed serious crimes. Now Sunu hopes to avenge his ancestor. This is why he has joined the Yin-ssu clique in order to destroy my state."[47] He also accused Sunu of "creating dissension among the Emperor's own children," and warned his children as well as the court ministers to "look out for him, because I myself have been always on guard against him."[48]

Despite the treachery of his forbears, before 1708, Sunu had always been treated kindly by K'ang-hsi, for he had proved himself a brave fighter in campaigns led by the emperor. Sunu was an official in the Imperial Clan Court, an organ that controlled all affairs relating to the imperial kindred, had judicial and disciplinary authority over them, and preserved the Imperial Genealogical Record.[49] As a senior director, he was the fourth ranking man in the Court. Typical of most of the Ch'ing administrative departments, this middle layer of bureaucrats really ran things, and since Sunu had occupied his position for a total of more than three decades (1673-1683, 1685-1708), his influence among the imperial clansmen was very great.

Sunu's power was also founded on the Lower Five Banners. Beginning in 1679, for thirty years he held the post of lieutenant general of the Manchu Bordered Red Banner. From 1699 to 1708 Sunu was also the military governor of Feng-t'ien, the capital of Manchuria. (Although publicly revealed only later, by the Yungcheng Emperor, Sunu's administration was corrupt. The morale of his soldiers was low, and instead of guarding the city, they all lived far out of town.)[50]

Thus, an imperial clansman such as Sunu had real power, and when he threw in his lot with Yin-ssu, the emperor was threatened and infuriated. With all these various sources of support, the Yin-ssu faction might easily—the emperor felt—decide to use violence to "force me to abdicate in Yin-ssu's favor!" The emperor feared that "even before I die, my children may have already been swinging their swords, wrestling for the throne."[51]

The emperor meted out severe punishments to Yin-ssu's adherents. Sunggayan, the emperor's son-in-law, was deprived of his title and submitted to his grandfather T'ung Kuo-wei for discipline; Maci was deprived of his high posts and submitted to Yin-ssu for house confinement. (This was the practice in dealing with convicted Manchus or bannermen; in entrusting an offender to a senior relative or a Manchu prince, who himself was often—but not always—a co-plotter, the emperor held the keeper responsible if the prisoner escaped. It seems doubly ironic by modern standards, because Yin-ssu himself was now under imprisonment.) Maci's brothers Ma-wu—the emperor's longtime close bodyguard—and Li Jung-pao were delivered to the Imperial Clan Court for imprisonment. The Chinese ministers Wang Hung-hsü and Li Chen-yü, in spite of long loyal service, were dismissed from their posts for their "bad reputation" and their irresponsible behavior in supporting the Yin-ssu nomination at the court conference.[52]

Behind these punishments, the retaliation of Yin-jeng is almost certain. Even the innocent Ts'ai Sheng-yüan, subchancellor of the Grand Secretariat, whose name was never connected with the Yin-ssu affair, was dismissed, for being "flippant"; the emperor later confessed that "the Heir Apparent disliked him" (probably because he was an independent loyalist).[53] K'ang-hsi, it is obvious, had returned to the policy of appeasement of Yin-jeng.

After punishing the Yin-ssu leaders, the emperor tried to soften the hard feelings among his children, and to that end even treated Yin-ssu with much kindness (Yin-shih, however, remained excluded from the family circle). Although confined to a house near the Imperial Villa outside Peking, Yin-ssu had his *pei-le* title restored in January 1709, and thereafter he occasionally performed official duties and sometimes accompanied the emperor to Jehol. He was set free in 1716, because of serious illness.[54]

K'ang-hsi chose to blame officials from the Lower Fiver Banners for the struggles among the brothers, accusing "outside rascals" as the source of all trouble. On April 19, 1709, K'ang-hsi elevated all his adult children except Yin-ssu to higher princely ranks.[55]

This was the day that the emperor reinstated Yin-jeng as his legitimate successor. He notified the people and then apprised Heaven and all relevant deities of his decision.[56] Concerning the joyous event, Father d'Entrecolles wrote from Peking, "The prince was reestablished in his dignity, with all the formalities that are usually observed in the empire. Proof of public joy was given everywhere, and the comedy that is still played now is drawn from a happening in ancient history, which has much in common with what has just happened."[57] None of the actors in this "comedy" realized that their play was part of a tragedy.

13
Life Confinement

SOON after his reinstatement as heir apparent, the old Yin-jeng reemerged. The Chinese sources vaguely describe his behavior as "persisting in his madness," but give no details. Court talk, however, suggested that the issues between the father and son remained the same: succession and immorality.

Impatient with his father's apparent intention of remaining on the throne indefinitely, Yin-jeng soon began to complain about it publicly. Rumors transmitted abroad through Korean envoys in Peking help illuminate the behavior of the heir apparent: "We have heard that the Heir Apparent is extremely rebellious and perverse. Frequently he complained: 'In the whole world, from ancient times to the present, has there ever been any person who had been designated heir apparent for forty years, yet was still not given the opportunity to become the emperor?' From this, one becomes aware of this man's character."

The Korean envoys also said that Yin-jeng showed hatred for the emperor, was immoral, and was a disruptive influence within the court:

We have carefully gathered the information that since the [1708] incident, the Emperor has been quite strict in restraining the Heir Apparent's movements—always trying to keep him around the Emperor. Seeing that his brothers are enjoying leisure and freedom outside the palace, he is so resentful about his lack of freedom and jealous about the ease of his brothers, that he vented his hatred and resentment directly to the Emperor himself.

Concerning Yin-jeng's immorality, the report added:

Furthermore, whenever the Emperor went to his Jehol summer palace with the Heir Apparent, Yin-jeng persisted in his old habit, lavishing upon himself wine and women. He sent his men to affluent places all over the thirteen provinces, where they extorted local officials and demanded a supply of beautiful ladies. If local officials failed slightly in meeting the demands, they were dismissed immediately through slander and [false] accusations.

"Though the Emperor knew all about his wrongdoings," the envoys also noted, "he was compelled to go along with them." K'ang-hsi later confirmed the truthfulness of this report.[1]

For three years after 1708, K'ang-hsi continued his policy of appeasement of Yin-jeng: enduring and concealing his crimes and yielding to his demands—always with the hope that paternal patience would eventually move the son's heart to repentance. Yet Yin-jeng's behavior was anything but encouraging to the father. The emperor's tolerance finally reached its limit when he received from Ching-hsi, the young Prince An's younger brother, a report that he could not ignore. K'ang-hsi learned that Yin-jeng's new factional leader, Tohoci, general commandant of the Gendarmerie of the Capital City, frequently held drinking parties with fellow Manchu officials to rally support for Yin-jeng. They planned to "recommend" Yin-jeng to the emperor—implying a coup that would force K'ang-hsi to abdicate in Yin-jeng's favor.[2] A look at the power wielded by the general commandant will help explain why Yin-jeng selected Tohoci as his new leader and why the emperor eventually imprisoned Tohoci. It will also contribute to our understanding of the emperor's definitive deposition of Yin-jeng as heir apparent.

Structurally, Peking was composed of four "cities."[3] In the center lay the Forbidden City, which comprised the emperor's living quarters, Throne Halls, and the Grand Secretariat's office. Outside this was the Imperial City, where most of the buildings and offices pertaining to the Imperial Household were to be found. Outside the Imperial City was the Inner (or Tartar) City, containing many shrines, banner garrisons, and central administrative buildings. Finally, the Outer (or Chinese) City, consisting of business districts and Chinese residential quarters, adjoined the Inner City on the south.

Up until the K'ang-hsi reign, the administration of Peking was decentralized. The Forbidden and Imperial Cities were guarded by banner forces—the Household Division guarded the former and the Outer Division the latter. The Household Division, which was under the control of the Imperial Household, contained not only guards performing various security functions, but also the Imperial Bodyguard. Deployed at strategic points within the Inner City was

the Division of the Gendarmerie. Composed only of banner soldiers selected from the Outer Division, it was known as "the Office
of Foot Soldiers of the Banners"; its commanding officer, chosen
from among the banner lieutenant generals or deputy lieutenant
generals, was called "General commander of the foot soldiers of the
banners." The Outer City was guarded and patrolled by traditional
Chinese Green Standard forces—not Chinese bannermen—known
as the Three Battalions for City Patrol and Arrests. The nine gates
of the Inner City were also guarded by Chinese forces, following
Ming practice, along with the seven gates of the Outer City. Thus,
at the beginning, the security of the capital city was maintained
under the joint command of Chinese troops and banner forces.

These combined forces composed what can be called the supreme
command of the military garrison of the capital city. In addition,
there was another organization, also under joint Manchu-Chinese
administration, that took charge of policing and judicial matters.
For this purpose Peking was originally divided into "five districts"
(*wu-ch'eng*, literally, "five cities"), under the supervision of two
police censors, one Manchu and one Chinese. Their role was similar to that of the judicial commissioners in the provinces—they
made arrests, conducted trials, and passed sentence, when the violation was considered a minor offense. From among the police censors, one police magistrate (*ssu-kuan*) and one assistant police
magistrate (*fang-kuan*) were appointed to each of the five districts.
The grass-roots level of the police structure was the Roadway Office, which was in charge of street maintenance and also the preser-
vation of public order, through the identification of undesirable
elements or suspicious strangers.

During the K'ang-hsi reign, this decentralized defense and law-
and-order structure underwent reorganization. All powers—military, judicial, police, and housing control—were put in the hands
of the commander of Foot Soldiers of the Banners. The first stage of
consolidation took place in 1674—undoubtedly to cope with the
local uprisings that were taking place simultaneously with the outbreak of the Rebellion of the Three Feudatories; K'ang-hsi ordered
the guarding of the nine gates taken over by the commander's office. In 1691 he ordered the Three Chinese Battalions also subordi-
nated to the commander. By the time Tohoci assumed the commander's post—which was now called general commandant of the
Gendarmerie of the Capital City—it had also acquired the police-
judicial functions originally assigned to the police censors. In place
of the police censors, two police commissioners were established,
one senior police provost and one junior police provost, who were
under the direct control of the commandant. These two were as-

sisted by two deputy provosts, who each took charge of half of the city—the western and the eastern districts—a division of Peking that replaced the five districts. Within the new power structure, the jurisdiction of the Roadway Office was enlarged.

Under Tohoci's direct command were 21,000 banner soldiers, including 1,737 musketeers, with more than a quarter of a million pounds of ammunition stored at the nine gates of the Inner City. In addition, the Chinese Three Battalions for City Patrol and Arrests had 1,470 cavalrymen and 3,630 foot soldiers.

Tohoci received his appointment in about 1705.[4] He had previously been a bond servant in the Imperial Household, in which his highest achievement was the low rank of controller (*ssu-k'u*) in the Department of the Privy Purse (of which Yin-jeng's confidant Ling-p'u had been made minister in 1704).[5] Given Tohoci's ultimate lofty position, one would expect him to have advanced in the banner hierarchy at least to the rank of deputy lieutenant general or imperial bodyguard of the first rank, ordinarily the minimum qualification necessary for appointment to a post such as general commandant of the Gendarmerie.

However, the emperor had his reasons for appointing Tohoci. Tohoci was a friend of the heir apparent's confidant Ling-p'u, through whom Tohoci might have made an agreement with the heir apparent concerning this new assignment; K'ang-hsi at this time was very much maintaining his policy of appeasing his son. Moreover, Tohoci's sister, who had particularly attracted K'ang-hsi, had been made an imperial concubine, officially named Ting-fei. She gave birth to K'ang-hsi's twelfth son, Yin-t'ao, in 1686 at the age of fourteen (she was to remain low in the harem hierarchy).[6]

Another indication that K'ang-hsi appointed Tohoci as part of his appeasement of Yin-jeng was his naming of Tohoci's eldest son, Shu-ch'i, to the key position of department director in the Board of Revenue. As Ling-p'u's appointment (to Minister of the Imperial Household, with special jurisdiction over the Department of the Privy Purse) had been intended to facilitate Yin-jeng's access to funds, so Shu-ch'i's was intended to cover up Yin-jeng's corruption of the Board of Revenue. This was corroborated by K'ang-hsi's instruction to Wang Hung-hsü when Wang was made president of the board, in 1708: Wang "must not be too strict in handling the board's affairs."[7]

Tohoci was known in court for his military and administrative competence, but he shared many of Songgotu's character traits: he was arrogant, dictatorial, and corrupt. Like Songgotu, he felt powerful enough to violate court etiquette—a crime punishable by death. He enhanced his image by having a mounted escort added to his retinue while traveling through the Peking streets, a prerogative enjoyed only by imperial princes.[8] Tohoci was a retainer of Ma-erh-hun, Prince An the Younger, maternal uncle of Yin-ssu's wife; but he often made a point of showing contempt for his prince-master. Whenever he met Ma-erh-hun on the street, instead of dismounting to salute him, as required by feudal etiquette, he simply rode on; and when Ma-erh-hun died, in late 1708, Tohoci forced the prince's family to cut short the regular mourning period from a hundred to forty days, so that he could partake of the festivities of the Chinese Lunar New Year season (he loved extravagant amusements).[9] Being the number-one confidant of Yin-jeng, as well as being close to the emperor, Tohoci of course attracted power seekers. People who sought political protection for selfish interests recognized Tohoci as their "adoptive grandfather"; one such "adopted grandson," named Chiang, a wealthy man from Soochow without much education, "passed" the metropolitan *chin-shih* competition and was ranked ninth on the list, thanks to the pressure exerted by his "grandfather" upon the chief examiners.[10] And yet, despite such flagrant behavior, Tohoci had been made a confidant of the emperor: since the powerful position of general commandant of the Gendarmerie could easily be the source of a military coup d'état (which he feared), K'ang-hsi worked to get the friendship and loyalty of Tohoci.

With the emperor's confidence, Tohoci took advantage of his opportunities for extortion. In this he allowed his deputies to conspire with local gang leaders and the heads of the illicit salt market. Innocent people were implicated in robbery cases; people who refused to yield to his, or his henchmen's, demands were tortured by the severest methods; officers and soldiers from the Three Battalions, in collaboration with local ruffians, frequently took part in blackmailing the common people.[11] Tohoci, who listed among his prominent followers K'ang-hsi's nephew Hai-shan (son of his half-brother Prince Kung—Ch'ang-ning), also gained control over key ministers on important boards in the central bureaucracy. This came to light when in 1708 he was accused of blackmailing a wealthy official named Li Yuan-lung for 120,000 taels. Although it was well known in court circles that Tohoci's son, using the alias Ch'i-ko, had constantly blackmailed both officials and common people through manipulation of law cases; it was not until Li made a direct appeal to the emperor that Tohoci for the first time had to defend his own lawless behavior.[12]

Tohoci now mobilized his henchmen in the central bureaucracy to cover up his crime. According to Wang Hung-hsü's secret reports, the charge laid against Tohoci was easily proved; however, the Manchu presidents of the Boards of Revenue and of Punishments, Hsi-fu-na and Ch'ao-k'o-t'o, were "longtime adherents of the General Commandant," and "the Manchu presidents and vice-presidents" of the Boards of Civil Appointments and of War "were all afraid of the General Commandant," so that during the trial these men were "unwilling to utter a single word if at all possible." Fu-ning-an, Manchu president of the Board of Rites, "was the only one among all the Manchu presidents who was not an adherent of the General Commandant." The emperor's problems with Yin-jeng also inspired silence. As in previous cases, such as the victimization of Ch'en Ju-pi in the Court of the Three Judiciaries, since K'ang-hsi did not want to confront the heir apparent—the power behind Tohoci—the only way for the Manchu ministers to protect themselves from retaliation from both the prosecution and the defendant was to be evasive.

Because of these dual considerations, the Manchu ministers left the whole Tohoci case to the Manchu department directors. But the directors, too, knew of the power behind Tohoci and shared the fears of the ministers if they were to insist on a fair trial; yet they also feared punishment if it were determined that they had participated in a cover-up. Thus, they in turn encouraged the Chinese directors to conduct the trial.

Tohoci's strategy was simply to claim that the money he extorted had been used to repay debts incurred by "an imperial prince," thus "putting the ministers of the joint tribunal in a delicate position so that they would not feel it feasible to pursue the case any further."[13] He also informed the court that he had asked "a very important personage" to defend him in the presence of the emperor. The intervention of this important personage (we do not know who), combined with the court's passivity, worked. The emperor took no action against Tohoci and the whole case was left off the official record.

Tohoci's name first appeared in the official record only in 1708, when a Chinese censor, Wang I, impeached him for "his lawlessness, deception of the Emperor, corruption, wickedness, and oppression of the common people." In response, K'ang-hsi handed the impeachment memorial to the deliberative bodies for comment, but after receiving their recommendations, he tabled the case for three years. When, at the same time, two supervising censors also impeached Tohoci for abusing his powers, K'ang-hsi rebuked the censors and defended Tohoci's innocence.[14]

K'ang-hsi's abortion of an investigation and just settlement in the Tohoci case was in line with his policy of appeasement of the heir apparent. As the emperor later confessed, he had exhausted his imagination to come up with ways to please Yin-jeng "in order that eventually his heart might be moved to follow good."[15] In court politics the emperor yielded to Yin-jeng's requests without any regard to justice: he would blame whomever Yin-jeng wanted him to blame; punish whomever Yin-jeng wanted him to; and dismiss whomever Yin-jeng wanted to get rid of; only when Yin-jeng wanted him to kill innocent officials did the emperor refuse him, because, he explained, "by nature I am not fond of killing."[16] His appeasement of Yin-jeng forced the court ministers into a worse dilemma: none felt easy about upholding justice in court conferences because they feared the retaliation of Yin-jeng and his henchmen; yet in not pursuing justice they risked severe punishment from the emperor for shirking their duty.

For Tohoci, however, the emperor's appeasement policy only served to build his sense of power. In 1710, for example, K'ang-hsi dismissed Chang T'ing-shu, Chinese president of the Board of Punishments, simply because he was "stubborn": he had refused to go along with Ch'i-shih-wu, Manchu president of the same board, in the sentencing to death of an official on the basis of fabricated charges. Ch'i-shih-wu was known in court circles to be a major henchman of Tohoci, whom the said official had offended.[17]

The emperor's tolerance of Tohoci reached its limit only when he believed that his own life was in danger. A series of events led to the demise of this man and eventually to the permanent confinement of Yin-jeng, on October 30, 1712.

The immediate cause of Yin-jeng's final confinement was the emperor's fear of another coup. As mentioned before, K'ang-hsi had been informed that Tohoci was rallying support for the "recommendation" of Yin-jeng to the emperor. Tohoci gathered his followers in drinking parties, which K'ang-hsi characterized as "seditious," to be "promptly quelled before they broke into open actions."[18] The emperor undoubtedly interpreted the word "recommendation" to mean forcing him to abdicate in Yin-jeng's favor.

Prior to the ultimate decision to depose Yin-jeng, the emperor had sent out warning signals by punishing his adherents instead of confronting the heir himself, still hoping that Yin-jeng might suddenly repent. By late 1711 K'ang-hsi no doubt felt the necessity of removing Tohoci from office. On November 29 of that year he released Tohoci from his post "because of sickness," a polite term signifying dismissal. The emperor then appointed his own cousin and brother-in-law, Lungkodo, of the T'ung family, to be the new general commandant of the Gendarmerie (Lungkodo held the position until K'ang-hsi's death).[19]

Five days after Tohoci's dismissal, K'ang-hsi again resorted to

innuendo to vent his displeasure at the unfilial behavior of his son
and the hostile behavior of his son's faction; he enjoined the leaders
of all the banner units to "recommend filial sons" to be publicly extolled as exemplars. Two days later, waxing uncharacteristically
forthright at a public audience with the entire court, the emperor
denounced a number of Manchu princes and ministers for "having
formed a clique for the Heir Apparent." He pointed out a few
notorious plotters in the group and protested, "I am amazed to see
that the elements in the Songgotu faction have never ceased to
exist; they all want revenge on behalf of Songgotu!"[20] He ordered
the arrest of several chief henchmen of the Yin-jeng clique, including Ch'i-shih-wu, Manchu president of the Board of Punishments;
Keng-o, Manchu president of the Board of War; and O-shan, a
lieutenant general in the metropolitan banner forces.

Meanwhile, the emperor was able to verify the charges laid
against Tohoci, and felt compelled, finally, to take action. By then
the privilege of submitting palace memorials had been granted to
high-ranking provincial officials, and now K'ang-hsi decided to ex-
pand his new information-gathering system to include the central
bureaucracy. On March 5, 1712, the emperor authorized all court
ministers to send him palace memorials, the target of the move explicitly being the Tohoci faction—and implicitly the heir apparent
himself. As the imperial edict explains, "For if anyone memorializes
on matters that cannot be made public, he is risking the safety of
his own life—How many officials can one find who are not afraid
of the consequence? This is why T'ao-ho-ch'i [Tohoci] and those
mean characters under him have constantly mustered adherents to
his clique without any fear of the imperial authority. Now their
activities are all made manifest."[21]

On May 14 the emperor submitted Wang I's original memorial of
impeachment of Tohoci to a court tribunal; the main charge was
corruption and the abuse of power. On May 16 the tribunal submitted its recommendation to the emperor, but the emperor rejected it as being too vague and because it contained no depositions
from the defendants Tohoci and Ch'i-shih-wu. The emperor ordered that the case be tried again, to be presided over by a new participant, a grand secretary. Meanwhile, on May 17, the Imperial
Clan Court memorialized the emperor that Tohoci and his chief
henchmen, Ch'i-shih-wu and Keng-o, had pleaded guilty to the
charge of gathering clique members in drinking parties. The emperor instructed that punishments for this particular crime be decided after the trial for corruption. He also for the first time openly
denounced Yin-jeng for "being unfilial and unkind" and for insti-
gating his "recommendation" by his henchmen to the emperor. On

May 20 the tribunal headed by the grand secretary memorialized K'ang-hsi that Tohoci, Ch'i-shih-wu, and Keng-o had been found guilty of corruption; the tribunal recommended that the three men be punished by strangulation after the Autumn Assizes (a judicial practice by which the emperor reviewed all capital cases of the year in the fall to decide which convicts would be executed; many executions were postponed from one fall to another), and the emperor approved the tribunal's recommendation.[22]

Soon after his conviction for corruption, Tohoci was further accused of additional crimes by Ching-hsi, the young Prince An's younger brother; Ching-hsi charged Tohoci with having held extravagant banquets during the mourning period for the young Prince An, who had died in late 1708. The emperor ordered the Imperial Clan Court, in conjunction with four of his children (Yin-chih, Yin-chen, Yin-ch'i, and Yin-yu), as well as Maci (now acting minister of the Imperial Household) and others, to try Tohoci on the new charge.[23] The court did not arrive at a decision until six months later.

On October 29, five months after Tohoci's arrest, the emperor ordered the arrest of Yin-jeng. The heir apparent was then fettered and imprisoned.[24] Father Ripa witnessed the sad scene:

> When we arrived at Chan-choon-yuen [Ch'ang-ch'un-yuan], the imperial residence near Peking, to our great terror we saw in the garden of that great palace eight or ten Mandarins and two eunuchs upon their knees, bare-headed, and with their hands tied behind them. At a small distance from them the sons of the Emperor were standing in a row, also with their heads bare, and their hands bound upon their breasts.

Ripa went on to say that, though "the sons of the Emperor" were standing in bondage, only the heir apparent was the target of the emperor's reproaches: "Shortly thereafter, the Emperor came out of his apartments in an open sedan, and proceeded to the place where the princes were under punishment. On reaching the spot he broke out with the fury of a tiger, loading the heir-apparent with reproaches, and confined him to his own palace, together with his family and court."

The next day, October 30, K'ang-hsi issued a "public manifesto," written in his own vermilion pen, to depose "the unfortunate prince as suspected of treason."[25] In his statement the emperor admitted that it was he who had pledged to be Yin-jeng's guarantor when he reinstated his son as heir apparent, but that Yin-jeng had persisted in committing his earlier crimes. The emperor now "felt ashamed," and he also "felt ashamed toward the people in the entire empire."[26]

He confessed that as a result of his efforts to appease his son he had placed his ministers in an awkward and unfair position. Now, since Yin-jeng's "madness" remained unaltered, he was forced to depose him permanently. On December 13, 1712, K'ang-hsi completed the procedure of deposition with a solemn report to Heaven, which expressed his deep regret.

Three days later, on December 16, the Imperial Clan Court memorialized the emperor that all charges laid against Tohoci by Ching-hsi had been found true. It recommended that Tohoci "be executed immediately by slow slicing" and that his son Shu-ch'i "be strangulated after the Autumn Assizes." The emperor did not act upon the recommendation until early the next year, by which time Tohoci had "died of illness in prison."[27] On February 27, 1713, the Imperial Clan Court again memorialized the emperor, proposing— and the emperor approved—that as further punishment Tohoci's corpse be chopped into pieces and burned, the ashes to be thrown into the air and not buried. His son Shu-ch'i was sentenced to death by strangulation after the Autumn Assizes. Tohoci's household servant Chou San—who had been implicated in the blackmailing of Li Yuan-lung—and Chou's son Chou Ch'i were beheaded on other charges.[28] It was as if K'ang-hsi were still trying to exorcise the evil spirits that had invaded his son Yin-jeng.

14
The New Contenders

THE designation of an heir plagued K'ang-hsi. The year 1712, when Yin-jeng was conclusively deposed, marked the beginning of a new search for a responsible successor. During the ensuing decade—the last of his reign—K'ang-hsi seemed determined never again to reveal his preference among his children for the heir apparentship. Even when his health became weak and officials had a legitimate excuse to urge him to establish a crown prince, they were forbidden to recommend a candidate. The restorationists were, of course, eager to see Yin-jeng in that position; the Yin-ssu faction first wanted to see Yin-ssu selected, and later backed another candidate; others began to speculate on new possibilities.

Many names, thus, were being circulated. Some of the candidates who previously had been weak were now strong; for example, Yin-t'i (the fourteenth imperial son) was only sixteen in 1703 —the time of the Songgotu plot—but now he was a vigorous young adult. On the other hand, some of the older contenders had been eclipsed.

In 1712 K'ang-hsi was fifty-eight and felt old. His years were made worse by ill health, brought on by the succession struggle and the disappointments he had recently suffered. His frailty only served to intensify the rivalry of the aspirants, whose jockeying for position also impaired the efficiency of the government. And it tarnished the image of a wise and powerful ruler.

THE RESTORATIONISTS WERE made up of pre-1712 supporters of Yin-jeng who continued to work toward his heir apparentship even after his deposition. They sought their goal in spite of the emperor's hostility toward them—as indicated by the harsh punishments meted out to Tohoci and his people—and gave up hope only at the very end of the K'ang-hsi reign. Yin-jeng maintained whole pockets of support in three of the central institutions: the Censorate, the Hanlin Academy, and the Grand Secretariat.

Early in 1713 a Yin-jeng sympathizer, the Chinese censor-general, Chao Shen-ch'iao, presented a memorial to the emperor, urging him to designate an heir apparent. The emperor said he could not do this, as he had not yet found a worthy candidate. He explained:

> For thirty years Jen-tsung of the Sung did not establish an heir apparent; neither did Emperor T'ai-tsu [Nurhaci] of our dynasty establish an heir. It was only after his death that Emperor T'ai-tsung [Hong Taiji] was enthroned as his successor by Manchu princes, *pei-le*, and ministers. [Likewise,] Emperor T'ai-tsung did not establish Emperor Shih-tsu [Shunchih] to be his successor *pre mortem* . . . All my children are inferior to no one either in learning or in judgment. But since they have grown up and received their princely titles, naturally their retainers would want to protect the interests of their respective lords. Even if it were possible for me to establish one of them as the heir apparent, who could guarantee then that nothing would happen in the future? Furthermore, it is not easy for anyone to enjoy this blessing, and none of them would want to harbor such an ambition. If anyone, however, should harbor such an ambition, he is surely an unworthy person . . . Now, if one wishes to establish an heir apparent, the candidate must be one who would take my heart as his heart. How can one do this lightly?[1]

In early 1714 the emperor approved a suggestion from Lungkodo, general commandant of the Gendarmerie of the Capital City, that sixty-eight guard posts surrounding the emperor's suburban villa be reinforced by troops selected from among the Chinese bannermen.[2] This signaled a general distrust of the Manchus—a paranoia fanned by the ruthlessness of the imperial sons.

In 1715 Ablan, nephew of Sunu and a member of the Yin-ssu faction, reported to the emperor that Yin-jeng had been engaged in secret communications (the letters were written in invisible ink) with P'u-ch'i, a prince and a lieutenant general of the Plain Red Banner. Originally a member of the Yin-shih faction, whom Yin-jeng had thrashed, P'u-ch'i now apparently had shifted his allegiance to Yin-jeng. The secret communications were transmitted by a physician who had been ordered by the emperor to attend Yin-jeng's sick wife. The letters revealed that Yin-jeng had requested P'u-ch'i to "recommend" him to the emperor for the post of generalissimo (supreme commander of the active combat troops). Both

P'u-ch'i and the physician were sentenced to be decapitated after the Autumn Assizes.[3]

Between late 1717 and early 1718 the restorationists made another attempt to reinstate him. In early 1717 Wang Shan, Chinese grand secretary and loyal supporter of Yin-jeng, had secretly memorialized the emperor to urge him to appoint an heir apparent. The emperor was displeased at Wang's suggestion and kept the memorial in the palace. Later that year, when the emperor was ill and appeared to be dying, eight censors jointly memorialized him, also entreating him to name an heir; they euphemistically suggested that an heir apparent be appointed in order to "share the Emperor's burden of ruling." The emperor again pigeonholed the memorial.[4]

According to a letter of 1718 that an anonymous Jesuit missionary wrote from Canton, there was talk at this time that K'ang-hsi, disgusted by his own sons, would choose a descendant of the Mongol Yuan dynasty as his heir. Though rumors of this sort probably originated with court officials who misinterpreted the emperor's political moves, it is nevertheless worthwhile quoting the letter, for it shows that the crisis of succession had become a major concern, not only within Chinese circles, but among foreigners as well. It reads:

> The Emperor had a sickness that caused some alarm, though it did not result in further complications. On the occasion of this sickness he showed some desire to name a successor. He kept everyone in suspense about whom he would take as his successor. He didn't want to name any of his children, nor anyone of Chinese descent. He thought both were too soft in character and would not be able to govern the empire. Besides, he thought, although the imperial houses of Han, T'ang, Sung, and Ming were all extinct, there did remain more than a thousand princes from the Yuan family. By saying this, he seemed to suggest that the thought of appointing a prince from among the descendants of the Yuan dynasty was a genuine possibility.

The missionary then injected his doubts, which probably expressed court sentiment: "But will the Chinese like this choice? Will the princes, sons of the Emperor, peacefully forfeit what their birth rights have entitled them to?"[5]

The remainder of the letter summarized how "the uncertainty about the Emperor's choice was cause for one of the first Mandarins to have his son present a memorial urging the Emperor to consider the importance of naming a successor and the stability it would create in the empire. He also suggested that the Emperor's second son be restored to his original status as the heir apparent." This item referred to the Chu-t'ien-pao case, of which we have the details in the *Veritable Records.*

Before Chu-t'ien-pao spoke to the emperor, and soon after Wang Shan and the censors had been reprimanded, K'ang-hsi's health further deteriorated, as a result of the Dowager Empress Hsiao-hui's falling seriously ill. Anxiety over her illness and then the shock and sorrow at her death, early in 1718, caused the emperor problems with his circulation. His feet bloated with dropsy and he fainted constantly, so that he had to stay in bed for nearly two months. K'ang-hsi completed his "valedictory" during what he thought were the last days of his life.[6]

At this juncture, Chu-t'ien-pao, a Manchu corrector in the Han-lin Academy, presented his secret memorial asking the emperor to reinstate Yin-jeng, saying that the prince was "virtuous and filial." Subsequently, court ministers also petitioned the emperor, stating that "a prospective heir apparent might be able to assist the Emperor until the Emperor's health is restored."[7]

Soon after reading Chu-t'ien-pao's memorial, K'ang-hsi ordered this man to stand trial in the presence of the court on February 19, 1718.

The Emperor: In your memorial you said my second son was both virtuous and filial. How did you come to know about that?

Chu-t'ien-pao: My father, Chu-tu-na, had mentioned it: that is how I heard.

The Emperor: When your father was in active government service, my second son was still in good health. His achievements—whether in learning, archery, horse riding, or any other skills—were all very impressive. But later he grew insane. Once this disease took hold, he lost his mind; his behavior was strange and wild. For example, once he stood with his back toward me and abusively cursed Hsü-yüan-meng; he even used unspeakably filthy language to curse his senior uncle [Prince Fu-ch'uan] and his uncle's children. Isn't this clear insanity? Did you know this also?

Chu: I did not know about it. I deserve a thousand deaths because of my stupid suggestion.

The Emperor: In your memorial, you said my second son was more sagacious day by day and more virtuous day by day. How do you know this?

Chu: This was what my father had heard from those who were guarding Yin-jeng at the place of confinement.

The Emperor: What are the names of those guards?

Chu-t'ien-pao could not answer. He just repeated, "I deserve death! I deserve death!"

The Emperor: Since you have memorialized me on such a weighty matter, I did not send anyone to question you because anyone else might overlook your good intentions. This is why I have personally interrogated you. You are a child who does not know anything. I have just asked you a few questions; and you are speechless. Someone else must have conspired with you and communicated with you. Tell me truthfully all about them.

Chu: Well, actually the memorial was written by my father, Chu-tu-na, and Tai-pao [Chu-tu-na's son-in-law]; they told me to present it.

The emperor then ordered Chu-tu-na and Tai-pao arrested and put in chains, to be tried immediately.

While waiting for the arrests, the emperor took the opportunity to assert that there were quite a few "mad" people among the imperial clansmen. He described their symptoms: "[Of Prince Ying:] He was a good fighter; but once he was seized by the disease of insanity, he lost self-control and behaved wildly. [Of P'u-ch'i:] Unable to make up his mind; totally unreliable. [Of San-kuan-pao:] Unstable, unpredictable like the blinking stars." He also mentioned an ordinary bannerman, Ch'i-shih (a common name), whom he later was to describe as:

A troublemaker by nature; like an ape. That was why Yin-jeng called him "the ape lieutenant general." But I think he was just like a hunting dog. When he saw a pigeon on the roadside, he jumped at it; when he saw a frog, he drove it; but when he saw a wild beast, which the hunter was really interested in capturing, he refused to make a move! . . . and whenever you see him lowering his eyebrows, you know he is contemplating betrayal through treacherous means![8]

Soon Chu-tu-na and his son-in-law Tai-pao were brought to the emperor's presence; K'ang-hsi then ordered that they be submitted to the imperial children and court ministers for trial.

The following day, the emperor personally examined Chu-tu-na and all the others involved in the memorial. The real motive behind Chu-t'ien-pao's move was simple and typical: he believed that if Yin-jeng could be reinstated, they all would "attain wealth and power."[9] They were punished severely: Chu-t'ien-pao was beheaded at once for being "disloyal and unfilial"—unfilial because "he implicated his own father in the trial" (though it was the emperor who had pressed him to confess). While Chu-tu-na was "leniently spared his life," along with others, he was submitted to the general commandant's office for "carrying a cangue permanently," and their wives and children were delivered to the *Sin jeku* to become "official slaves" in the Imperial Household.[10]

The same day, the court ministers jointly memorialized the emperor, asking that he reconsider the nature of the position of heir apparent, preparatory to making his appointment. The emperor took the opportunity to reiterate his deep regret about having allowed Songgotu to determine the rules governing the heir apparent's insignia and rituals. He said: "Today you ministers have come to see me about the matter of an heir apparent. When Yin-jeng was the Heir Apparent, all the protocol concerning the heir apparent was established by Songgotu. The designated garments and insignia all violated the established proprieties, and were almost identical with mine! This caused Yin-jeng to change his nature and he began to indulge in rebellious behavior."[11]

K'ang-hsi ordered his ministers to look into the precedents set in the *Collected Statutes* of the Ming, as well as those of the Han, T'ang, and Sung. Then they were to present their ideas, based on their research, for new protocol concerning rituals and insignia, as a step toward the naming of an heir apparent. The emperor was later pleased with the ministers' proposals, for they reduced the usurping aspects in the existing protocol and conformed with the precedents set by the previous dynasties.

By this time—February 1718—K'ang-hsi had been ill for more than two months and there was no sign that he would regain his health. He openly confessed that he was afraid that some of the Yin-jeng followers might take advantage of his weakness, using force to push for the release of their leader.

The restorationists' wishful thinking lingered on. In early 1721, when K'ang-hsi's reign entered its sixtieth year of the Chinese *seculum* (or period of sixty years, carrying the significance of a centennial in the West), Wang Shan presented a secret palace memorial to the emperor: to commemorate this auspicious year of the reign—the longest in the imperial history of China—K'ang-hsi should reestablish Yin-jeng as heir apparent. Soon afterwards, twelve censors, three of whom had collaborated with Wang Shan in in 1717, memorialized the emperor to the same effect. Influenced by reports from his secret informant Wang Hung-hsü, K'ang-hsi publicly denounced Wang Shan and the censors for their malicious intentions and ordered harsh punishments. Wang Shan was sentenced to banishment to the northwest, where he was to fight in the army that was campaigning against the Western Mongols (since he was too old to withstand such treatment, his son Wang I-ch'ing was allowed to serve as his substitute).[12]

Compared with the relative leniency K'ang-hsi had shown in reprimanding other Chinese senior ministers, the severity of Wang Shan's sentence was designed to demonstrate that support of Yin-jeng was not to be tolerated, that Yin-jeng had been unequivocally dropped from consideration for the heir apparentship.[13]

YIN-SSU, THE OTHER conspicuous contender so far, also re-mained in the emperor's disfavor in the post-1712 years, mostly because of his aggressive behavior. Immediately after Yin-jeng was deposed for the second time, Yin-ssu went to the emperor and said, "I just don't know what kind of attitude I should take now. I would rather pretend that I am sick." The emperor saw through Yin-ssu, who was trying to discover his father's plans: "You are merely a *pei-le* [third-rank prince]; how could you dare overstep propriety by saying this to me? How could you have dared to test my intentions with such a statement?" Later, K'ang-hsi told his ministers: "Being a mere *pei-le*, Yin-ssu suggested such an idea without due regard to propriety. He recklessly said this to me simply to tempt me to divulge my intentions. Does this not prove that he is utterly treach-erous and totally wicked?"[14]

Toward the end of 1714 another confrontation occurred, which served to seal Yin-ssu's fate. K'ang-hsi made a second trip to his Jehol summer palace, after his usual retreat, on which he had plan-ned to take Yin-ssu along. But Yin-ssu was unable to go with him, because he had to offer sacrifices at the tomb of his mother on the second anniversary of her death; he was to meet the emperor at Jehol soon after he had completed the ceremony. However, with-out securing his father's approval, he never arrived at the summer palace. This was considered a deliberate act of provocation. (Ac-companying the emperor to Jehol was viewed by the Yin-ssu fac-tion as something better avoided, as this would restrict their free activity. Once, in order to avoid the emperor's company, Yin-t'i feigned illness, thus angering his father.)[15]

Yin-ssu further provoked the emperor. On December 29, the day after the imperial party had arrived at Yao-t'ing—north of Peking on the way to Jehol—Yin-ssu sent two of his men, a eunuch and a bodyguard, to extend his "greetings" to his father; accompanying the greetings was a gift—two dying eagles. He asked his messengers to tell the emperor that he would like to join the party at T'ang-ch'üan (the site of an imperial lodge, a place known for its hot springs) for the return trip to Peking. The emperor took great of-fense at all this, seeing it as a mockery—that Yin-ssu likened his father's fate to that of the dying eagles.

Enraged at Yin-ssu's behavior, which the emperor described as both "unfilial and unrighteous," K'ang-hsi summoned the eunuch and bodyguard to an area in front of his tent to be interrogated. Forcing his ministers and children to watch, he used the squeezing rods to inflict agonizing pain in the messengers' ankles, under which torture, they revealed the names of the chief henchmen in the Yin-ssu faction; the most important ones were Olondai and Alingga.

Three days later, on January 1, 1715, at T'ang-ch'üan, the emperor summoned the sons who were with him—Yin-o (his tenth), Yin-t'ao (twelfth), Yin-wu (fifteenth), Yin-lu (sixteenth), and Yin-li (seventeenth). He then formally denounced Yin-ssu. He said that three days earlier, when he had received the dying eagles, he was so angry that he thought he would have a heart attack. He went on to express his feelings about Yin-ssu. First he said that he did not want to name Yin-ssu as his heir because of both his family background and his dangerous character: "Yin-ssu was born of a woman of low birth from the *Sin jeku*. Treacherous and ambitious as a child, Yin-ssu began to act most disloyally after he had heard the comment of the physiognomist Chang Ming-te [about his future honor]. He hired people to assassinate my second son [Yin-jeng]. This matter was known to the entire court. I am afraid that when he made an attempt on the life of my second son, he did not care at all what it would do to me!"

Then the emperor explained that he had decided to release the convicted Yin-jeng in 1709 because he thought Yin-ssu would be worse than Yin-jeng as the heir apparent: "When I was seriously ill [in late 1708], court ministers recommended Yin-ssu for the heir apparentship. I was caught in a dilemma. I decided to release Yin-jeng, who I knew was not supposed to be released!" He described how he had felt ever since the release: "For the past few years, I have been extremely depressed and unhappy. Yin-ssu still hoped to realize his original ambition. He continued to form a faction with treacherous elements, secretly engaging in adventurous conspiracies. The faction spread rumors saying that since I am old, my days are not many, and since Yin-ssu had been formerly recommended by court ministers, who would dare to challenge him? Hence, he felt assured [that he would be my successor]."

The emperor then declared: "From now on, my relationship with Yin-ssu as father and son is severed," because "I am afraid that some of my children, who behave no better than dogs and pigs, will want to use military means to force me to abdicate in his favor, in order to show their gratitude toward Yin-ssu." Sarcastically, the emperor added, "If this should indeed happen to me, I would accept death with gladness and with a smile on my face!"

He warned his children: "I am very indignant. This is why I have made this statement to you. I hope all my children will remember my kindness and obey my instructions—this is indeed an appropriate thing for all of you to do as my children and as my subjects. Otherwise, at my death bed, I am afraid some of you will fight each other for the throne, swinging your swords over my corpse!"

The emperor concluded with strong words about Yin-ssu's character: "Yin-ssu harbored deep hatred against me because he had failed to become the heir apparent. My second son lost respect because of his rebellious acts; but Yin-ssu has always been successful in winning people's hearts. He is a hundred times more dangerous than Yin-jeng!"

The following day, the emperor again expressed his fear of Yin-ssu. He told his children how he had exiled Yin-ssu's nurse and her husband, Ya-ch'i-pu, to the Manchurian frontier for their role in assisting Yin-ssu, but that later they had secretly returned to Peking, for which the emperor had them put to death. After the execution, Yin-ssu had had the audacity to present a memorial to the emperor saying that he had been unfairly judged by his imperial father. "In short," the emperor concluded, "this man had numerous wicked adherents, extremely dangerous and treacherous. Even I myself am afraid of him. Someday, he will avenge the death of Ya-ch'i-pu!"[16]

During 1715 Yin-ssu was further disgraced. His princely allowances and those of his subordinates were terminated. By the end of the year, his former Chinese resident tutor Ho Cho had also fallen into disgrace, because of his alliance with Yin-ssu, as documented by two letters from Yin-ssu to Ho, found in a search of Ho's house. The emperor was particularly irritated by the fact that Yin-ssu, though without a son by his wife had not taken additional concubines, and yet he allowed Ho Cho's daughter to be brought up by his wife in his own house. Earlier, the emperor had issued explicit orders forbidding such a personal relationship between a Manchu prince and a Chinese, in order to keep Chinese literati out of the emperor's family affairs.[17]

In late 1716 the emperor learned that Yin-ssu was suffering from typhoid fever (an influential eunuch, Wei Chu, was bribed to convey the exaggerated report of Yin-ssu's illness). This brought out K'ang-hsi's sympathy, and he ordered Yin-ssu released from confinement forever and permitted to return home. Thereafter, from time to time Yin-ssu would attempt to evoke his father's compassion with feigned illness, but to no effect. By now it was plain that Yin-ssu had been eliminated from the succession race.[18]

The Yin-ssu faction was thus in need of a new candidate.

BEFORE 1712 YIN-CHIH had never expressed an ambition to become heir apparent. But when the heir apparentship was vacated by Yin-jeng's final deposition, Yin-chih was regarded as the most probable candidate, for several reasons. First, after Yin-shih (the eldest brother) and Yin-jeng (the second) had been ruled out of the contest, Yin-chih, the third brother, was now the highest-ranking of the remaining sons of K'ang-hsi: court officials "all speculated that Prince Ch'eng [Yin-chih], because of his age, will certainly be the most likely person to be selected as the heir apparent."[19] Second, he had been commissioned by the emperor to supervise literary projects in the Wu-ying Hall and later in the Meng-yang Study —an office where Jesuit missionaries and Chinese scientists engaged in the compilation of works on music, mathematics, and astronomy. On his staff were such renowned scholars as Fang Pao, Ch'en Meng-lei, and Ho Kuo-tsung, and under his supervision an important compendium on music, mathematics, and astronomy was completed, in 1714.[20] Yin-chih's appointment to this prestigious position created the impression that he was now the favorite son of the emperor. Thirdly, because of his intellectual inclination, Yin-chih was liked by Chinese scholars, especially the Southern literati and various of the Fukien people, perhaps including the famous Li Kuang-ti and some of Li's disciples. Their friendship added to Yin-chih's standing.[21]

Later the Yung-cheng Emperor related that during this time his brother Yin-chih "considered himself as the designated heir apparent." When, in 1718, K'ang-hsi ordered his court ministers to suggest rites and insignia for the future heir apparent, Yin-chih scolded the officials for having reduced the splendor of the crown prince.[22]

As early as 1707, K'ang-hsi had begun to accept invitations to visit Yin-chih's garden. This friendly interaction between Yin-chih and his father was viewed as a sign of Yin-chih's good fortune— even recent historians see it as a favorable indication. However, a similar relationship was also growing between the emperor and Yin-chen, the fourth son. In fact, official records suggest that it was Yin-chen who initiated this practice—at the Jehol summer palace— of inviting the emperor to visit his garden; Yin-chih was merely appropriating Yin-chen's idea. And in contrast with Yin-chen, Yin-chih's lack of filial piety made him an unlikely choice of the filial emperor. In 1690 he had shared Yin-jeng's secret joy at the emperor's seemingly impending death; and in 1699 he had shaved his head before the expiration of the hundred-day mourning period for his mother's death, for which offense he was punished by demotion to a lower princely rank.[23]

Nevertheless, Yin-chih's prestige at court, whatever it actually was, was felt by the officials. It was sensed even more in the provinces, where, for lack of accurate information, rumors often inflated reality. This condition is illustrated by the Meng Kuang-tsu incident of late 1716 and early 1717.[24]

It was usual for imperial princes frequently to send gifts to their retainers who were serving as provincial officials. From this custom developed the opportunity for the princes to extort money from their officials. In late 1716 a certain bannerman (he appears in the record as Meng Kuang-tsu, a "fugitive rowdy") left Peking to visit provincial officials, on whom he bestowed gifts, claiming that he was Prince Ch'eng (that is, Yin-chih). Governors and governors-general received him with great reverence; some went so far as to kneel before him. Nien Keng-yao, governor of Szechwan, in turn presented Meng with "horses and silver taels," and T'ung Kuo-jang, governor of Kiangsi, gave him "silver taels and satin." Civil and military officers solemnly welcomed the "prince," and transmitted news of his visit to the next province through the post. All the officials in the empire seemed to believe this man to be Yin-chih.

The governor of Chihli, Chao Hung-hsieh, suspected imposture and secretly memorialized the emperor on this unusual event; for without K'ang-hsi's authorization, no imperial princes were allowed to leave the capital.[25] The emperor accordingly issued a decree to all provincials demanding that they "report to the Emperor by secret palace memorials" about these visits, and he ordered the arrest of the impostor. Meng Kuang-tsu was apprehended and immediately executed. The Board of Punishments recommended that Nien Keng-yao and T'ung Kuo-jang be deprived of their governorships for greeting the impostor with gifts. (The emperor, however, commuted Nien's sentence to "dismissal with special permission to remain in post to carry out the governor's duties," probably because of the intervention of Nien's master, Yin-chen, now Prince Yung. Nien defended his innocence in a secret memorial to the emperor, which was full of lies, but it either fooled K'ang-hsi or else he chose to tolerate it, in view of Nien's importance in the strategic Szechwan region.)[26]

The Meng Kuang-tsu scandal perhaps affected Yin-chih's image, for after it he was no longer regarded as the most promising candidate for heir apparent. One contemporary observer remarked that despite Yin-chih's self-assurance, he was in fact no more than a "single-handed"[27] faction, without a strong power base among either the Manchus or the Chinese.

AMONG ALL THE imperial sons, Yin-chen was the only one K'ang-hsi had praised for being able to understand him. There is much evidence that Yin-chen indeed shared his father's concerns and had tried to fulfill the emperor's heartfelt hopes for both the father-son and the brotherly relationships.

Yin-chen was probably the most learned of all of the brothers. He demonstrated great interest in Chinese scholarship and was a knowledgeable devotee of Ch'an (Zen) Buddhism. In 1703, a month and ten days before Songgotu's arrest, the twenty-five-year-old Yin-chen invited the renowned Confucian scholar Yen Jo-chü to his residence in Peking where he showed Yen great honor.[28]

K'ang-hsi much admired Yin-chen's calligraphy. Many of the scrolls allegedly written in the emperor's hand were actually done by Yin-chen. Judging from the elegant characters of Yin-chen's vermilion endorsements and the learned essays full of classical allusions that flowed artistically from his writing brush, his literary achievement was nothing less than exceptional.[29] As noted earlier, Yin-ssu's writing was so bad that his imperial father had ordered him to do exercises to improve it.)

K'ang-hsi asserted that he had paid a great deal of attention to Yin-chen's early education. While most of his children were cared for by nurses or relatives, the emperor personally raised Yin-chen. This is probably because Yin-chen's mother, the concubine Te-fei, was K'ang-hsi's favorite consort during the boy's childhood. Though K'ang-hsi felt that the teenaged Yin-chen behaved "slightly temperamentally" (literally, "slightly unstable in joy and anger"), he outgrew this phase;[30] Yin-chen's intense interest in Ch'an meditation may have originated in his determination to control his emotions.

The *Veritable Records* contain a number of passages in which K'ang-hsi praises Yin-chen for being modest, sincere, and filial. He also describes Yin-chen's sensitivity to his father's feelings: "As regards his understanding of intentions and desires, and his love for me, as well as his diligence and earnestness, he is truly a man of sincerity and filial piety."[31]

On another occasion the emperor extolled him as a "truly great man" because of his magnanimity toward Yin-jeng. Before Yin-jeng's arrest in 1708, the two brothers' relationship had not been congenial; Yin-jeng treated Yin-chen insultingly—obviously he was resentful of Yin-chen's moral superiority,[32] for the contrast in their personalities was conspicuous. But Yin-chen turned the other cheek. According to K'ang-hsi, "When Yin-jeng was arrested earlier [in 1708], no one came to me to defend him. Only my fourth son, extremely broadminded and conscientious, repeatedly pleaded secretly for mercy in Yin-jeng's behalf. One who possessed such a motive is truly a great man."[33] Because of his intervention, K'ang-hsi even suspected that Yin-chen, too, belonged to the Yin-jeng faction, and in 1712 had him arrested along with Yin-jeng and the other brothers, as noted by Father Ripa.[34] After the 1708 incident, Yin-chen faithfully followed his father's injunction to "stop any socializing activities among brothers," in order to demonstrate his nonpartisan stance.[35]

In 1709, on the day of Yin-jeng's reinstatement, K'ang-hsi elevated Yin-chen's rank to the highest level, *ch'in-wang*, prince of the blood of the first degree; other brothers, such as Yin-t'ang and Yin-t'i, were raised only to *pei-tzu*, prince of the blood of the fourth degree, while Yin-ssu was allowed to retain his *pei-le*, prince of the blood of the third degree, without elevation. Yin-t'ang and Yin-t'i were greatly offended by this action, and Yin-chen again generously pleaded that his own rank be "lowered one degree and the ranks of Yin-t'ang and Yin-t'i be raised by one degree so that we brothers might live together peacefully."[36] For this reason, all his brothers respected—though not necessarily loved—Yin-chen up until 1722 (when their father's death sparked the most bitter stage of their competition); even Yin-t'ang, who actively worked first for Yin-ssu's candidacy and then for Yin-t'i's, praised Yin-chen for his noble attitude toward the deposed Yin-jeng.[37]

Yin-chen was cautious about entering the contest for succession, since he had seen how his father reacted to his more aggressive brothers. But some of Yin-chen's retainers were less discreet, as can be seen from the example of Tai To, a local official who was a bannerman under Yin-chen's lordship. In 1713 Tai sent a secret memorial to Yin-chen urging him to change his passive attitude, to "cultivate the influence of the Prince Yung [Yin-chen's princely title] family":

> As to your family, there must be a few talents. But they are like pearls buried in the sea . . . How could their talents be discovered? Since I have received Your Excellency's instruction that members of our family are allowed to make contributions to the government in exchange for official posts,[38] this clearly proves that Your Excellency wants to help talented members [of our family] be promoted. I therefore urge Your Excellency to pay special attention to this matter, namely to discover new talents and to help those already in the government be promoted. Then gradually members of our family will be magnified even though they are now insignificant; and those who occupy only small offices will

become high officials. Those who are serving in the provinces eventually will become governors-general, governors, commanders in chief, and brigade generals; and those serving in the capital will become grand secretaries, presidents, and vice presidents of the boards or members of the nine ministries. Although one cannot expect that all of them will be helpful in the future, yet even just two or three talents would be of great help.

At the end of the memorial, Tai warned Yin-chen of the danger of "maintaining neutrality" in the struggle:

At this critical juncture, Your Excellency should not relax your guard even for a moment. Otherwise, if some swift feet get ahead of you in the race, and seeing that Your Excellency is ten thousand times superior to others in talent, wisdom, virtues, and learning, it would be impossible for you to maintain neutrality. [Whoever wins the race] may feel envious [of your superior qualities] and harbor malicious intentions toward you [to eliminate you]. If you wait for that to happen, it will be too late for you to regret.

Yin-chen's response to this memorial shows his extreme cautiousness even at this point; it reads: "Your advice is extremely valuable, but it is useless to me. Had I such an intention, I would not have behaved this way. Furthermore, such a troublesome job I wish to avoid, much less aspire to it . . . You need not worry about it for me. You should never allow this kind of motive to rise in your mind. Be careful! Be careful!"[39]

The memorial and Yin-chen's reply suggest two things: First, up to now Yin-chen had yet to muster significant support either in the court or in the provinces—few of his retainers held important positions. Second, Tai To's memorial perhaps spurred Yin-chen to reconsider his future and that of the throne; his subsequent behavior suggests that, in part, he adopted Tai's advice, despite his declared lack of interest in the heir apparentship.

Meanwhile, Yin-chen continued to rise in his father's esteem. In early 1715, while staying with the emperor at Jehol, Yin-chen and Yin-chih were invited by their father to advise on the projected campaign against the Eleuth Mongols in the west.[40] In suggesting the hard-line policy of "extinguishing the renegades by force" (with which the emperor agreed), Yin-chen impressed his father with his sound judgment.

Yin-chen's changing attitude toward the succession is revealed in his response to the second secret memorial from Tai To, sent in 1716. This memorial was submitted after the two had conferred in Peking, at which time Yin-chen had entrusted Tai to proffer gifts on his behalf to Man-pao, Yin-chen's bannerman who was governor-general of Fukien and Chekiang; this was a common practice among imperial princes: to show special favor to a high-ranking retainer in exchange for monetary support. The memorial reads:

> Your slave Tai To extends his hearty greetings to Your Excellency, my master. I set out in the middle of the seventh month from Hangchow and arrived at my post at Fukien in the ninth month. All the things that you wanted me to submit to Man-pao have been secretly delivered to Ch'ien Lao-ko and T'u-pa-li [probably Tai's subordinates]. I asked the latter to transmit them to Man-pao. I will report to you again when Man-pao has delivered the silver taels to me.

Tai's memorial then rambles in different directions:

> I would like to report on another matter. When I passed by the Wu-i Mountain, I met a Taoist monk, whose behavior was quite unusual. After I talked with him, I discovered that his words were quite extraordinary. I will report to you separately on this matter.
>
> Being a foolish person, I really have very little interest in official advancement. Also, because I am not used to the food and water and climate in Fukien, I have been ill ever since I arrived here. In the future I intend to return to the capital on the grounds of poor health.

Yin-chen's response contains remarks that imply his growing desire to rule:

> I am fine. How are you feeling? I am very displeased with your letter. Why did you display such a discouraging spirit in your letter, saying you wanted to come back on grounds of poor health? You ought to have enough ambition to become a governor-general or a governor, then you can be proud of yourself. If you are satisfied with remaining subordinate to others, how can you be happy about it? By saying this, I mean it to be true for the entire empire, not just Fukien province. As to the words you have heard from the Taoist monk, write me again in detail.[41]

Tai supplied these details in his next secret memorial, submitted later in 1716: "Regarding that Taoist monk, I asked him to tell the fortune of my master. He arrived at the conclusion that your future may be described by the character *wan* [an abbreviation of *wan-sui*, literally, "ten thousand years," a term synonymous with the word *huang-ti*, "the Emperor"]. Upon hearing this, my heart leaped for joy. I will tell you all the rest after I have returned to the capital."[42]

In his reply Yin-chen commended Tai: "You have handled the

matter quite properly, showing your conscientiousness [in sending me the letter]. Concerning the words the Taoist monk exchanged with you, you must relate them to me in greater detail. You are indeed quite fortunate to have been able to meet this kind of person."[43] By now Yin-chen's interest in the heir apparentship is evident, but only to us—not to court ministers. He made no overt actions that would divulge his changed intentions.

The year 1717 was crucial for all the aspirants to the throne. By the end of that year "many rumors were flying about the capital," Tai To said in a memorial of 1717 to Yin-chen.[44] It was the fatal illness of the Dowager Empress Hsiao-hui that had precipitated the rumors. People believed that, as an act of filial piety for Hsiao-hui, K'ang-hsi would choose his heir apparent, so that the old empress could see the prince crowned before her death.

But, all the speculation focused on active contenders rather than the quiet Yin-chen. In the court, Yin-chen was not considered likely to be selected as the next heir apparent. This view, though misguided, caused such great concern in Tai To that he made some wild suggestions to Yin-chen in his next memorial. It reads:

> I have earnestly prayed day and night for Your Excellency, expecting good news to come. Recently, however, I have heard that many rumors are flying about the capital. I find that the island of Taiwan is situated in the sea far away from the mainland. It is a separate realm with vast fertile soil. The post of Intendant in Taiwan is empowered to take charge of military affairs. If I could be appointed to this post, I would be able to muster military forces and train them on your behalf. This is also a precautionary measure for your future in the event that you have to retreat from the mainland.

In response, Yin-chen reproved Tai To: "If you have such an intention, you will certainly encounter an unexpected punishment from Heaven. I advise you to stay in your present intendantship [and not harbor any wild ideas]!"

In early 1718 Li Kuang-ti was summoned to Peking by the emperor (Li had been on sick leave in Fukien since late 1715). Since Li was now regarded as the emperor's chief adviser, the court ministers deduced that K'ang-hsi had recalled him to the capital in order to obtain his opinion on the choice of a successor.[45]

Before Li left Fukien, Tai To went to see him. They discussed the matter of the heir apparentship, and Tai made Li an offer. Tai reported:

> Recently the grand secretary Li Kuang-ti had been on sick leave here in Fukien, but he received the Emperor's special order to return to the

Capital promptly, even though he was still in poor health. Rumors say that his recall is connected with the matter of appointing an heir apparent, and that the Emperor wished to have secret consultations with him on the matter. It was a great shock to me to hear this. I therefore paid a special visit to him in order to detect his intention. He told me that "at the present time, the eighth son of the Emperor [Yin-ssu] is the most worthy one," and so forth. I told him: "Yin-ssu is a coward and is incompetent; he can hardly be compared with my master, [Yin-chen] the fourth son of the Emperor, who is both talented and virtuous . . . If you, sir, are willing to cooperate, you will share wealth and power [with us]." He nodded his consent to my proposal.

The rest of Tai's memorial recounted Yin-chih and Yin-t'i's recruitment of Southern scholars (such as Yang Tao-sheng, styled Wen-yen, a famous astronomer, and Ch'eng Wan-ts'e, a disciple of Li Kuang-ti), to show Yin-chen how actively the other imperial contenders were working.

Yin-chen lit into Tai To for his suggestions to Li: "Did I ever mention a single word about this while you were here in the capital? How have you, an insignificant official in the provinces, dared to behave so audaciously and outrageously? Your life is no heavier than a goose feather, but my reputation may be stained by you for ages. I regret being your master. Perhaps this is something predestined in our previous lives."[46]

It seems strange that among all the names put forward as a possible heir apparent, Yin-chen's was never publicly proposed. For Yin-chen, more than any of his brothers, stayed on excellent terms with his father, and he was a unifying influence within the imperial family. In 1709 K'ang-hsi had built a garden palace for him, naming it Yuan-ming yuan (it was the nucleus of the later, more famous palace that French and English soliders looted and burned in 1860); Yin-chen often invited his brothers to this palace, even his rivals for the throne. Yin-t'i, who had been made generalissimo to lead the campaign in the west, and who sought the heir apparentship, had dinner many times with Yin-chen in late 1718, before leaving for the front. Other brothers whom Yin-chen invited either for dinner or to enjoy his garden included Yin-lu (the sixteenth son), Yin-t'ao (the twelfth), Yin-ch'i (the fifth), and Yin-hsiang (the thirteenth). Yin-chih was also invited, but he declined on grounds of illness (he perhaps felt too competitive with Yin-chen for their father's favor). In 1722 the emperor three times accepted Yin-chen's invitation, and once all the brothers (except for Yin-jeng and Yin-shih, who were in confinement) were gathered at Yin-chen's palace.[47]

Thus it appears that Yin-chen had succeeded in maintaining harmonious relationships with most of his brothers.[48] His efforts to bring the imperial children together strongly qualified him for the heir apparentship, and it is difficult to accept the allegation posited by Yin-chen's enemies after 1722—which was believed even by twentieth-century scholars—that Yin-chen was the most unfavored son among his brothers. Why, then, did K'ang-hsi frequently assign him the task of performing important sacrificial ceremonies? In 1721 and 1722, for instance, the emperor asked Yin-chen to represent him at the solemn winter-solstice sacrifice at the Altar of Heaven;[49] such a request could only signify K'ang-hsi's great confidence in Yin-chen's sincerity and filiality.

THE YEAR 1718 WAS a bad one for both the restorationists and those who favored Yin-chih. But meanwhile, the Yin-ssu faction, which had lost Yin-ssu as a viable contender, had found a new candidate—Yin-t'i—for the throne. Yin-ssu remained the leader of the faction but now directed Yin-t'i's campaign behind the scenes.

By 1718 the K'ang-hsi regime was at war again with the Western Mongols, who in 1717 had invaded Tibet, a vassal state of the Ch'ing court. At the end of 1718 the imperial armies suffered a serious setback, and in an attempt to boost their morale, the emperor appointed the thirty-two-year-old Yin-t'i (his fourteenth son) as their supreme commander, with the title generalissimo, the highest military rank. When the new commander left the capital in 1719, the emperor ordered his brothers and the entire court to see him off.[50] This impressive honor prompted people to think that it was Yin-t'i who was being groomed for the heir apparentship. Yin-t'i's supporters, at least, thus interpreted the emperor's act, and they began to work toward its fulfillment.[51]

The thirty-seven-year-old Yin-t'ang (the ninth son) was Yin-t'i's major contact in the capital (the two had earlier been allied in the Yin-ssu effort). Before Yin-t'i departed, he told Yin-t'ang, "It appears that this position [heir apparent] will most probably be mine." And Yin-t'ang confided to his former tutor Ch'in Tao-jan: "In the event that the fourteenth prince be made the heir apparent, he will certainly desire my advice."[52] Yin-t'ang then began a publicity campaign in behalf of Yin-t'i; to the Portuguese missionary Jean Mourao (João Mourão), who was thought to have some influence with the emperor, Yin-t'ang said, "This time, the fourteenth prince has been made the supreme commander of the expeditionary forces; my imperial father thinks very highly of him. I think in the future the heir apparentship must necessarily be his!"[53]

Despite Yin-t'ang's declared certainty, the Yin-ssu faction remained as unsure as ever about the emperor's intentions. They displayed their uncertainty in the ways they used to bring their influence on K'ang-hsi. First, they attempted to keep him under constant surveillance; Yin-t'ang was said to have "lavishly bribed two eunuchs named Ch'en Fu and Li K'un to observe and report on the Emperor's daily mood and movement, and asked them to keep him informed of all such matters constantly."[54] Yin-t'ang also worked to establish good relations with the influential director of the eunuchs, Wei Chu—head of the Inner Chancery of Memorials to the Emperor. Wei Chu occupied a strategic position in the line of communication between K'ang-hsi and the outer court; even the emperor's children had to ask Wei Chu to transmit their messages to their father.

Wei Chu's relationship to the Yin-ssu faction can be traced back at least to 1716. It was he who, that year, helped Yin-ssu secure K'ang-hsi's sympathy by exaggerating the seriousness of Yin-ssu's typhoid fever; Yin-ssu's previously terminated annual allowances were restored thanks to Wei Chu's adroitness. For his efforts, Yin-ssu knelt in gratitude before Wei Chu.[55]

Yin-t'ang went even further in cultivating good relations with Wei Chu: he had his son Hung-cheng acknowledge Wei Chu as his "adoptive uncle"—for a eunuch, the word father was not applicable. Wei Chu and another influential eunuch Liang Chiu-kung (who had both attended K'ang-hsi since his youth) were to meet with tragic downfalls soon after the emperor's death, for their collaboration with the Yin-ssu faction.[56]

The Yin-ssu faction also attempted to win the support of Li Kuang-ti and other Chinese scholars. After 1703 Li's influence on K'ang-hsi's decision making had increased steadily; when Yin-jeng was deposed, K'ang-hsi held a private meeting with Li to discuss the problem of the heir apparent. K'ang-hsi's confidence in the Manchus had declined so sharply that even Sung-chu, a Manchu grand secretary, tried to flatter the Chinese Li in the hope that Li might "say some good words for him" to the emperor. After Li died, in late 1718, Yin-t'i continued his public-relations campaign by exhibiting great interest in Chinese learning and by patronizing Chinese scholars. When he invited Li's disciple Ch'eng Wan-ts'e to be his literary adviser, he addressed Ch'eng as "sir." He also succeeded in attracting to his advisory staff some of the associates of one of the most prominent scholars of the early Ch'ing, Li Kung. Having made these connections, Yin-t'i twice—in 1720 and 1721—sent "carts and horses" to Li Kung himself, to invite him to be his mentor. Li, however, declined, and fled to a hideout to avoid Yin-t'i's messengers: he was said to have trembled upon receiving Yin-t'i's invitation, because he was terrified of becoming involved with any faction in the struggle for succession.[57]

Yin-t'i also had his eyes on a strong figure in the southwest, Nien Keng-yao, governor of Szechwan (for whom the rank governor-general of that province was created in 1720). Nien was also a generalissimo, appointed to lead a section of the expeditionary forces against the Eleuth Mongols. He was approached by the Yin-ssu faction in 1720, through the Portuguese Missionary Mourao. Yin-t'ang wished to get a military-campaign post for his Chinese confidant Ho T'u, so he sent Mourao to ask Nien for the favor; Mourao offered to return Nien's kindness with "any foreign-made articles he wished." Nien cooperated, for which he received thirty or forty "European-made purses."[58]

Finally, Yin-t'i also enlisted the service of fortune-tellers. In 1719 he invited a Shensi man, Chang Hsia-tzu (meaning "Chang the Blind"; his real name was Chang K'ai), to determine his chances for the heir apparentship. Chang predicted that "he would be the future Emperor," for which he was awarded twenty taels. Later Chang confessed that he had lied to Yin-t'i, "simply to get some silver."[59]

Yin-t'i's reputation was fairly good when, as generalissimo, he arrived at the northwest front. Soon, however, after establishing his power there—with the help of a large sum of money sent to him by Yin-t'ang—he began to accept bribes, extort money, and blackmail his subordinates; by 1721 he had accumulated enough wealth to repay his debts to his collaborators: 200,000 taels went back to Yin-ssu and 60,000 to Yin-t'ang. In addition, sexual debauchery and drunkenness had also become a part of Yin-t'i's life on the front. Yin-t'i's new behavior, according to the Yung-cheng Emperor, was "known practically to all."[60]

It is quite possible that hostile channels carried these matters to the emperor's attention. On November 17, 1721, Yin-t'i was recalled to Peking for "consultation on strategy." Yin-t'ang interpreted the action as the emperor's deliberate hindrance of Yin-t'i: K'ang-hsi was "obviously unwilling to let Yin-t'i succeed in the expedition, lest Yin-t'i should become too difficult to handle in the future."[61] The emperor kept Yin-t'i in Peking until May 29, 1722.[62] There was, thus, logic to Yin-t'ang's interpretation, for emergency consultations would not ordinarily last six months.

That K'ang-hsi decided to send Yin-t'i back to the front reinforced the misgivings within the Yin-ssu faction; the emperor's action seemed to show that Yin-t'i was in fact not a leading candidate for the heir apparentship. For, if K'ang-hsi had indeed chosen him as his successor, he would certainly have kept him close by, rather than sending him thousands of miles away while his own health steadily deteriorated. Amidst the rivalry of his sons K'ang-hsi must have seen the need of the presence of a strong heir apparent. Furthermore, since K'ang-hsi had previously denounced Yin-ssu's brotherly adherents as "dogs and pigs" who might venture to force him to abdicate in Yin-ssu's favor, it was hardly likely that he would install Yin-t'i, Yin-ssu's collaborator, as his heir.

Finally, the most important clue to understanding K'ang-hsi's feelings about Yin-t'i is the incompatibility of K'ang-hsi's values and those of the Yin-ssu faction. The faction's guiding principles, *i-ch'i* and the importance of clandestine action, diametrically opposed K'ang-hsi's reverence of loyalty and filial piety. As early as 1713 K'ang-hsi had hinted at the sole criterion for choosing an heir: he "must take my heart as his heart."[63] Yin-t'i simply did not fit this role. The rumors raged on.

PART V

Decision

15
The New Emperor

THE last image we have of the "good old Emperor" (as John Bell, a Scottish visitor to the court, called him in 1721) is not that of the scholar in repose, but that of the hunter in action.[1] The scene is the imperial hunting park Nan-yuan, the vast forest six miles southwest of the capital. For K'ang-hsi, the style of the hunt—symbol of the military prowess of the Manchus—had had to change. Just as over the century the Manchus' absorption of Chinese culture had eroded their military ability, so a lifetime of worries had diminished K'ang-hsi's vitality. Nevertheless, he strove to embody the valor of the Manchu race until the very last of his days. He could not forget his grandmother's exhortation never to fail his ancestors.

On November 29, 1722, K'ang-hsi arrived at the park and settled into his favorite lodge, only a mile from the main gate. It was a "small but neat building," as Bell described it, "having a double row of galleries, open to the forest, on all sides . . . On the south side of the house is a canal, filled with clear water, and several large fish ponds . . . At a convenient distance from the house stood about a thousand tents, where the courtiers and grandees had lodged the night before."

Breakfast was at four in the morning, and the old emperor was ready for action before dawn. At the signal heralding the emperor, all men "drew up in lines . . . dressed in their hunting habits, the same as those used by officers and cavalry of the army, when in the field, and armed with bows and arrows." As the emperor approached, one could see him sitting on "an open machine"—having been unable to ride for some years—"cross-legged"; the litter was carried by four men supporting the long poles on their shoulders.

179

Before the emperor lay a fowling piece (not a traditional Manchu weapon), a bow, and a sheaf of arrows.

The imperial retinue was impressive as it marched out to the chase. The company mounted and followed the emperor, at some distance, till they came into "the open forest where they all formed a semicircle, in the center of which was the Emperor . . . close by him were the master of the chase, with some greyhounds, and the grand falconer with his hawks." These beautiful Siberian birds were as white as doves, but with one or two black feathers in their wings and tails.

As the flanks of the imperial army moved out, the chase began. First K'ang-hsi hunted hares, taking delight in hitting his mark with the skill of an accurate archer as the creatures darted past him. Then with his hawks he went after pheasants, partridges, and quails in the thickets and tall reeds. Next the emperor pursued a variety of deer—recalling the hunt at Mulan, where stags were his favorite target—killing them "very dexterously with a broad-headed bow." In hunting he would resort to his fowling piece only when dealing with the most dangerous prey: wild boars and tigers. For two weeks K'ang-hsi thus enjoyed himself.

On December 14 he suddenly fell ill. He commanded his train to transport him back to the Suburban Villa. The official record does not provide the nature of this illness, but private sources supply details. An unidentified Jesuit wrote that the emperor was taken ill "with a cold and shivering"; the cold was caused by coagulation of the blood, and "no remedy did him any service."[2] Another Jesuit observer, Father Ripa, described the emperor as having been "seized with an inflammation"; he deemed it a rather uncommon ailment, for it was usually caused by sudden changes of weather, and in Peking "the cold increases in uniform gradation."[3]

K'ang-hsi's illness came as no surprise to the court or himself. He had frequently complained about his poor health over the past ten years; the prolonged illness of 1708, characterized by abnormally fast heart palpitations, had permanently affected him. By early 1717 he started to have dizzy spells and to lose a great deal of weight—as the two portraits from this period testify. K'ang-hsi had always resented being helped, but now his weakness forced him to rely on others, even to walk. By early 1718 his feet had become inflamed and bloated, his general health had further deteriorated, and death seemed imminent. It was on this occasion that he articulated his aforementioned valediction in front of his sons and the Manchu ministers.[4] He urged the listeners to heed this as his final statement, specifically as it related to the matter of his successor, and concluded with a crisp "I will say no more!"

The valediction was given in response to the court ministers' urging that he appoint an heir to "share the . . . ruling," in case of his "sudden death." Three points stand out in his last testament.

First, the prospective ruler had to fulfill two requirements: he had to possess reverence for Heaven and demonstrate emulation of his parents and ancestors. Second, the emperor was fully aware of the danger that could arise if an heir apparent were not designated *pre mortem*. Taking advantage of the chaos that would accompany his sudden death, "mean characters," as he put it, might attempt to establish their own candidate among the imperial children. He vowed, "As long as I have my last breath, I will never allow these sorts of people to prevail." And third, the reason he delayed naming an heir was the bitter experience he had with the former heir apparent, Yin-jeng; this had convinced him that "state powers must be vested in the hand of one man," which precluded the assistance of a crown prince "sharing" the rule. He was therefore not prepared to reveal his choice until it appeared certain that he was about to die.

As late as 1719, while complaining about the rapid loss of his health ("my inner pneuma and my blood strength are slipping away and my spirit is diminishing"), the emperor again warned his ministers of what "unfilial people" might want to do—take advantage of his frailty to establish their own man as the heir apparent.[5] In 1722, once more seriously ill, K'ang-hsi must have been preoccupied with the question, "Who will succeed me when I die?"

K'ang-hsi lay in bed for seven days as his condition worsened; yet he made no mention of a successor. Up to this point, the prospects of the candidates for heir apparent compared thus:

Though regarded at court as the strongest contender, Yin-t'i was kept thousands of miles away, at the northwestern front; furthermore, K'ang-hsi had not promoted Yin-t'i beyond "prince of the blood of the second degree" (*chün-wang*). Now three of Yin-t'i's older brothers had achieved the title "prince of the blood of the first degree" (*ch'in-wang*); these sons were Yin-chih (the third brother, oldest of the qualified candidates—Yin-shih and Yin-jeng were both imprisoned), Yin-chen (the fourth brother), and Yin-ch'i (the fifth).

As with Yin-t'i, Yin-ch'i was apparently not the emperor's choice either. A month before his illness, K'ang-hsi had sent Yin-ch'i to the Imperial Mausolea, forty miles northeast of Peking, to offer sacrifices to the emperor's deceased stepmother the Dowager Empress Hsiao-hui. During the critical seven days, K'ang-hsi did not recall Yin-ch'i (who returned to Peking only after his father's death); the emperor seemed content to leave him at the Mausolea to continue the filial rituals on his behalf.[6] In fact, neither Yin-ch'i nor anyone else had ever claimed that he was K'ang-hsi's choice for heir apparent.

This narrowed the candidates to two, Yin-chih and Yin-chen. As noted before, however, after the Meng Kuang-tsu scandal of 1716, Yin-chih was no longer considered the front-runner; his former close relationship with Yin-jeng also did not help his cause. But the most important reason for the unlikelihood of his being chosen heir apparent was his lack of filial piety toward both his father and his deceased mother.

Yin-chen's filial piety, his concern for his brothers, and his intellectual accomplishments make it seem that he must have long been on K'ang-hsi's mind as the heir apparent. In 1722 a private source states that Yin-chen was once "openly commended" by the emperor "in front of the imperial consorts" for his "filial affection and care" for his father.[7] Perhaps overimpressed by the rumors favorable to Yin-t'i, few linked Yin-chen's filial behavior to the heirship.

The last task that K'ang-hsi assigned to Yin-chen, two days after he fell ill, tells us much. On December 16 the emperor appointed Yin-chen his representative in the very solemn sacrifice to Heaven on the winter solstice (December 22), a ceremony that was preceded by a week of fasting and prayers. As the Son of Heaven, K'ang-hsi had always claimed that it was his sole prerogative to sacrifice at the Altar of Heaven on that day, and the only son he had ever asked to substitute for him on this occasion was Yin-jeng, while still the heir apparent. K'ang-hsi compromised his principle only when he was too weak to perform the Three Kneelings and Nine Prostrations to Heaven, at which times in recent years (1708, 1717, 1718, and 1720) he had appointed his trusted chief chamberlain of the Imperial Bodyguard, Ma-erh-sai (concurrently chief minister of the Imperial Equipage Department), to perform the sacrifice (K'ang-hsi had been able to observe the fast and prayer period).[8] That the emperor had not, since Yin-jeng, appointed any of his sons as his representative, was presumably owing to his desire to conceal his preference for the heir apparent.

But in 1720 K'ang-hsi started to demonstrate his favor, by having Yin-chen represent him at the sacrifice at the Imperial Ancestral Hall on his sixty-seventh birthday (he rejected a recommendation from court ministers that a high-ranking Manchu official be named to perform this function).[9] Although that year Ma-erh-sai was again appointed to represent the emperor at the Altar of Heaven on the winter solstice, in 1721 K'ang-hsi finally asked one of his sons to substitute for him at this ceremony. The son he chose was Yin-chen.[10]

K'ang-hsi's illness had caused him by 1722 to be more conscious of his relationship with Heaven and of the need of divine sanction for his empire, as well as his own health (he had testified to such beliefs repeatedly during his lifetime, and they appear in his Family Instructions). With this in mind, he again assigned Yin-chen to represent him, on the winter solstice, first "fasting in sincerity and reverence" and then performing the ritual at the Altar of Heaven. When Yin-chen requested to be permitted to stay near his father, in order to attend to his needs, K'ang-hsi asserted that the ceremony was the most important matter—more important to him than having Yin-chen close at hand.[11]

On December 17 Yin-chen sent his bodyguards and eunuchs three times to inquire after the emperor's well-being. The emperor told them, "I am feeling slightly better." Yin-chen did the same on the next two days, and received the same response from his imperial father.

On December 20, at about two in the morning, the emperor's condition drastically declined. He then sent for Yin-chen, who, at the Palace for Fast and Prayer (Chai-kung) in the southern suburb of Peking, was two to three hours away from the Suburban Villa, where K'ang-hsi lay. The emperor did not summon Yin-ch'i, who was forty miles away—let alone Yin-t'i, who was far off on the western front.

At about four o'clock the emperor called in the sons who were gathered outside his bedroom—Yin-chih (the third), Yin-yu (the seventh), Yin-ssu (the eighth), Yin-t'ang (the ninth), Yin-o (the tenth), Yin-t'ao (the twelfth), and Yin-hsiang (the thirteenth)—as well as Lungkodo, the emperor's cousin and brother-in-law, now the general commandant of the Gendarmerie of the Capital City.[12] From his deathbed, K'ang-hsi issued a terse decree: "My fourth son, Yin-chen, is a person with honorable character, resembling me. He will certainly be able to continue my task as the Emperor. Let him be enthroned!"

Yin-chen probably arrived about eight o'clock that morning. Around ten o'clock he entered his father's bedroom. The emperor discussed his worsening condition—which would suggest that his mind was still alert—but he did not tell Yin-chen of his selection of a successor. After the short conversation, Yin-chen left to wait outside his father's chamber.[13] Yin-chen entered the room three more times that day to comfort the emperor. On the last occasion, the dying K'ang-hsi gave Yin-chen the rosary he wore around his neck, given him by his late father, Shun-chih. This was a token of religious sanction of Yin-chen's succession—and yet still the emperor said nothing about his decision.[14]

At approximately eight o'clock that night, December 20, 1722, K'ang-hsi died. Only then was Yin-chen told by Lungkodo,[15] in the presence of his brothers, that he was the new emperor.

Epilogue

Y IN-CHEN inherited the imperial throne, and with it all the old problems. As the Emperor Yung-cheng he proved himself a worthy successor of his father. Within his thirteen-year reign (1723-1735), Yung-cheng regenerated the K'ang-hsi bureaucracy—low in morale, faction-ridden, corrupt, and verging on bankruptcy—and transformed it into a most efficient imperial administration, which featured ingenious innovations. Profiting from the fruits of Yung-cheng's rule, China under his successor, the Ch'ien-lung Emperor (r. 1736-1795), was to witness unprecedented peace and prosperity, lasting until the end of the eighteenth century.

But Yung-cheng's political success came at a high human cost. Because of the threat posed by his ambitious brothers, Yung-cheng was forced at times to be ruthless. Of the brothers, Yin-jeng presented few problems, for K'ang-hsi had ordered him permanently confined and the influence of the restorationists had evaporated. (Yung-cheng treated the ex-heir apparent with kindness, for which Yin-jeng, before he died, on January 27, 1724, expressed his gratitude.) But the Yin-ssu faction was a source of great difficulties for Yung-cheng, despite his efforts to win Yin-ssu's good will by conferring on him numerous honors.[1] The disappointed Yin-ssu, along with his ally brothers, refused to concede defeat, transferring their anger from their deceased father to their imperial sibling, and a new round of struggles and secret maneuvers was resumed. Dutiful and uncompromising, Yung-cheng met the challenges with skill: he made effective use of the palace memorial system for investigation of his brothers' hostile activities, and to rehabilitate the crumbling administration he purged his recalcitrant brothers, influential

185

eunuchs and dishonest officials. He was especially disgusted with the Southern intellectuals, so that few of his top confidants were recruited through the regular channels of the civil-service examination system.

In these ways Yung-cheng made a large number of enemies among the princes, officials, and eunuchs, who were accustomed to K'ang-hsi's leniency. They countered the new emperor's reforming zeal with vilifications of his character and rumors of his "illegitimate" claim to the throne. Within a few years this conflict ended in a confrontation that sent shock waves out from the imperial court; the ripples extended in wider and wider circles both in space and in time.

Allegations of Yung-cheng's usurpation spread to remote parts of the Chinese empire, and the stories were even told abroad—they are to be found in Korean and Japanese records.[2] In the course of time these ripples so distorted Yung-cheng's image that he became a monstrous stock villain in popular fiction and drama. Twentieth-century writers in China have created sensational details, attributed outrageous motives, and finally produced a synthetic Yung-cheng much larger than life. The study of the Emperor Yung-cheng would provide an excellent opportunity to probe the mystery of power and personality and to illuminate the relationship between fiction and history.

Appendix
Notes
Bibliography
Glossary
Index

Appendix

Chinese Dynasties	Ch'ing Reigns
Ch'in 221-207 B.C.	(In Manchuria)
Han 202 B.C.-A.D. 220	Nurhaci 1616-1626
(Period of disunion 220-589)	Hong Taiji 1627-1643
Sui 589-618	(In Peking)
T'ang 618-906	Shun-chih 1644-1661
(Period of disunion 907-960)	K'ang-hsi 1661-1722
Sung 960-1279	Yung-cheng 1723-1735
Yuan (Mongols) 1260-1368	Ch'ien-lung 1736-1795
Ming 1368-1644	Chia-ch'ing 1796-1820
Ch'ing (Manchus) 1644-1912	Tao-kuang 1821-1850
	Hsien-feng 1851-1861
	T'ung-chih 1862-1874
	Kuang-hsü 1875-1908
	Hsüan-t'ung 1909-1911

Imperial Government under K'ang-hsi

Except for special regions (such as Manchuria, Chinese Turkestan, and Mongolia), the local government of China during the K'ang-hsi period was overseen by governors-general and governors. Governors-general were usually military officials, whose jurisdiction covered more than one province; the governors were civil officials, whose jurisdiction covered one province only. The jurisdiction of the governor-general of Liang-Kiang, for example, included Kiangsi and Chiang-nan (Chiang-nan consisted of Kiangsu and Anhwei), and each of these three provinces had a governor. Each provincial governor was assisted by a financial commissioner and a judicial commissioner.

A province was divided into prefectures, under prefects. For different purposes various prefectures or sections of the provincial government were grouped in a *tao* (circuit), under the administrative control of an intendant (for example, *liang-tao*, a grain intendant who collected grain taxes). Each prefecture was divided into departments or subprefectures, under subprefects, and each department or subprefecture was broken up into districts, under district magistrates. The districts constituted the lowest level of local government; within them were towns and villages. The latter were ruled by an informal power group, the local "gentry," consisting of degree holders, retired officials, and other influential people in the rural communities.

The central government in Peking was composed of four kinds of offices: (1) the Grand Secretariat, staffed by grand secretaries and lesser officials, in charge of reviewing provincial memorials and making recommendations, as well as the drafting and promulgating of imperial edicts; (2) the Six Boards (or Ministries) in charge of deliberating routine governmental business according to administrative regulations and precedents—the core of the imperial bureaucracy; the Mongolian Superintendency, which had a status equivalent to that of the Six Boards, handled relations with the Mongols; (3) nonadministrative organs, such as the Censorate and the Court of Judicature and Revision (which, along with the Board of Punishments, constituted the Three Judiciaries), the Hanlin (National) Academy, the Department of Astronomy, and so forth; (4) the emperor's personal bureaucracy, consisting of the Imperial Clan Court, the disciplinary body that supervised the conduct of the imperial clansmen; the Imperial Household Department; the Supervisorate of Imperial Instruction; and the Imperial Bodyguard, as well as other offices in charge of ceremonial and practical (medical and the like) functions.

A characteristic of the imperial government under the Manchus was the simultaneous appointment of a Manchu and a Chinese to all the ministerial Ch'ing positions. Thus, on each of the Six Boards, for instance, there were a Manchu and a Chinese president, senior vice-president, junior vice-president, and so forth. The term "inner court," which appears frequently in this book, refers to the living quarters of the emperor, as well as to the emperor's entourage—eunuchs, bodyguards, and intellectual advisers. The Grand Secretariat, the Six Boards, and the nonadministrative organs all belonged to the "outer court." (The emperor's personal bureaucracy, hard to categorize, fits under neither of these headings.)

K'ang-hsi's Consorts and Sons

The Emperor K'ang-hsi had forty consorts, among whom thirty bore him children, a total of fifty-six: twenty daughters and thirty-six sons. Of the thirty-six sons, only twenty-four were ranked in the imperial genealogy; the others had died in infancy or early childhood. In the following chart imperial consorts, the mothers of the twenty-four sons, are listed according to their hierarchical status. These women's personal names are not known; the official genealogy gives only the canonized title and rank of each consort. For example, Ching-min, the canonized title, and Huang-kuei-fei, her rank, together serve as the name for the mother of the thirteenth son, Yin-hsiang. Huang-kuei-fei means "imperial concubine of the first rank"; Kuei-fei, that of the second rank; Fei, that of the third rank; and Pin, that of the fourth rank. The number within a parenthesis preceding a son's name signifies his seniority. Note that the fifth and twenty-third sons share the Romanized syllable *-ch'i*; this syllable in fact represents two Chinese characters, distinguished by tones in pronunciation. The original name of the fourteenth son was Yin-cheng, which he changed to Yin-t'i in 1722 after Yin-chen became the Yung-cheng Emperor. This chart is based on *Ch'ing Huang-shih ssu-p'u* (Four genealogies of the Ch'ing imperial family), compiled by T'ang Pang-chih and published in Shanghai in 1923.

Imperial Consorts	Their Sons
Empress Hsiao-Ch'eng	(2) Yin-jeng (June 6, 1674-Jan. 27, 1725) 51 *sui*
Empress Hsiao-kung (Te-fei)	(4) Yin-chen (Dec. 13, 1678-Oct. 8, 1735) 58 *sui*
	(6) Yin-tso (Mar. 5, 1680-June 15, 1685) 6 *sui*
	(14) Yin-t'i (Yin-cheng) (Feb. 10, 1668-Feb. 16, 1755) 68 *sui*
Ching-min Huang-kuei-fei (Min-fei)	(13) Yin-hsiang (Nov. 16, 1686-June 18, 1730) 45 *sui*
Wen-hsi Huang-kuei-fei	(10) Yin-o (Nov. 28, 1683-Oct. 18, 1741) 59 *sui*
Mi-fei (Lady Wang)	(15) Yin-wu (Dec. 24, 1693-Mar. 8, 1731) 39 *sui*
	(16) Yin-lu (July 28, 1695-Mar. 20, 1767) 73 *sui*
	(18) Yin-chieh (Sept. 10, 1701-Oct. 17, 1708) 8 *sui*
Chin-fei	(17) Yin-li (Mar. 24, 1697-Mar. 21, 1738) 42 *sui*
Hui-fei	(1) Yin-shih (Mar. 12, 1672-Nov. 25, 1734) 63 *sui*
I-fei	(5) Yin-ch'i (Feb. 14, 1679-July 10, 1732) 54 *sui*
	(9) Yin-t'ang (Oct. 17, 1683-Sept. 22, 1726) 44 *sui*
	(11) Yin-tzu (June 8, 1685-Aug. 22, 1696) 12 *sui*
Jung-fei	(3) Yin-chih (Mar. 23, 1677-July 10, 1732) 56 *sui*
Ch'eng-fei	(7) Yin-yu (Aug. 19, 1680-May 18, 1730) 51 *sui*
Liang-fei	(8) Yin-ssu (Mar. 29, 1681-Sept. 30, 1726) 46 *sui*
Ting-fei	(12) Yin-t'ao (June 18, 1686-Aug. 22, 1753) 79 *sui*
Hsiang-pin	(19) Yin-chi (Oct. 25, 1702-Mar. 28, 1704) 3 *sui*
	(20) Yin-i (Sept. 1, 1706-Feb. 19, 1755) 50 *sui*
Chin-pin	(22) Yin-hu (Jan. 10, 1712-Feb. 12, 1744) 33 *sui*

Imperial Consorts	Their Sons
Ching-pin	(23) Yin-ch'i (Jan. 14, 1714-Aug. 31, 1785) 73 *sui*
Hsi-pin	(21) Yin-hsi (Feb. 27, 1711-June 26, 1758) 48 *sui*
Mu-pin	(24) Yin-pi (July 5, 1716-Dec. 3, 1773) 58 *sui*

Notes

Abbreviations

CCC	Sheng-tsu Jen Huang-ti ch'i-chü chu
CKTP	*Chang-ku ts'ung-pien*
CPYC	*Chu-p'i yü-chih*
CSL	*Ta-Ch'ing Sheng-tsu Jen-huang-ti shih-lu*
CSL:YC	*Ta-Ch'ing Shih-tsung Hsien-huang-ti shih-lu*
HTSL	*Ta-Ch'ing hui-tien shih-li* (1899)
HTTL	*Hsiao-t'ing tsa-lu*
KH	K'ang-hsi reign
KHHT	*Ta-Ch'ing hui-tien* (1690)
KHTC	*Kung-chung tang K'ang-hsi ch'ao tsou-che*
KHWC	*K'ang-hsi ti yü-chih wen-chi*
KKWH	*Ku-kung wen-hsien*
MHMCC	*Man-Han ming-ch'en chuan*
NWF	*Manchu Archives* *Nei-wu fu Man-wen-tsou-hsiao tang*
PCTP	*Pa-ch'i Man-chou shih-tsu t'ung-p'u*
SLHK	*Shih-liao hsün-k'an*
SLTKCP	*Shih-liao ts'ung-k'an ch'u-pien*
SLTP	*Shih-liao ts'ung-pien*
SYNK	*Shang-yü Nei-ko*
TCTA	*Kuan-yü Chiang-ning che-tsao Ts'ao-chia tang-an*
WHCN	*Sheng-tsu wu-hsing Chiang-nan ch'üan-lu*
WHTP	*Wen-hsien ts'ung-pien*
YC	Yung-cheng reign

Prologue

1. Hsiao I-shan, *Ch'ing-tai t'ung-shih*, p. 12. Cf. Mo Tung-yin, p. 83.

2. Emperor T'ai-tsung's personal name was Hong Taiji. The use of the name Abahai originated in Erich Hauser's translation of (*Huang-Ch'ing*) *k'ai-kuo fang-lüeh* (Berlin, 1926) and was later adopted by Arthur Hummel, editor of the influential biographical work *Eminent Chinese of the Ch'ing Dynasty, 1644-1912* (Washington, 1943-44), and it has been widely used as his personal name in Western literature. However, I have not yet found any original Chinese or Manchu documents that give a source for the use of this name. The only person I have found whose personal name was Abahai was the mother of Dorgon (Hong Taiji's half brother). See Okada Hidehiro, "Ch'ing Tai-tsung chi-wei k'ao-shih" (A study of Hong Taiji's succession to the throne), *KKWH*, vol. 3, no. 2, p. 32.

3. For Manchu atrocities and Chinese resistance, see *Chiang-nan wen-chien lu* (Taipei, 1967). As late as 1712 K'ang-hsi was still suspicious of Southern motives: see his endorsement of Wang Tu-chao's (governor of Chekiang) memorial, which reads: "With respect to the hearts and customs of the Southerners, you naturally know them well. Never treat things lightly." See Wang Tu-chao's memorial dated 51/2/-, in *KKWH*, vol. 1, no. 1, p. 66 (December, 1969).

4. Economically, the Soochow prefecture alone would have been able to provide annual tax revenue equivalent to that produced by the entire province of Chekiang. And "during the last six centuries of imperial rule in China, from Yuan through the Ch'ing, the current of Chinese culture always flew north from the South." For more discussion of the so-called Soochow culture, see Miyazaki Ichisada, *Ajia shi kenkyū*, (Kyoto, 1964), IV, 322, 469-470.

5. Cf. Arthur F. Wright, "Sui Yang-ti: Personality and Stereotype," in Arthur F. Wright, ed., *Confucian Persuasion* (Stanford, 1960), pp. 47-76.

6. Cf. Ho Ping-ti, "The Salt Merchants of Yang-chou: A Study of Commercial Capitalism in Eighteenth-Century China," *Harvard Journal of Asiatic Studies* 27:130-168 (1954). Though Ho's article essentially deals with the life-style of salt merchants during the eighteenth century, his descriptions equally apply to the latter half of the seventeenth century. For evidence, see chapter eight with respect to An San and other rich salt merchants.

7. For political implications of this play, which had to do with K'ung's abrupt dismissal, see Ch'en Wan-nai, "Lun K'ung Shan-jen 'Yin-shih pa-kuan' i-an" (A study of the puzzling case of K'ung Shan-jen's "dismissal for certain causes"), in *KKWH*, vol. 1, no. 2, pp. 35-41.

8. For reference to "Yang-chou brand," see *Yang-chou fu-chih* (1733), 60:2b-3b.

9. *K'o-she ou-wen*, 15b, and *HTTL*, 5:23 (Mingju and Songgotu).

10. The villa was completed in 1686. Also motivated by filial piety, K'ang-hsi's grandson the Emperor Ch'ien-lung (r. 1736-1795) constructed a "Soochow street" in his suburban villa near Peking, because his mother loved the scenery of the South. *HTTL*, 1:21a-b.

11. *Yung-hsien lu* (Shanghai, 1959), pp. 137-138.

12. For an analysis of the evolution of the early-Manchu power structure, see Silas H.L. Wu, *Communication and Imperial Control in China: Evolution of the Palace Memorial System, 1693-1735* (Cambridge, Mass., 1970), pp. 2-3, 7-8.

13. Cf. Yoshio Hosoya, "Ch'ing tai pa-ch'i chih-tu chih yen-pien," in *KKWH*, vol. 3, no. 3, pp. 37-60.

14. For the *pao-i* system, see Cheng T'ien-t'ing, *Ch'ing-shih t'an-wei* (K'un-

ming, 1936), pp. 59-80; for special references to *pao-i*, see *CSL*, 82:20, 83:6b-9b; 108:7a-b; *HTTL*, 5:16b-17.

15. For the official translation of *Sin jeku*, see *HTSL*, 1219:1b. For their low social status compared with regular *pao-i* in the Imperial Household, see *CSL*, 62:9, 10; 236:12b. The mother of Yin-ssu (K'ang-hsi's eighth son) was characterized in the official records as a woman from "mean background" (*CSL*, 236:9), or from "criminal background in the *Sin jeku*" (*Ch'ing huang-shih ssu-p'u*, 2:14); cf. *SYNK* 3/9/30 (8a-b).

16. Few scholars have applied modern psychological concepts and techniques to the study of Chinese historical figures in imperial China. Jonathan D. Spence's *Emperor of China* (New York, 1974) presents K'ang-hsi's self-image as centering on several major issues that lasted throughout his life. For a discussion of filial piety by a contemporary anthropologist, see Francis L. K. Hsü, *Americans and Chinese* (New York, 1970), pp. 76-78, 304-305. Also see Benjamin I. Schwartz's critical essay, "On Filial Piety and Revolution: China," in *Journal of Interdisciplinary History*, vol. 3, no. 3, pp. 569-580 (winter 1973).

17. Harold D. Lasswell, *Power and Personality* (New York, 1963), p. 20. Cf. also Silas H. L. Wu, "Value Demands and Value Fulfillment: An Approach to the Study of the Ch'ing Emperor-Official Relationship," in *Ch'ing-shih wen-t'i*, vol. 1, no. 8, pp. 27-37 (May 1968).

18. Dison Hsüeh-feng Poe, "Imperial Succession and Attendant Crisis in Dynastic China," *Tsing Hua Journal of Chinese Studies*, New Series, vol. 8, nos. 1 and 2: pp. 87-88 (August 1970).

1. The Grandmother

1. *CSL*, 8:9b-10. For a portrait of the young K'ang-hsi see *Ch'ing-tai ti-hou hsiang*, ts'e 1. On the subject of K'ang-hsi's garments, E. Ysbrants Ides wrote: "His dress consisted of a common dark-colored damask waist-coat, a coat of deep blue satin, adorned with ermines, besides which he had a string of coral hanging about his neck and down on his breast. He had a warm cap on, turned up with sable, to which was added a red silk knot, and some peacocks' feathers hanging down backwards. His hair, plaited into one lock, hung behind him. He had no gold nor jewels about him. He had boots on, which were made of black velvet." See Ides's *Three Years Travels from Moscow Over-land to China* (London, 1706), pp. 72-73.

2. *CSL*, 8:9b-10.

3. *HTSL*, 416:2.

4. K'ang-hsi's entire adult behavior demonstrated a consistent pattern of filial devotion manifested toward senior relatives—grandmother, stepmother, and elder brother; private sources corroborate official records on K'ang-hsi's early filial piety. Cf. Joachim Bouvet, *The History of Cang-Hy the Present Emperor of China* (London, 1699), p. 85; "The old Empress his Grand-mother . . . was always both in her life time, and after her death, the true object of his filial Respect."

5. According to Manchu custom, when a Manchu nobleman died, one of his concubines had to die with him. An unwilling concubine was strangled to death "by the multitudes" to enforce compliance with this custom. When Nurhaci died, his empress, as well as two concubines, committed suicide so that they might be buried with him. The system was slightly modified in 1634, when it was decreed that upon a nobleman's death only his legitimate wife would be "allowed" (expected) to die with him; concubines were permitted to do so if they chose. After the death of Hong Taiji (K'ang-hsi's grandfather), in 1643, a

consort of his was forced to commit suicide. (For this custom see Mo Tung-yin, p. 143.)

When Shun-chih died, one of his consorts committed suicide the same day, because she "felt deeply grateful to the emperor and became extremely sorrowful and heartbroken, so she died." Her exemplary act of fidelity was recognized: she was posthumously given the title *fei* (imperial concubine of the third rank) (*CSL*, 1:20b-21). As late as 1722, when K'ang-hsi died, the Empress Hsiao-kung, mother of the Yung-cheng Emperor, insisted that she "must go with the K'ang-hsi Emperor." It was said that only at the earnest request of Yung-cheng, who claimed that he still needed her guidance, did she consent to delay her decision. She died less than two years later (of asthma?), with strong hints in the record that she had refused medication. See *CSL:YC*, 7:21; *Ta-i chüeh-mi lu* (1730), 1:19b-20. For *hsün-tsang*, see Cheng T'ien-t'ing, pp. 46-47; d'Orléans, *History of the Two Tartar Conquerors of China*, p. 45.

6. For Hsiao-chuang's case, see *CSL*, 132:8b.

7. Shun-chih died of smallpox; see *CSL:Shun-chih reign*, 59:18, *Ch'ing huang-shih ssu-p'u*, 1:6b. For the death of K'ang-hsi's mother, see *CSL*, 8:13.

8. *CSL*, 290:12b-13.

9. When his grandmother died, in 1688, K'ang-hsi repeatedly referred to his infinite debt to her: that she had nurtured him and raised him when he was orphaned in childhood. See *CSL*, 132:1-8, and passim.

10. For Hsiao-chuang, see *Eminent Chinese*, pp. 300-301. For her relationship with the Jesuits at the Shun-chih court, see Rachel Attwater, *Adam Schall*, p. 104.

11. For Dorgon, see *Eminent Chinese*, p. 215; *Ch'ing-shih* (Taipei, 1961), p. 3539. For his relationship with Hsiao-chuang, see Ch'en Chieh-hsien, "To-erh-kun ch'eng 'Huang-fu she-cheng wang' chih yen-chiu" (A study of the question of Dorgon's being entitled as the Shun-chih Emperor's "Imperial Father the Prince-Regent"), in *KKWH*, vol. 1, no. 2, pp. 1-19 (March, 1970).

12. For Donggo, see *Eminent Chinese*, p. 257; d'Orléans, pp. 42-43; *Ch'ing-lieh-ch'ao hou-fei chuan kao*, 1:69b, 147, 148, 159; and *Ch'ing Huang-shih ssu-p'u*, 1:6b.

13. The custom of early marriage in traditional China lasted into the twentieth century. The average age of marriage for a boy in a Northern Chinese community in the 1930s was fourteen. See Sidney D. Gamble, *Ting Hsien* (New York, 1954), p. 385. For the wet-nurse institution, see *HTSL*, 1219:2b.

14. "The nostrils," he wrote, "are like trenches of the field where one sows the seeds of smallpox." He also thought that this practice was an indigenous Chinese method, not influenced by tobacco smoking, which had been introduced to China only a short time before. Commenting on the length of time before the appearance of the pustules following the initial fever, he added, "If the pustules do not appear before the third day, one can be sure that out of ten children eight or nine will be saved. But when they break out on the second day, half of them will incur a great risk. Finally, if they break out on the very first day of the fever, one cannot be assured of the life of any of them." See *Lettres édifiantes et curieuses concernant l'Asie, l'Afrique et l'Amérique* (Paris, 1843), III, 535-538.

Chinese handbooks on smallpox inoculation state that the best time for the pustules to break out is eight to nine days following the fever; and they describe the vulnerability to smallpox epidemics of those children who fail to show a positive reaction to the inoculation. They attribute the source of the latent "poison of the smallpox pustules" to the child's parents: "The poison is a result of the solidification of the lustful fires of a father and mother at the time of conception." See Chang Hsün-yü, *Chung-tou hsin-shu* (Shanghai, 1912), 3:22-23.

15. *CSL*, 290:12b; *PCTP*, 43:61-62. The temple was Fu-yu Ssu (The Temple of Divine Protection).

16. See *Yung-hsien lu*, pp. 304 and 390. A third nurse, named Lady Kua-erh-chia, to whom K'ang-hsi was indebted for her care, probably during late childhood, was granted an honorific title when she died, in 1699. See *CSL*, 194:11b.

17. *KHWC*, vol. 5, chüan 40, pp. 1-5.

18. *Eminent Chinese*, p. 257; Attwater, p. 104.

19. *CSL*, 1:3b-4.

20. *CSL*, 1:3b-4 (compare this with K'ang-hsi's answer to the same question when asked by his grandmother: *CSL*, 244:2b). This same tale, after many oral transmissions at court during the K'ang-hsi reign, was eventually told to the Scottish physician John Bell during his stay in Peking while he was associated with the Russian embassy, between 1719 and 1722. When Bell published his account more than forty years later, in 1763, the story, "drawn from the best information I could procure," was presented thus: "Xungtsti [Shun-chih] died a young man, and left his second son, Kamhi [K'ang-hsi], to succeed him. On finding himself at the point of death, he called for his eldest son, and asked him whether he would take upon him the government. But, being young and modest, he was unwilling to accept, and begged his father would excuse him on that account. Then Kamhi was called, and asked the same question. He was better instructed, and briskly answered, he was ready to obey his father's commands, and would take the weight of the government upon him. This answer so pleased the Emperor, that he named him his successor; and, accordingly, on the death of his father, he was proclaimed Emperor." (See Bell's *A Journey from St. Petersburg to Pekin, 1719-1722* [Edinburgh, 1965], pp. 175, 178-179.)

This account inevitably contains inaccuracies, because Bell heard the story sixty years after the event had occurred. Nevertheless, Bell confirms the basic idea that K'ang-hsi was "better instructed."

21. *CSL*, 1:2. These are probably the only hagiographic elements in the *CSL*; they invariably concern miraculous signs that anticipated the birth of the new ruler.

22. Despite the exotic tales about Shun-chih's death, he did die of smallpox. See d'Orléans, p. 44. For an evaluation of the official Manchu record that deals with Shun-chih's deathbed designation of K'ang-hsi as heir apparent, see Ch'en Chieh-hsien, "Ch'ing-ch'ao huang-ti ti Man-wen pen-chi," in *KKWH*, vol. 2, no. 2, p. 18 (March, 1972).

23. For Oboi, see *Eminent Chinese*, p. 599, and Robert B. Oxnam, *Ruling from Horseback: Manchu Politics in the Oboi Regency, 1661-1669* (Chicago, 1975).

24. *CSL* KH, 244:2b. That K'ang-hsi remembered this statement in 1710, nearly fifty years after his enthronement, clearly suggests that "harmony" has been the principal value in his political philosophy since childhood. For more discussion of K'ang-hsi's value system, see Silas H. L. Wu, *Communication and Imperial Control*, pp. 111-112.

25. *KHWC*, 2.40:1.

26. Bouvet, pp. 85-88. For K'ang-hsi's own testimonies, see *T'ing-hsün ko-yen*, 8b-9, 23b, 53b-54.

2. The First Empress

1. The *CSL*, in simplifying the description of the ceremony, introduced occasional time confusion; compare *CSL*, 16:16b-18, with *HTSL*, 324:17-19b, and *KHHT*, 49:7-10.

2. For Gabula, see *PCTP*, p. 92, and *Eminent Chinese*, p. 664.

3. *CSL*, 16:18-19b.

4. *CSL*, 16:19.

5. The most recent study on the succession of Hong Taiji is Okada Hide-hiro, "Ch'ing T'ai-tsung chi-wei k'ao-shih," *KKWH*, vol. 3, no. 2, pp. 31-38 (March, 1972). Earlier studies on the succession crises before the Shun-chih reign include Chao Kuang-hsien's "Ch'ing-ch'u chu-wang cheng-kuo chi," *Fu-jen hsüeh-chih*, vol. 12, nos. 1-2, pp. 1-9 (1944)—Chao maintains that K'ang-hsi's adoption of the Chinese system of establishing an heir apparent was a reaction to this earlier experience—and Li Kuang-t'ao, "Ch'ing T'ai-tsung to-wei k'ao," in his *Ming-Ch'ing-shih lun-chi* (Taipei, 1970), pp. 437-439.

6. *CSL*, 48:15. This was also implied in K'ang-hsi's statement about Yin-ssu's mother's coming from a "mean" family background, namely, having been a bond servant in the *Sin jeku* of the Imperial Household. See *CSL*, 235:20.

7. Ebilun had long been related to the imperial family; his mother was either a sister or a cousin of Nurhaci. Official records state that K'ang-hsi took one of Ebilun's daughters as concubine during "her childhood," and in 1677 after she fell seriously ill, she was elevated to the status of empress (three years after the Empress Hsiao-ch'eng's death); she died the following year and was canonized as the Empress Hsiao-chao. So she was probably about the same age as the Empress Hsiao-ch'eng, if not younger (ten or eleven). For Ebilun, see *Eminent Chinese*, pp. 219-221, and for Hsiao-chao, see *Ch'ing lieh-ch'ao hou-fei chuan kao*, p. 174, and *Ch'ing huang-shih ssu-p'u*, 2:10.

8. *CSL*, 29:9b-10.

9. *Eminent Chinese*, pp. 577-579. The compiler of the *Yung-hsien lu* noted that Mingju's younger sister was "an Imperial concubine of the second degree who gave birth to K'ang-hsi's eldest son, Yin-shih" (p. 191). This was not supported by the imperial genealogy, *Ch'ing huang-shih ssu-p'u*. Both Mingju and Yin-shih's mother were from the Nara clan. Cf. *Ch'ing-shih*, pp. 3469 and 3931.

10. For biographical information on Songgotu, Mingju, and Hsiung Tz'u-li, see *Eminent Chinese*, pp. 563, 577, 308.

11. *HTTL*, 1:4b; *CSL*, 31:6b-7; *Ch'ing-shih*, p. 68.

12. *CSL*, 22:11b-17; *Ch'ing-shih*, p. 3892.

13. *Ch'ing-shih*, p. 3892; Wu Hsiu-liang [Silas H. L.], "Nan-shu-fang chih chien-chih chi-ch'i ch'ien-ch'i chih fa-chan," *Ssu yü-yen* 5:6-7 (March 1968).

14. For Ch'eng-hu, see *Ch'ing huang-shih ssu-p'u*, 3:12; for his death, see *CSL*, 38:9.

15. *CSL*, 38:9-10. Such self-control may seem impossible to modern Westerners; but one needs to remember that Chinese—and Manchu—child rearing taught the restraint of emotional expression.

16. For illness, see *CSL*, 39:28b; 40:7b-9. For K'ang-hsi's distress, see *CSL*, 42:4b, 8-9.

17. *Ch'ing huang-shih ssu-p'u*, 3:18-19.

18. For Wu San-kuei and the rebellion, see *Eminent Chinese*, p. 678, and Lawrence D. Kessler, *K'ang-hsi and the Consolidation of Ch'ing Rule, 1661-1684* (Chicago, 1976), pp. 74-90.

19. *CSL*, 42:19; 43:3-4; 44:12b.

20. This was his own testimony; see *T'ing-hsün ko-yen*, pp. 11, 17-19; d'Orléans, p. 57.

21. *Ch'ing huang-shih ssu-p'u*, 3:12b.

22. *CSL*, 47:20-20b; *Ch'ing-shih*, p. 3295.

23. *CSL*, 234:4 and 13.

3. The Heir

1. *CSL*, 58:19b-21; 56:1b-2; *Ch'ing-shih*, pp. 72-73.

2. Wu Hsiu-liang, "Nan-shu-fang," pp. 6-7; cf. Kessler, chaps. 4, 6.

3. *Ch'ing-shih*, pp. 72-73.

4. *CSL*, 56:1b-2; 58:21.

5. *Ch'ing-shih*, p. 73.

6. *CSL*, 58:13a-b.

7. *CSL*, 234:13.

8. *CSL*, 59:5a-b. Except for minor modifications, this ceremonial procedure followed that of the Ming. For rituals of similar nature, the *Ta-Ming hui-tien* (1505) was still consulted by Ch'ing rulers as late as the Yung-cheng reign. See *Ch'ing-shih*, p. 3496. For the investiture, see *KHHT*, 43:21b-25.

9. For this description, see Bell, p. 135.

10. Bell described the system: "The master of the ceremonies . . . ordered all the company to kneel, and make obeisance nine times to the Emperor. At every third time we stood up, and kneeled again . . . The master of the ceremonies stood by, and delivered his orders in the Tartar language, by pronouncing the words *morgu* and *boss*; the first meaning to bow, and the other to stand." See Bell, p. 134.

11. *CSL*, 58:19-21.

12. Bouvet, p. 17.

13. *T'ing-hsün ko-yen*, 11b, 17-19. The San-fan Rebellion had caused both mental and physical stress in K'ang-hsi. On occasion the tension was so great that he fell ill for several months. *CSL*, 82:20b-21; 87:4b-5.

14. *CSL*, 234:3.

15. Ibid.

16. Yin-jeng's attachment to Songgotu in his youth and adulthood suggests that he must have had a close relationship with him in his childhood (cf. *Ch'ing-shih*, p. 3932). Songgotu was so intensely hated in the imperial court that he was nearly assassinated (cf. *HTTL*, 5:23a-b). While disliked by his fellow officials, Songgotu was friendly with the Jesuits and often intervened in their behalf to win imperial favor (P. J. B. Du Halde, *The General History of China*, tr. R. Brookes [Paris, 1735], pp. 495-497). In 1680 Songgotu was released from active duty in the outer court; however, the emperor reassigned him to duty in the inner court as junior chamberlain of the Imperial Bodyguard (*CSL*, 90:18).

17. She began to suffer poor health after 1685. See *Ch'ing-shih*, p. 3492.

18. *T'ing-hsün ko-yen*, p. 23.

19. For Yin-shih's relationship with Hsiao-hui, see *CSL*, 237:14. K'ang-hsi termed Yin-shih "a wanton and rebellious person." (*T'ing-hsün ko-yen*, p. 37.)

20. For Chang Feng-yang, see *HTTL*, 5:17. In 1686 K'ang-hsi ordered that a certain bond servant of Prince Giyesu's be severely punished because the bond servant had publicly cursed and scolded the vice-major of Peking. This person might well have been Chang Feng-yang (*CSL*, 123:22). At any rate, Chang's conduct was typical of the behavior displayed by many of the bond servants of Manchu princes. (Cf. *CSL*, 82:20b-21.)

21. *HTTL*, 5:17. CCC 24/2/10, in *SLTP*, II, 9.

22. *Ch'ing-shih*, p. 3493.

23. For her contacts with palace nurses, see *Yung-hsien lu*, p. 304; *HTTL*, 5:25.

24. For K'ang-hsi's sons and daughters, see *Ch'ing huang-shih ssu-p'u*, chüan 3. For reference to his personal attention to Yin-chen's rearing, see *CSL*, 235:24b-25. Yin-shih was raised by the wife of Ko-lu (a minister of the Imperial

Household); Yin-chih, by the wife of Cho-erh-chi (junior chamberlain of the Imperial Bodyguard); Yin-ssu, by the wife of Ya-ch'i-pu. See *CSL*, 235:2b. For Yin-jeng's hostility toward Yin-chen, see *Ta-i chüeh-mi lu*, 1:21b-22b; *HTTL*, 1:8-8b.

25. For Te-fei, see *Ch'ing huang-shih ssu-p'u*, 2:12.

26. For the Manchu system of selecting ladies-in-waiting, see *HTSL*, 1114: 11b; *HTTL*, 2:51b; Shan Shih-yuan, "Kuan-yü Ch'ing-kung chih hsiu-nü ho kung-nü" (Concerning the ladies-in-waiting in the Ch'ing court), in *Ku-kung po-wu yuan yuan-k'an* (Peiping, 1935), pp. 97-103. Candidates were chosen from a group ranging in age from thirteen *sui* (about twelve years old) to eighteen *sui* (about seventeen). A palace lady could be elevated to the status of imperial concubine in her teens once she had given birth to a male child.

27. *CSL*, 234:11; *Eminent Chinese*, p. 924; *Ch'ing-shih*, p. 3908. Chang Ying served as Yin-jeng's tutor probably when the South Library was first established, when he was appointed to the library's staff.

28. Kao Shih-ch'i, *Hu-ts'ung tung-hsün jih-lu*, in *Hsiao-fang-hu chai yü-ti ts'ung-ch'ao*, ts'e 4, p. 245 (1877); *CSL*, 234:11; *Ch'ing-shih*, p. 3555; d'Orléans, pp. 69-70.

29. *KHWC*, vol. 1, chüan 40, pp. 8b-9.

30. *CSL*, 234:11b.

31. Wang Shih-chen, *Chü-i lu*, 31:1b-2. This piece was probably composed in 1689 as a farewell present to Hsü Ch'ien-hsüeh, his onetime tutor, when Hsü was leaving the capital for his home in the South after his dismissal. Cf. *Ch'ing-shih*, p. 3916, and *HTTL*, 6:46b; also see *Eminent Chinese*, p. 832.

4. The Southern Literati

1. For Yin-jeng's relationship with Hsiung, see Li Kuang-ti, 14:17b; and that with Kao, see Kao Shih-ch'i, *P'eng-shan mi-chi* in *Ku-hsüeh hui-k'an*, comp. Teng shih (Shanghai, 1912), 1st ser., no. 12, p. 4b. For political involvement, see *Eminent Chinese*, p. 413 (for Kao), p. 308 (for Hsiung), and p. 311 (for Hsü Ch'ien-hsüeh).

2. For Hsiung's dismissal, see *CSL*, 62:6; for Songgotu's role in Hsiung's dismissal, see Li Kuang-ti, *Jung-ts'un yü-lu hsü chi*, 14:15-16b. Li noted that though Hsiung "believed that he had been betrayed by Songgotu," "later they became good friends; and they always recommended each other to the Emperor." After Hsiung's return to power, in 1688, he was again made an imperial tutor to the heir apparent. The relationship between Songgotu and Hsiung demonstrated the intricate nature of imperial court politics.

3. For a brief survey of the early history of the South Library, see Wu Hsiu-liang, "Nan-shu-fang."

4. *Eminent Chinese*, p. 664. Songgotu was dismissed under the euphemistic pretext that he "requested to be discharged voluntarily from the office of grand secretary because of poor health," and he was allowed "to be present at court audiences in the capacity of junior chamberlain." (*CSL*, 90:18.) For Mingju's role in the San-fan Rebellion, see *MHMCC*, 14:4-16, 19:45b-52; *CSL*, 244:21; *HTTL*, 1:12. For factional struggles between Songgotu and Mingju, see *Fang Wang-ch'i ch'uan-chi* (Shanghai, 1936), p. 344; *HTTL*, 5:9.

5. For Kao's biography, see *Eminent Chinese*, p. 413. My description is based largely on an early-eighteenth-century entry by Wang Ching-ch'i, *Tu-shu t'ang hsi-cheng sui-pi*, in *CKTP*, p. 130. For further information on the complex factional relationships between Kao and Songgotu, Mingju, Hsü Ch'ien-hsüeh, and others, see Fang Wang-ch'i, pp. 338-339, Kuo Hsiu, *Kuo Hua-yeh hsien-sheng shu-kao*, I, 3-7b; *Eminent Chinese*, p. 710.

6. For the *Ching-yen* system under K'ang-hsi, see *CSL*, 35:7, 9b; *HTSL*, 1047:20. It was in 1673, when the San-fan Rebellion broke out, that K'ang-hsi ordered Daily Lectures to be held to further his knowledge of Confucian classics. *CSL*, 41:9.

7. *CSL*, 70:6, *Man-Han ming-ch'en chuan*, 26:34.

8. *Ch'ing-shih*, p. 3942.

9. According to Fang Pao, Chang Ying did not want to have a "conspicuous name" at court because he was modest and unassuming. He was friendly with his colleagues and never joined a faction. See *Kuo-ch'ao ch'i-hsien lei-cheng ch'u-pien*, comp. Li Huan (1884-1890), 9:32-34. The only substantial record Chang left was a brief account of his accompanying the emperor on his second Southern tour (1689). See Chang's *Nan-hsün hu-ts'ung chi-lüeh*, in *Tu-su t'ang wen-chi*, chüan 13.

10. See *HTTL*, 5:14. The official record contains a very terse reference to this incident, mentioning only the verse that K'ang-hsi composed. See *CSL*, 117:10.

11. For Hsü's and Wang's appointments to the South Library, see *Kuo-ch'ao ch'i-hsien*, chüan 57-59. For their factional activities, see Wu Hsiu-liang, "Nan-shu-fang," 11-12, and *Eminent Chinese*, pp. 311-312. One of Hsü's "students," a Mr. Yen, described Hsü's appearance rather sarcastically: "He is sixty [in 1689, when he was dismissed], fat, with a light complexion, delicate skin, no mustache; nearsighted, narrow eyes as if they were two lines; short-necked, and bald like a monk or a eunuch. Even at a quick glance, one would know immediately that he is an extraordinary man." Yen suspected that Hsü had secretly betrayed him while pretending to be sympathetic about his dismissal. See Hung Yeh, "Yen Cheng-hsien hsien-sheng i-kao wu-chung," in *Shih-hsüeh nien-pao*, vol. 2, no. 5, pp. 1-15. Hsü's corruption at court and the oppressive and extortionary behavior of his family toward the people in his native district, K'un-shan, in the South, were supported by the NPM(P) archives. Some of the complaints filed by the local people against the Hsüs were presented to the emperor through the governor-general of Liang-Kiang, but the emperor simply pigeonholed them in the palace archives. See "Hsü Ch'ien-hsüeh teng pei k'ung chuang" (Complaints filed against Hsü Ch'ien-hsüeh and others), in *WHTP*, pp. 112-129. Hsü's downfall was said to have been brought about by Mingju, who allegedly had been betrayed by Hsü. See *Kuo-ch'ao ch'i-hsien*, 8:52b; *CSL*, 146:13; *Ch'ing-shih*, p. 3939.

12. *CSL*, 125:8b.

13. *Fang Wang-chi*, pp. 338-339. For Mingju's and Yü Kuo-chu's corrupt behavior, see *Kuo-ch'ao ch'i-hsien*, 314:28b; *CSL*, 125:8b. T'ang Pin's integrity and reputation were supported by the Yung-cheng Emperor. See *SYNK*, edict dated YC 6/9/6 (no. 2).

14. *Fang Wang-ch'i*, p. 388.

15. *Ch'ing-shih*, p. 3908.

16. *Eminent Chinese*, p. 671.

17. In Ming times the heir apparent held audiences in the Wen-hua Hall to accept congratulations from court officials as well as to receive his lessons from official tutors.

18. For a description of the opening session, see *KHHT*, 44:18-20; compare it with the Ming precedents in *Ta-Ming hui-tien*, 52:8-11.

19. T'ang was made chief supervisor of instruction on KH 25/3/20; see *CSL*, 125:8b.

20. Kuo was one of the supervisors of instruction. For the entire membership of the supervisorate, see *CSL*, 125:8. Whether daily study sessions were always

held in the heir apparent's residence is not clear. On another occasion T'ang Pin indicated that the sessions were held in the outer court: see *T'ang-tzu i-shu*, 4:76-77.

21. *T'ang-tzu i-shu*, 4:76-77. T'ang indicated that Yin-jeng had practiced calligraphy "since six."

22. Hsü Ch'ien-hsüeh, *Tan-yüan wen-chi*, 12:2b-4 ("nine years old"; cf. note 21).

23. Ibid., 35:1-4. Cf. CCC 24/2/30, in *SLTP*, II:22-23.

24. My description of the T'ang Pin tragedy is based on Li Kuang-ti, 15:2-4 (the death of T'ang Pin caused by the betrayal of Kao Shih-ch'i and his colleagues), and Meng Sen, *Ch'ing-tai shih* (Taipei, 1960), pp. 175-178. Also, see *Ch'ing-shih*, pp. 3940 and 4002; *CSL*, 133:24; 130:11; 134:18b. Cf. *CSL*, 82: 20b-21; 83:8-9 (evidence of bond servants' influence).

25. *Fang Wang-ch'i*, p. 344.

26. Meng Sen, *Ch'ing-tai shih*, p. 177.

27. *Ch'ing-shih kao* (Hong Kong, n.d.), p. 1466.

28. In 1707 K'ang-hsi conceded that he had been aware of the heir apparent's undesirable traits for a long time and "had tolerated" him for "twenty years," since about 1687. See *CSL*, 234:26.

29. *CSL*, 141:5a-b.

30. For K'ang-hsi's manifestation of filial piety at the death of his grandmother, see *CSL*, 131:28-133:1b.

31. *CSL*, 131:29b; 132:1b-2b.

32. *CSL*, 133:7b-8.

5. Signs of Conflict

1. For Mingju's downfall, see *CSL*, 133:17-20; *Kuo-ch'ao ch'i-hsien*, 8:5-7, 9:24-27. For Galdan, see Mark Mancall, *Russia and China: Their Diplomatic Relations to 1728* (Cambridge, Mass., 1971), pp. 146-149, 158.

2. *CSL*, 235:21-21b.

3. See Gerbillon, *The Second Journey of P. P. Gerbillon and Pereyra in Tartary, in 1689*, in Du Halde, *A Description of the Empire of China and Chinese Tartary*, II, 301-333. Also quoted in G.N. Wright, I, 57-59.

4. *CSL*, 147:18b, 20, 22b-24.

5. Ibid.; Bouvet, pp. 73-74.

6. For his examplary act, see *CSL*, 149:8b-9.

7. For the downfall, of the Hsü faction, see *Man-Han ming-ch'en chuan*, 3:4-12b (Hsü); 3:26-34 (Kao); 3:22-26; for the close relationship between Hsiung and the heir apparent, see Li Kuang-ti, 14:17a-b; Le Comte, *Memoirs*, p. 33.

8. For Songgotu's military adherents, see Chapter 7. In 1683 K'ang-hsi testified to the court that Songgotu was "haughty, lacked self-control," and that "all court ministers feared him." (*CSL*, 108:6.) Songgotu's brother Ch'ang-t'ai, through his relationship with Yin-jeng, also wielded disproportionate power at court. (*Yung-hsien lu*, p. 359.)

9. CCC 52/2/2. That K'ang-hsi called the power-hungry Songgotu the "greatest sinner" of the Ch'ing dynasty suggests how strongly he must have felt about the arrogation of imperial prerogatives by his son; such usurpation had caused Yin-jeng "to suffer rapid deterioration in character" and to become "wanton and rebellious." See *CSL*, 277:9.

10. For the festival, see Doolittle, *Social Life of the Chinese*, II, 44; for the Ming ceremony, see *Ta-Ming hui-tien*, chüan 89; for the ceremony adopted by K'ang-hsi, see *HTSL*, 162:19b-20b; 179:10b.

11. According to Ch'ing administrative regulations, an incumbent official might be tried for criminal offenses only after he had been removed from his post. For the incident, see *CSL*, 162:19b.

12. *CSL*, 162:21b, 27; 164:19b.

13. *CSL*, 164:11.

14. *CSL*, 164:7b; *Ch'ing-shih*, p. 3555.

6. Regency

1. Later K'ang-hsi charged Songgotu with having "criticized state affairs," a cryptic way of saying that Songgotu had criticized the emperor on the matter of abdication. See *CSL*, 211:13b-14.

2. For the Sung emperor Hsiao-tsung, see *Sung-shih*, pp. 4537-5564.

3. For Kao-tsung's abdication, ibid. For a study of Hui-tsung see Betty Tseng Ecke, "Emperor Hui Tsung, The Artist: 1082-1136," Ph.D. dissertation, New York University, 1972.

4. *CSL*, 235:6.

5. As he recalled in 1708, see *CSL*, 235:21b.

6. The term *t'ing-li* means to be the emperor's "regent," "deputy," or "co-ruler" during the emperor's absence from the capital. See *CSL*, 235:19.

7. *CSL*, 171:24b; 173:23b; 162:17a-b.

8. For Fu-lun and Maci's relationship with Mingju, see *Kuo Hua-yeh hsien-sheng shu-kao*, I, 3-7b, 20-22.

9. *KHWC*, I, 29:5.

10. *KHWC*, II, 19:3b.

11. *KHWC*, II, 19:6b-18. It is interesting to compare the writing styles of Yin-jeng and the emperor. Yin-jeng was formal and brief, the emperor personal and long. A memorial sent by Yin-jeng to the emperor dated KH 35/3/- includes a terse greeting to his father and "best regards" to his brothers, and then moves on to political matters. In contrast, the emperor responded with feeling: "I am in peace and my health is good. How are you, my Heir Apparent? All your brothers are well. All ministers, officials, and soldiers are well. The only thing [that I regret] is that it continues to sleet and snow. It really doesn't matter much, but since it is still going on, I am a bit worried." See P'an Shu-pi, "K'ang-hsi san-shih-wu nien san-yüeh Huang-t'ai-tzu Man-wen tsou-che," in *KKWH*, vol. 5, no. 1, pp. 65-76; cf. also "Yin-jeng's brief Manchu memorial dated 35/5/-," no. 40, in *KHTC*, 8:177.

12. For K'ang-hsi's personal command of the army, see *CSL*, 173:19-24b.

13. *CSL*, 173:19-20b; "Yin-jeng's Manchu memorial dated 35/5/18," no. 49, *KHTC*, 8:231. It seemed pure luck that K'ang-hsi found water and grass at the Kerlon River region. According to a Jesuit account, "The Kerlon is not deep, but almost everywhere fordable on a sandy Bottom, is of a good Water, and of about sixty common foot in breadth; its Meadows on each side are the richest Pastures in Tartary." (Du Halde, IV, 119-120.)

14. For the decisive victory scored by Fei-yang-ku at Tchao Modo, see *CSL*, 173:24-28. For a personal account of the battle at Tchao Modo, see Yin Hua-hsing, *Hsi-cheng chi-lüeh* (A brief account of the western campaign, 1696), pp. 10-13; the brigade general of Ninghsia, Yin played a leading role in the defeat of the enemy. For general coverage of the campaign, see Chang Yü-shu, *P'ing-ting shu-mo fang-lüeh* (The official account of the pacification of the northern deserts, 1696). See also Du Halde, *General History*, IV, 177-178, and *Eminent Chinese*, pp. 265-268, 757-759.

15. For the celebration and the letter to the dowager empress, see *CSL*, 173: 28-29. For K'ang-hsi's letter to Yin-jeng, see *KHWC*, vol. 2 chüan 29, pp. 8b-11;

for the old captive, see Hsiao I-shan, p. 831.

16. See the Manchu memorial translated by P'an Shu-pi, cited in note 11.

17. K'ang-hsi recalled in 1708, see *CSL*, 235:25.

18. For the audience, see *CSL*, 175:18b; *SLTKCP*, pp. 992-993, 999, and 1005.

19. *CSL*, 179:8b-9b and 180:4b-5b; cf. charges against Songgotu in *CSL*, 212:13b.

20. For the 1697 campaign, see *CSL*, 180:2b-183:22b; the imperial army left the capital on KH 36/2/6 (February 26, 1697) and returned on KH 36/5/16 (July 4, 1697). See *CSL*, 181:2b-3 (for the capture of Galdan's son), 181:12 (letter to dowager empress), and 183:7-9 (death of Galdan). Also see Yin Hua-hsing, *Hsi-cheng chih-lüeh*, pp. 14b-15; Du Halde, I, 178; *Eminent Chinese*, p. 665.

21. *Ch'ing Sheng-tsu yü-chih*, in *CKTP*, p. 36.

22. Ibid., p. 38.

23. Ibid., p. 38.

7. Bad Omens

1. *CSL*, 183:22a-b; 184:21; 185:9 (executions); 253:23 (Yin-jeng's character).

2. *CSL*, 185:9.

3. In 1708 K'ang-hsi charged Yin-jeng with having allowed "outside women" to appear in his palace (*CSL*, 234:7). It appears that the maintaining of pretty boys for sex by upper-class Manchu and Chinese officials and literati was prevalent at the time. See Wang Shu-nu, *Chung-kuo ch'ang-chi shih* (History of prostitution in China), pp. 318-320, and Wang Ching-ch'i, *Tu-shu t'ang hsi-cheng sui-pi*, in *CKTP*, pp. 131 and 133.

4. *CSL*, 235:23.

5. *CSL*, 212:13b, 16.

6. *CSL*, 201:20b-21b (Li Kuang-ti and others); 203:16 (P'eng P'eng).

7. *PCTP*, 6:19b-21 (Hsü-yüan-meng); also *Fang Wang-ch'i ch'üan-chi*, p. 345.

8. *CSL*, 210:3b.

9. *T'ing-hsün ko-yen*, p. 36.

10. *CSL*, 196:2b-3 (Yin-chih).

11. *CSL*, 201:18-19 (presents to dowager empress).

12. *Ch'ing-shih*, p. 4029; *CSL*, 209:14b. Olondai was later demoted to First Rank Imperial Bodyguard, possibly owing to Yin-jeng.

13. *CSL*, 206:8b.

14. *CSL*, 205:16.

15. *Ch'ing-shih*, pp. 4028-29 (Alingga and Olondai's hostility toward Yin-jeng); *CSL*, 192:2, 205:18 (Songgotu and Hsin-yü).

16. For Hsiung as the chief examiner, see *Eminent Chinese*, p. 309, and *Ch'ing-pi shu-wen*, 3:9b-18. Hsiung and Songgotu were originally enemies. It was under Songgotu's influence that Hsiung was removed from office in 1676 (*CSL*, 62:6), but the two became friends after Hsiung was recalled to Peking in 1688. Li Kuang-ti criticized Hsiung for his lack of moral principles in associating with Songgotu by saying, "How can anyone regard him [Hsiung] as a decent person?" See Li Kuang-ti, 14:11b-16.

17. For the role of the chief examiner, see Ichisada Miyazaki, *Kakyo* (Osaka, 1946), pp. 138-139, and Shang Yen-liu, *Ch'ing-tai k'o-chü k'ao-shih shu-lu* (Peking, 1958), p. 103.

18. *CSL*, 206:5; 212:8b (Li Kuang-ti's praise); for Wang Hung-hsü as the secret informant, see chapters 8 and 9.

19. For the examination scandal, see *CSL*, 200:8b-9b, 201:20b-21, 202:6b. The scandal was preceded by a similar case in the provincial examination held a year earlier. The metropolitan scandal almost certainly was the doing of very powerful figures, as many "young boys" were among the successful competitors. The emperor ordered that all successful candidates be reexamined, but court ministers evaded the task of making up the new test; they requested that the emperor himself propose the questions (they obviously feared the consequences of "successful" candidates failing). The emperor was also compelled to assign his own children, senior ministers, and imperial bodyguards to proctor the examination, after which the court ministers requested that the emperor grade the papers. Such fear within the court implies that Yin-jeng might well have been the source of the corruption of the examination system. Evidence corroborating this suspicion includes Yin-jeng's being the only adult imperial son in Peking at the time of the scandal (all his adult brothers were with the emperor in Jehol) (*CSL*, 194:13); in addition, twelve years later, in 1712, when a provincial examination scandal occurred in Chiang-nan, it was established that Yin-jeng was behind it. For the 1700 metropolitan scandal, see *CSL*, 196:2, 197:8-9, and Hsiao I-shan, pp. 807-808. For the 1712 provincial scandal, see Jonathan D. Spence, *Ts'ao Yin and the K'ang-hsi Emperor*, pp. 240-252, and Silas H. L. Wu, *Communication and Imperial Control*, pp. 142-148.

20. For a list of the independents Li Kuang-ti recommended to the emperor, see *Li Wen-chen kung nien-p'u*, ts'e 2, 15-17b; these included Hsü-yüan-meng, Ch'en P'eng-nien, Chang Po-hsing (governor of Kiangsu in 1712), Ch'en Ju-pi, Fang Pao, and others. Li's independence annoyed the powerful court partisans: see *Kuo-ch'ao ch'i-hsien*, 10:37a-b; *Fang Wang-ch'i ch'üan-chi*, pp. 341 and 344.

21. For Ho Cho's biography, see *Kuo-ch'ao ch'i-hsien*, 57:5b, and *Eminent Chinese*, pp. 283-285. Also see *Ch'ing-shih*, p. 5244 (Hsü Ch'ien-hsüeh), and *I-meng hsien-sheng chi*, comp. Wu Yin-p'ei (P'ing-chiang, 1909), 4:7 (Li's recommendation).

22. For Ho's character, see *I-meng hsien-sheng chi*, 5:5, and *fu-lu* (appendix), pp. 5-6; *Yung-hsien lu*, p. 35.

23. *I-meng hsien-sheng chi*, 2:13, 5:5.

24. For letter to Ho Huang, see ibid., 4:6-7.

25. *I-meng hsien-sheng chi*, 11:17b.

26. *I-meng hsien-sheng chi*, 11:17-18; *Eminent Chinese*, p. 284.

27. See *CSL*, 211:26 and 212:4b. It is worthwhile noting that of the successfull *chin-shih* candidates that year, two were later to participate in factional activities: Wang Shih-tan, the top candidate, was then dismissed by the emperor for "evil conduct" and Chao Chin, ranking second, was proved a key member of the heir apparent's faction. See also *CSL*, 267:8a-b; *Yung-hsien lu*, p. 306.

28. *I-meng hsien-sheng chi*, 11:17b.

29. For Wang and Yin-jeng, see *Ch'ing-shih*, p. 5390; Wang Hao, *Sui-lien chi-en*, in *Hsiao-fang-hu chai yü-ti ts'ung-ch'ao*, 1st ser., ts'e 4, pp. 286-289.

30. For Hsiung, see *CSL*, 212:4.

31. *CSL*, 212:3b (Hsin-yü); 212:6b-8 (*Ming History*); 212:8a-b, 10. (Li and K'uei-hsü); 212:13b (Songgotu arrested).

32. For the 1702 tour, see *CSL*, 210:1, 2b-3, 3b, 5-13b.

33. For Yin-jeng on the 1700, 1701, 1702, and 1703 tours, see *CSL*, 200:11b;

204:16; 208:12b; 209:23; 211:3b-4, 18.

34. In response to a memorial, dated KH 41/10/-, from the textile commissioner Li Hsü, the emperor wrote, "The Heir Apparent suddenly caught a bad cold and fell seriously ill." (*WHTP*, p. 858.)

35. The emperor later recalled how he had exhorted the heir apparent, saying, "When we rulers become ill, we have many people around to assist and attend us. Can we still feel dissatisfied with such privileges, when we consider the conditions of the eunuchs and poor people? To whom can they pour out their anger?" *T'ing-hsün ko-yen*, p. 43.

36. See *CSL*, 212:15b.

37. *CSL*, 210:6a-b (pretenders).

38. *CSL*, 210:15b; 212:3b.

39. *CSL*, 211:2-3 (K'ang-hsi's birthday).

40. For the 1703 tour, see *CSL*, 211:3b-21, and Spence, *Ts'ao Yin*, p. 132.

41. For Kao's account of this experience, see his *P'eng-shan mi-chi*, in *Ku-hsüeh hui-k'an*, comp. Teng shih (Shang, 1912), 1st ser., no. 12. See also *Eminent Chinese*, p. 414, and *Ch'ing-shih*, p. 3942.

42. *CSL*, 212:13b-14b. The emperor publicly denounced Songgotu thus: "As to the charges that your household servant formerly brought to my attention in a secret report, I have kept that report without taking any action against you. I did so because I intended to treat you leniently. But you have shown no sign of regret; instead you complain about me behind my back, criticizing state affairs and forming factions for lawless acts . . . If I don't expose your plot, you will certainly make your move. This is something I have given thorough consideration. If I point out just one single wrongdoing of yours, it will constitute sufficient grounds to have you executed immediately . . ." The last sentence reveals the seriousness of the offense; undoubtedly it referred either to Songgotu's attempted coup or his criticism of K'ang-hsi's failure to carry out his promise to abdicate. See *CSL*, 212:15-16b.

43. For these Manchu names, see *CSL*, 212:13-17. Among the military adherents were: (1) T'ung-pao, then a deputy lieutenant general (cf. *Ch'ing-shih*, pp. 82, 87). He was absent from the capital at the time of the incident. (2) Weng-o-li, a deputy lieutenant general. Among board ministers who had been exiled and later recalled to Peking were: (1) Ma-er-t'u, president of the Board of Revenue (1690). (*Ch'ing-shih*, pp. 2566-72.) (2) O-k'u-li, junior president of the Board of Revenue (1683). (*Ch'ing-shih*, pp. 2560-61.) (3) Wen-tai, junior president of the Board of Rites (1684). Among officials whose status cannot be identified were Shao-kan and A-mi-ta.

44. *CSL*, 212:16b-17.

45. The opera's title varies: in some parts of China it is called *Sou-so-fu* (Searching Songgotu's residence); elsewhere it is called *San-sou-fu* (Three searches of Songgotu's residence); see T'ao Chün-ch'i, *Ching-chü chü-mu ch'u t'an* (Peking, 1963), p. 392.

The opera opens with Shih Shih-lun on his way home from an inspection trip to Nanking. He captures two bandits, Shan-ssu and Shan-wu, and from them he learns that the "Grand Tutor" (Songgotu's honorary title) has secretly made an imperial crown and robe to use after usurping the throne. Shih takes the two bandits to Peking and reports all this to the emperor. The emperor then authorizes Shih to make a search of Songgotu's residence, but Shih finds no evidence to substantiate his charge. For this, he is heartily insulted by Songgotu, and the emperor also becomes enraged and threatens to execute Shih.

At this point Chang Ming-ko (Chang P'eng-ko), former president of the Board of Punishments, memorializes the throne that he will vouch for Shih's integrity, offering the lives of his whole family as a guarantee. The emperor accordingly orders Shih to make a second search, but again nothing is discovered. Chang advises Shih to use torture to interrogate the two bandits, and by this means Shih learns where Songgotu has concealed the crown and robe. After a third search, Shih finds the evidence, and the emperor "demotes Songgotu to commoner's status." See Liu Ch'eng-fu, ed., *Yin-yüeh tz'u-tien* (A dictionary of music) (Shanghai, 1935), p. 62.

There might be some basis for the role ascribed to Shih Shih-lun. Shih had been known as a staunch opponent of the heir apparent's henchman Tohoci, who, as Yin-jeng's chief representative at court, later worked toward Yin-jeng's takeover of the throne. (*Ch'ing-shih*, p. 3974.) Also, when the emperor received the first report of Songgotu's plot, in 1700, Shih was serving as an intendant in Chiang-nan, in which role his only fault, according to the emperor, was that he was "too stubborn" and "uncompromising." (*Ch'ing-shih*, p. 3974.)

46. For the official record, see *CSL*, 212:15b; for an unofficial account, see Wang Ching-ch'i, *Tu-shu-t'ang hsi-cheng sui-pi* in *CKTP*, p. 131. According to Wang, Kao was originally very grateful to Songgotu, for it was Songgotu who had recommended him to the emperor and thus changed his life. But after Kao had achieved prestige, Songgotu failed to show him any courtesy—having met Kao through his chief household servant, Songgotu regarded him as his inferior. Even after Kao became the emperor's most favored court official, Songgotu continued to treat him "like a slave," and when Kao visited Songgotu, Songgotu would ask him to kneel while talking, no matter how long the conversation. (When Songgotu was in a bad mood, he would let Kao kneel for hours while he cursed him mercilessly.) He never addressed Kao formally, but simply said, "You, Kao Shih-ch'i!" and Songgotu's servants called him "Hsiang-kung," equivalent to "mister," rather than "Your Honor," or something similarly appropriate. Kao was also harassed by Songgotu's family tutor and collaborator Chiang Huang, who demonstrated much contempt for Kao.

In 1703, Wang asserts, when Kao returned to Peking with the emperor, Kao had decided finally to betray Songgotu—and Chiang—and to form an alliance with Mingju, who still held great power behind the scenes. Wang's account inevitably contains hearsay, but it does corroborate the outline given in the official record, and it reconciles the "household servant" theory with that of Kao Shih-ch'i.

47. For Yin-jeng's deference to Kao, see Kao Shih-ch'i, *P'eng-shan mi-chi*, p. 4b.

48. Wang Ching-ch'i, *Tu-shu t'ang hsi-cheng sui-pi*, in *CKTP*, p. 131; *Yung-hsien lu*, p. 57.

49. Sung Lao's two memorials dated 42/6/- and 42/7/- in *KKWH*, vol. 1, no. 2, pp. 183-84; Li Hsü's memorial dated 42/7/-, in *WHTP*, p. 858.

50. *CSL*, 234:3b-4.

51. For the 1703 western tour, see *CSL*, 213:23b-214:8, and *Sheng-tsu hsi-hsün jih-lu*, in *SLTP*, ts'e 1.

52. Li Kuang-ti, 18:9b.

53. *CSL*, 213:16-17 (court martial).

54. Li Kuang-ti, 18:9b.

8. The Lure of the South

1. Southern tours: see Spence, *Ts'ao Yin*, chap. 4.

2. K'ang-hsi's deep concern about the South was evident when he wrote to Wang Tu-chao in 1712, "The hearts of the Southerners and their customs you know very well. Never take things lightly at any time"; Wang was then gover-

nor of both Chekiang and Kiangsu. See Wang Tu-chao's memorial dated 51/2/- in *KHTC*, vol. 3, pp. 514-516. K'ang-hsi so feared the danger from the sea that he appointed—reluctantly—Wang Yuan, who had "the background of a pirate," to the position of brigade general. See the special edict to Liang Nai, governor-general of Fukien and Chekiang, attached to Liang's memorial dated 47/3/4, in *KKWH*, vol. 2, no. 2, p. 154; the edict was not written in K'ang-hsi's hand, but probably in that of Yin-chen, his fourth son. For spying on Japan, see Li Hsü's memorials dated 40/3/- and 40/10/- in *WHPT*, pp. 856 and 857.

3. For details on the Chu San T'ai-tzu case, see next chapter.

4. Ts'ao Yin's memorials dated 48/9/-, 48/10/-, in *WHTP*, pp. 290-291.

5. *CSL*, 234:18.

6. Ts'ao Yin's memorial dated 43/7/29, in *KKWH*, vol. 2, no. 1, p. 138, where K'ang-hsi's response is not printed in full; the last three *"hsiao-hsin"* 's ("Be careful!" 's) are left out (cf. the entry in *WHTP*, p. 290). Ts'ao Yin seemed to be an independent who was loyal only to the emperor. His son-in-law was Prince Na-erh-su, a member of the imperial clan and a close bodyguard of the emperor; the marriage tie was established by K'ang-hsi. Although Ts'ao Yin was later found to have given money to Ling-p'u, the heir apparent's henchman, there is evidence that he disapproved of Yin-jeng's conduct, as shown in his intervention in the later Ch'en P'eng-nien case. Ts'ao Yin and Li Hsü were granted honorary official titles to reward them for the fabulous temporary palaces they built for the emperor on his Southern tours; see *NWF Manchu Archives* (2). For the marriage tie, see Ts'ao Yin's memorials dated 45/8/4 and 48/2/8 in *KKWH*, vol. 1, no. 2, pp. 148 and 163; for giving money to Ling-p'u, see *NWF Manchu Archives* (4). For Prince Na-erh-su, see "Yu-kuan Na-erh-su ti shih-hsi" in *NWF Manchu Archives* (1).

7. *CSL*, 119:4a-b.

8. Spence, *Ts'ao Yin*, chap. 4.

9. *WHCN*.

10. Ibid., p. 9.

11. Chang Yün-i was the second son of Chang Yung (1616-1684), a native of Shensi, who defected to the Manchus in the early days of the Manchu conquest, and scored brilliant military victories. Chang Yung moved to Peking in 1649. His son Chang Yün-i was appointed Peking police commissioner, commander of the metropolitan guard division at the capital city. In 1693 Chang Yün-i was made director of the Court of Imperial Stud (ranked 3B). He served as Chinese commander in chief in Chekiang from 1696 to 1709. For Chang Yung's biography, see *Eminent Chinese*, pp. 66-67, and *Ch'ing-shih*, pp. 3841-43, where several references are made to Chang Yün-i. For the latter's biography, see *Chiang-nan t'ung chih*, comp. Huang Chih-chien and Yin-chi-shan (1736), 111:17.

12. For this anecdote about Chang Yün-i, cf. *CSL*, 192:12, and *WHCN*, p. 19.

13. Ibid., p. 9.

14. Ibid., pp. 8b-9.

15. Ibid., p. 32.

16. Ibid., p. 49.

17. Ibid., pp. 45b-46.

18. Li Hsü: see his memorial dated 32/12/- in *WHTP*, p. 854; Ch'eng Wei-kao: *WHCN*, pp. 45b-46. There is evidence of a close connection between Yin-jeng and members of the Ch'eng clan. Ch'eng Wei-kao, head salt merchant in Yangchow, was prominent in entertaining the imperial party when Yin-jeng was accompanying the emperor in the 1705 tour of the South. (See *WHCN*, pp.

45b-46.) In 1730 Ch'eng Han-chan, also of Yangchow, was found to have been connected with Chang Yun-ju, a renowned underground hero who attempted to avenge Yin-jeng's deposition. (See Li Wei Archives, no. 07722, dated YC 8/1/6.) Ch'eng Lien, a censor, was among those who petitioned the emperor to reinstate Yin-jeng as heir apparent after he had been deposed. (See *Yung-hsien lu*, p. 105.) This Ch'eng Lien might be the same one who is mentioned in note 50 of this chapter, but the Chinese character for the *lien* differs in the two names.

Chang Ying, then grand secretary, vividly recorded a scene during the 1689 Southern tour, in which the emperor's ministers had to dash out of their favorite play upon receiving word that K'ang-hsi wanted them to join him at a local opera performance. The favorite play they were forced to miss was the famous love story *Hui-chen chi* (The story of Yin-ying), by the T'ang novelist Yuan Chen (778-831). (For a good translation of the play, see James R. Hightower, "Yuan Chen and the Story of Ying-ying," *HJAS* 33:93-103 [1973].) See Chang Ying, *Nan-hsün hu-ts'ung chih-lüeh* in *Hsiao-fang-hu chai yü-ti ts'ung-ch'ao*, ts'e 4, p. 283.

19. The places where the emperor made long stops included: Yangchow— four days (while going south); Chin-shan (Chiang-t'ien Temple)—seven days (three on trip south, four returning); Sung-chiang fu—six days (going south only); Hangchow—four days (farthest point on the trip); Chiang-ning—six days (returning only). See *CSL*, 219:13b-22:20b.

20. Li's expenses. *Su-chou fu-chih*, 148:34b-35. Although Li also was found to have used money to gain the friendship of Yin-jeng's confidant Ling-p'u, he actually belonged to the Yin-ssu faction. See *NWT Manchu Archives* (3) and *Yung hsien-lu*, p. 352. Effects on local finance: for example, the embezzlement by Huang Ming, financial commissioner of Chekiang, of more than half a million taels in public funds, a common occurrence in the Southern provinces. For Huang's case, see the secret report supplied to the emperor by Liang Nai, governor-general of Chekiang and Fukien, in Liang Nai's memorial dated 47/8/10 in *KKWH*, vol. 2, no. 2, pp. 176-177. More information on Huang Ming will be given later in this chapter.

21. *WHCN*, pp. 6b-7.

22. Ibid., p. 10.

23. Ibid., p. 10.

24. Li Hsü: Su-chou fu-chih (1748), 148:34b-35; for the *Romance* see Herbert A. Giles, *A History of Chinese Literature* (New York, 1923), p. 168; also cf. A. E. Zucker, *The Chinese Theater* (Boston, 1925), pp. 70-71.

25. For the poem's complete translation by Herbert A. Giles, see his *A History of Chinese Literature* (New York, 1923).

26. For preface and poem, see *WHCN*, pp. 7b-8.

27. Visits: ibid., pp. 10b-11, 26b.

28. *Su-chou fu-chih*, 3:30.

29. Ibid., 3:34b-35.

30. Ibid., 3:30b-31.

31. *CSL*, 234:3.

32. Ibid.

33. *CSL*, 234:7.

34. For Korean reports, see Kuksa p'yǒnch'an Wiwǒnhoe, comp., *Chosǒn wangjo sillok*, Sukchong reign (Seoul, 1955-58), 47:20.

35. Ibid., 52:42.

36. For Ch'en P'eng-nien, see *Kuo-ch'ao ch'i-hsien*, 164:18, and translation in Silas Wu, *Communication and Imperial Control*, pp. 56-58. For Ch'en's dismissal, see *CSL*, 224:16b-17, and *Ch'ing-shih lieh-chuan* (Shanghai, 1928),

13:23. For Fang Pao, see *Fang Wang-ch'i*, p. 248 (about earthworms).

37. *WHTP*, pp. 79-80; *CSL*, 220:12b; 221:1b, 3, 6b.

38. Li Hsü's memorial dated 45/2/- in *WHTP*, p. 859.

39. For Soochow rice smuggling, see Li Hsü's memorial dated 45/3/-, in *WHTP*, p. 859; for earthquake and Taiwan, see *CSL*, 224:16b, 227:3b.

40. *CSL*, 222:7b; Ts'ao Yin's memorial dated 48/3/-, in *WHTP*, p. 290.

41. For the three tours, see *CSL*, 224:11b; 225:15b; and 227:21. Yin-shih (K'ang-hsi's eldest son) and Yin-hsiang (his thirteenth) went on these three tours, and on the spring tour they were joined by Yin-chen (the fourth son) and Yin-t'ang (the ninth).

42. For K'ang-hsi's refusal to decide, see *CSL*, 244:4-6b; for Asan's new appointment, *CSL*, 227:21; for Keng-o and Ch'ao-k'o-t'o as his successors to the presidency of the Board of Punishments, *CSL*, 231:23. For Ch'ao-k'o-t'o's connections with the heir apparent's faction, see Wang Hung-hsü's memorial of 1708, no. 25, in *WHTP*, p. 91, in which Wang said that Ch'ao-k'o-t'o was a follower of Tohoci, leader of the heir apparent's faction. Keng-o was Songgotu's "household bond servant" (personal retainer) and die-hard adherent (*CSL*, 248:17).

43. Final acceptance of suggestion and dowager empress's intervention: *CSL*, 227:28-29b.

44. *CSL*, 228:10-13.

45. *CSL*, 229:17.

46. Li Yü held the title Eunuch of the Imperial Presence (*yü-ch'ien t'ai-chien*). He seemed to be a key figure in the line of communication between the emperor and the court, and he was particularly entrusted with the duty of dealing with foreigners. On 41/3/30 (April 26, 1702) he and He-shih-heng, probably department director in the Imperial Household, and Chao Ch'ang, of the Office of Imperial Inscriptions (Yü-shu ch'u), transmitted to the Jesuit missionaries the "Imperial Mandate, April 26, 1702" (see Antonio Sisto Rosso, O.F.M., *Apostolic legations to China of the Eighteenth Century* [South Pasadena, 1948], p. 234). In addition, the emperor's eldest son, Yin-shih, received an imperial order to join Li Yü in handling the missionaries. He-shih-heng was of the Sunu family, and they and Yin-shih were later found to be key members of the anti-Yin-jeng coalition and Li Yü was later discovered to be a Yin-ssu adherent). (*CSL:YC*, 45:11.) K'ang-hsi's assignment of Li Yü to be the liaison between himself and Wang Hung-hsü in an investigation that would probably implicate Yin-jeng seemed logical. For Li Yü's relationship with Yin-shih, see the document dated 47/4/16 in Rosso, p. 250.

47. Wang Hung-hsü's memorial no. 20, in *WHTP*, p. 90.

48. Ibid.

49. For *k'un-ch'ü* as a vogue, see Ch'en Wan-nai, *Yuan-Ming-Ch'ing hsi-ch'ü shih* (Taipei, 1966), pp. 404-414.

50. Cf. Li Hsü's memorial dated 32/12/-, in *WHTP*, p. 854, and imperial response to Li Hsü's memorial, dated 46/8/-: "The harvest is bad this year; by all means, you must avoid buying any more people for me!" Cf. also *Yang-chi-chai ts'ung-lu*, 13:8b (Soochow actresses in the Imperial Household).

51. Ling-p'u: *CSL*, 219:6b, 324:17b-20.

52. Fan P'u: Biographical note in *Hui-chou fu-chih* (1827) and *Tung-p'ing chou chih* (1771), 12:49. Also cf. Wang Hung-hsü's memorials nos. 20, 21, and 22, in *WHTP*, pp. 90-91, and Li Hsü's memorial dated 48/12/2, in *WHTP*, p. 866. In 1726 the Yung-cheng Emperor, in response to a memorial from O-erh-t'ai, governor of Yunnan, dated YC 4/3/20 (no. 3) in *CPYC*, characterized Fan P'u as "a disgusting and mean person."

53. For Ch'eng clansmen from Hui-chou prefecture and their role in the salt and copper monopolies, see Yamawaki Teizirō, *Nagasaki to Tojin bōeki* (Nagasaki and the China trade) (Tokyo, 1964), pp. 185-194. Some of the powerful members of the Ch'eng clan migrated to Hsin-an, in Kiangsu; see *Ch'eng-shih tsu-p'u ssu-chung* (1895, Toyo Bunko ed.). In connection with the Southern tours, Ch'eng Lien—who probably received his appointment as grain intendant of Chekiang province through voluntary contributions to the government —took principal charge of building the temporary palace at West Lake, in Hangchow. According to Wang Hung-shü's report (his memorial no. 23, in *WHTP*, p. 91), Ch'eng Lien's father, Ch'eng Tseng, was an influential "head salt merchant," who engaged in the salt monopoly in the Liang-Huai region. Ch'eng Lien was dismissed in 1711 for mishandling tribute grains. (*CSL,* 248: 12.) Ch'eng Kuang-k'uei, also son of a salt merchant, was involved in the 1712 examination scandal in Chiang-nan; though "ignorant about the principles of literature," he passed the provincial examination by cheating (*CSL*, 248:8b); cf. Ts'ao Yin's memorials of 1711 and 1712 (nos. 1-6), in *WHTP*, pp. 291-293. Ts'ao Yin Archives, no 2757 (enclosed in a greetings memorial dated 51/4/22); no. 2758 (enclosed in a weather report dated 51/5/3); no. 2759 (enclosed in a memorial on the publication of the imperially sponsored literary project *P'ei-wen yün-fu*, dated 51/4/3); no. 2760 (enclosed in a weather report dated 51/5/ 22); and no. 2762 (enclosed in a memorial dated 51/3/27 on the arrival in Chiang-ning of Lang T'ing-chi, to be the acting governor-general of Liang-Kiang). These memorials were published in *WHTP*, pp. 291-93, and again in *KKWH*, vol. 2, no. 1, pp. 182-187, but in neither case is there a clear indication of the dates. For salt merchants' contributions, see Saeki Tomi, *Shindai ensei no kenkyū*, p. 9. Cf. *Yung-hsien lu*, pp. 150, 259-260, 397-398, 378.

54. *Huang-ch'ao wen-hsien t'ung-k'ao*, chüan 14 (p. 4976); Saeki Tomi, "Shincho no kōki to Sansei shōnin," in *Shakai bunka shigaku* (Tokyo, 1966), p. 13.

55. Fan P'u and Ch'a Sheng: Wang Hung-hsü's memorials nos. 20 and 21, *WHTP*, p. 90.

56. Ma I-tzu: *CSL*, 229:7b, and *Yung-hsien lu*, p. 306. Chang Po-hsing: *CSL*, 229:7b, 251:15b.

57. Wang Hung-hsü's memorial no. 20, *WHTP*, p. 90.

58. Cf. Wang Shu-nu, *Chung-kuo ch'ang-chi shih* (Shanghai, 1935), p. 322.

59. Wu-ko, written in the two characters 五 哥 , was undoubtedly the correct form, as found in official K'ang-hsi documents: see, for example, CCC 51/4/23 and 54/7/6, where the same characters were used and where he was referred to as "imperial bodyguard of the first rank at the Ch'ien-ch'ing Gate, concurrently serving as deputy-general." There are two other names with the homophones Wu-ko, one written 武 格 , which appears in *CSL*, 221:22b, and the other written 伍 格 , which appears in *CSL:YC*, 47:13b, and *Yung-hsien lu*, p. 206.

60. Cf. Yin-chi-shan Archives, undated: The report was submitted by Yin-chi-shan, governor of Kiangsu (1728-1731), at the request of the Yung-cheng Emperor. Based on information submitted by Wu Ts'un-li's household servant, it listed at least 137 names—ministers, guard officers, banner officials, and others—who had accepted money from Wu Ts'un-li; the total value of "presents" he gave out exceeded a half million taels of silver. Mai Kung received "1,800 taels" from him.

61. At Yangchow: *CSL*, 229:12b, and Wang Hung-hsü's memorial, no. 21, *WHTP*, p. 90.

62. This is Wang's memorial no. 21, in *WHTP*, p. 90.

63. This should properly be written *kang-shang*. See Wang's memorial no. 24, in *WHTP*, p. 92. For the meaning of *kang*, see Ts'ao Yin's memorials dated 43/11/22 and 50/3/9, in *WHTP*, p. 295; *CSL*, 233:3b; *Ch'ing-shih*, p. 1497; and *HTSL* 223:3b.

64. Fan P'u: Wang's charge was corroborated by another secret report sent to the emperor; see Li Hsü's memorial dated 48/12/2, in *WHTP*, p. 866.

65. In response to Wang's request that the emperor return his memorials in sealed envelopes, K'ang-hsi enclosed Wang's memorial in an envelope on the back seam of which he wrote, "Nan shu-fang chin-feng" (securely sealed by the South Library), and on the left side of the front of the envelope he noted, "tz'u-shu tsung-kuan ch'in-shou chiao-yü Wang Shang-shu" (Let the chief eunuch [Li Yü] hand this letter to the board president Wang in person). For Wang's request, see his memorial dated 46/6/15, no. 21, in *WHTP*, p. 90. I examined this envelope at the NPM(T). The NPM(T) has nine memorials submitted by Wang during the period between 46/4/24 and 46/9/23, four of which were routine greetings memorials; see Wang Hung-hsü archives, dated above.

66. Wang's memorial no. 22, in *WHTP*, pp. 91-92.

67. Edict dated 46/11/19, in *KHWC*, vol. 4.

9. A Pretender

1. *CSL*, 234:8a-b.

2. Wang Hung-hsü's memorial dated 46/6/17, no. 22, in *WHTP*, pp. 90-91.

3. Wang Hung-hsü's memorial no. 23, dated 46/9/23, in *WHTP*, pp. 90-91. On another occasion, Huang Ming was characterized by Liang Nai, governor-general of Chekiang and Fukien, as a "wicked ruffian." Huang boasted that "although I had been earlier sentenced to death [on criminal charges], I felt no fear about it. Is there anyone in the whole nation who doesn't know this man Huang Ming? Concerning financial matters, I can say publicly that I do like to receive a little more money!" Huang openly practiced blackmail, gathering more than half a million taels (which amounted to ten percent of the entire annual tax of Chekiang province); despite Liang Nai's "earnest exhortation and warning," Huang "responded with deaf ears." See Liang Nai's memorial dated 47/8/10, in *KKWH*, vol. 2, no. 2, pp. 174-177.

In the same memorial, Wang revealed how the emperor's Southern tours had affected rivalries among local politicians. During the 1705 tour the governor of Chekiang was Chang T'ai-chiao, who entrusted Ch'eng Lien (of note 53 in chapter 8) with the weighty task of entertaining the imperial party. Wang Jan took over the governorship from Chang in 1706, and he then gave Kao Ch'i-p'ei, circuit intendant, the honor of preparing the reception for the imperial party during the 1707 tour. Ch'eng Lien, needless to say, complained about this appointment, contending that Kao did not make any contribution to the costs of the reception. (Since the money for these entertainments was derived from local officials' contributions, these officials in turn had to find ways to meet their extra expenses, and, being meagerly paid, they had to resort to corruption.)

4. Imperial endorsement of Li Hsü's memorial dated 46/6/-, in *WHTP*, p. 860.

5. Ts'ao Yin's memorial dated 46/6/20, in *KKWH*, vol. 2, no. 1, p. 150.

6. Li Hsü's memorial dated 40/8/-, in *WHTP*, p. 860.

7. Li Hsü's memorial dated 46/12/7, in *WHTP*, p. 860.

8. Liang Nai's memorial dated 47/2/13, in *KKWH*, vol. 2, no. 2, p. 143.

9. *CSL*, 232:11b.

10. Imperial endorsement of Li Hsü's memorial dated 46/12/-, in *WHTP*, p. 862; of Liang Nai's greetings memorial (undated, but attached to his memo-

rial dated 47/2/16), in *KKWH*, vol. 2, no. 2, p. 146.

11. Imperial endorsement noted on Li's memorial dated 42/2/-, in *WHTP*, pp. 862-63; Japanese report: *Ka i hentai*, p. 2548; I-nien's execution: *CSL*, 233: 19b-20, and *Ka i hentai*, p. 2610.

12. For references to Chu San T'ai-tzu and Chang Nien-i, see *CSL*, 232:9-10b, 11-11b; Li Hsü's memorial dated 47/2/-, in *WHTP*, pp. 862-63. For a general study of the Chu San T'ai-tzu case, see Meng Sen, "Ming Lieh-huang hsün-kuo hou-chi," in his *Ming-Ch'ing shih lun-chu chi-k'an* (Peking, 1959), pp. 28-77. Meng Sen quotes a number of rare works, including manuscript sources.

13. The trial of and deposition given by Wang Shih-yuan (Chu San T'ai-tzu) was included in Chao Hung-hsieh's memorial, in *SLHK*, pp. 20-22. See also Ts'ao Yin's memorial dated 47/3/26, in *KKWH*, vol. 2, no. 1, pp. 152 and 154, and the appendix: "A brief account of the Chekiang trial."

14. Meng Sen, p. 48.

15. *CSL*, 232:22b.

16. Meng Sen, "Ming Leih-huang," pp. 47, 48. The manuscript account was written by Li Fang-yuan, who was sentenced to exile on the Manchurian frontier for having employed Chu as a tutor for his grandchildren in Shantung. Chu San T'ai-tzu was charged by the Board of Punishments with being an "impostor" of the Ming prince (*CSL*, 235:9a-b).

17. Controlling the Three Judiciaries were three of Yin-jeng's henchmen: Wang Shan, Chinese president of the Board of Punishments; Shu-lu, Manchu senior censor-general; and Lao Chih-pien, Chinese president of the Court of Judicature and Revision. See *WHTP*, pp. 95, 106-109; *Kuo-ch'ao ch'i-hsien*, 20:13-16b.

In addition to this obvious situation, there is indirect evidence derived from the *Nan-shan chi* case that Yin-jeng was behind the Chu San T'ai-tzu victimization. The execution in 1655 of the eunuchs who had recognized the Ming heir apparent was recorded in a work entitled *Nan-shan chi*, written by Tai Ming-shih. Later, in 1711, Yin-jeng "picked out phrases here and there in the *Nan-shan chi*" that he deemed hostile to the dynasty, and he persuaded Chao Shen-ch'ao, then senior censor-general, to impeach Tai for seditious intentions (after Yin-jeng's deposition, Chao would be a loyal restorationist). Tai was tried, and he and many members of his family were executed, by slow slicing. The charge was that while collecting late-Ming materials to prepare a history of the period, Tai had used the Ming reign titles instead of the Ch'ing—this was treasonable because it implied that the rule of the Ch'ing was illegitimate. The episode is well known in Chinese history as "The case of literary persecution concerning the *Nan-shan chi*." For Tai's biography, see *Eminent Chinese*, p. 701; for *Nan-shan chi* on the first Ming heir apparent, see Meng Sen, p. 42; for Yin-jeng's role in the *Nan-shan chi* case, see *CSL*, 249:3a-b, and *Yung-hsien lu*, p. 69.

18. Ts'ao Yin's memorial dated 47/5/25, in *KKWH*, vol. 2, no. 1, p. 159.

19. Ibid.

20. Ts'ao Yin's memorial dated 47/7/15, in *KKWH*, vol. 2, no. 1, pp. 161-162.

21. *Chosŏn wangjo sillok*, 47:20.

22. *Ka i hentai*, p. 2610.

23. *CSL*, 234:8a-b.

10. Dismissal

1. For a description of the beauty of the Jehol summer palace and its surroundings, as well as glimpses of K'ang-hsi's private life at Jehol, see Matteo Ripa, *Memoirs of Father Ripa* (London, 1846), pp. 72-75, 76-79, 115-116.

2. Other sons accompanying the emperor on this trip were Yin-shih (the eldest, aged thirty-seven), Yin-hsiang (the thirteenth, twenty-three), Yin-t'i (the fourteenth, twenty-one), and the teenagers Yin-yu (the fifteenth, sixteen), Yin-lu (the sixteenth, fourteen), and Yin-li (the seventeenth, twelve). See *CSL*, 233:3.

3. Analysis of imperial concubines and their sons is based on *Ch'ing Huang-shih ssu-p'u*, compiled by T'ang Pang-chih. Also, cf. biographies of the empresses and concubines in *Ch'ing lieh-ch'ao hou-fei chuan kao*, compiled by Chang Ts'ai-t'ien (1929).

4. See *I-men hsien-sheng chi*, 4:13.

5. Father P. d'Entrecolles's letter to "Fr. Procurator General of the Indian and Chinese Missions," dated July 17, 1707 (*sic*; it should be 1709), in *Lettres édifiantes*, III, 161. Ripa, p. 115.

6. Kao Shih-ch'i, *P'eng-shan mi-chi*, p. 4.

7. Ripa, pp. 73, 115-116. Though Ripa's account concerned the 1711 trip to Jehol, his description must represent the pattern of imperial life there: as he noted (p. 116), "Such were frequently the recreations of his Imperial Majesty, and particularly in the cool of the summer evenings."

8. For an interesting description of the 1711 autumn hunt, see Ripa, pp. 75-76, 78-79.

9. Yin-chieh's illness: *CSL*, 233:24a-b.

10. For warnings to those persons guilty of physical assault, see *CSL*, 233:26b-27b. For references to Yin-shih and Yin-ssu, see *CSL*, 234:22b; 235:2a-b.

11. *CSL*, 233:24b, 234:1b, 3b.

12. *CSL*, 234:1b.

13. For Yin-shih, *CSL*, 234:4b; K'ang-hsi's vigilance, *CSL*, 234:2b; Yin-jeng's motive for revenge, *CSL*, 234:19b.

14. *Li Wen-cheng kung nien-p'u*, ts'e 1, 27b-39b.

15. *Hsiao-t'ing hsü-lu*, 1:2b-3; Ripa, p. 75.

16. See Wang Hao, *Sui-lien chi-en*, p. 287b, where Wang stated that "the Heir Apparent's tent" was close to that of the emperor's. At the Jehol summer palace, "the Heir Apparent's study" was located to the west of the emperor's residence; see Chang Yü-shu, *Hu-ts'ung tz'u-yu chi*, pp. 299a-b.

17. *CSL*, 234:5b.

18. Yin-jeng's crimes: *CSL*, 234:5-9, 15b-20. One of his crimes—corruption —is independently recorded by the European traders at Canton. A certain Chinese broker, Leanqua, told the supercargoes of the ship *Kent* in 1704 about "The Emperor's Merchant." The supercargoes recounted: "As to the news we have heard of a thing called an Emperor's Merchant, it is but too true; that he is a man who formerly sold Salt at Canton, and was Whip't out of the Province for being caught defrauding the Emperor of his duties on that commodity, but not being whip't out of all his money, he had found means to be introduced to the Emperor's Son and Successor, who for a sum of money, reported to be 42,000 taels, has given him a Patent to trade with all Europeans in Canton, exclusive of all other Merchants, forbidding any one to interfere with him, without his special Licence first obtained; and that *this is done without the Emperor's knowledge*" (italics mine). (Hosea Ballou Morse, *The Chronicles of the East India Company Trading to China, 1635-1834* [Oxford, 1925], p. 138.) This source suggests how pervasive Yin-jeng's corruption had become four years before his first deposition, in 1708.

19. *CSL*, 234:2b-3.

20. *CSL*, 234:4, 19b.

21. *CSL*, 234:4b-5. Cf. *Lettres édifiantes*, III, 161-162: Yin-jeng's attempted

coup was partly prompted by a fortune-teller's prediction that he "must attain the throne by a certain date or never."

22. *CSL*, 234:5-5b.

23. *Lettres édifiantes*, III, 161-163.

24. For K'ang-hsi's health, see *CSL*, 234:7b; 275:10.

25. *CSL*, 234:10b-11.

11. The Yin-ssu Faction

1. *CSL*, 235:25; also see Ch'in Tao-jan's deposition in *WHTP*, p. 4.

2. For K'ang-hsi's reference to the mean status of Yin-ssu's mother, see *CSL*, 261:8b, and *Ch'ing Huang-shih ssu-p'u*, 2:14. It was not until 1701 that his mother's status was elevated to *pin* (imperial concubine of the fourth rank), which was second lowest in the harem hierarchy (*CSL*, 202:17b).

3. Prince An, Yolo, was a son of Hong Taiji. Yolo fathered at least three sons, namely, Ma-erh-hun, Ching-hsi, and Wu-erh-chan, and a daughter of unknown name (whose daughter, also of unknown name, was Yin-ssu's wife). See *CSL*, 235:8b-9; 202:24b-25.

4. Yin-ssu's wife: *CSL*, 235:9; *WHTP*, p. 14; *Eminent Chinese*, p. 934.

5. *I-men hsien-sheng chi*, 4:13.

6. Ch'in Tao-jan was the only one among the three who had not yet acquired the *chin-shih* degree; he would receive it in 1709. During the intervening six years, he was very close to Yin-t'ang, and because of his involvement in the succession struggle, he was later charged by the Yung-cheng Emperor with improper association with Yin-t'ang for which he was imprisoned for fourteen years. He was not released until the early years of the Ch'ien-lung reign, and he died at age ninety. (*Kuo-ch'ao ch'i-hsien*, 135:3b; *Yung-hsien lu*, p. 285.) Ch'in was a descendant of the noted Sung poet Ch'in Kuan (1049-1100); his father, Ch'in Sung-ling (1637-1714, *chin-shih* of 1655), was a successful competitor in the special examination given to noted Confucian scholars (*po-hsüeh hung-tz'u*) in 1679. (*Eminent Chinese*, pp. 167-168; *Yung-hsien lu*, pp. 64-65.) According to Fang Pao, Wei Fang-t'ai was assigned as tutor to Prince Ch'un (Yin-yü), the seventh son of the emperor. (*Fang Wang-ch'i*, p. 135.) Yin-t'i's tutor was Hsü Lan (*Yung-hsien lu*, p. 102).

7. Ch'in Tao-jan's deposition, in *WHTP*, p. 3.

8. Ho was charged with conspiring with Yin-ssu in the succession struggle and with being unduly close to him, to the extent that he had entrusted his daughter's care to Yin-ssu's wife. K'ang-hsi made a special notation on the letter: "This is the letter from Yin-ssu to Ho Cho. It must be kept very carefully and not misplaced by any chance." Ten years later, the Yung-cheng Emperor used this letter to substantiate Yin-ssu's complicity in the succession struggle, though he did heed Yin-ssu's request never to publish the letter, to save him from embarrassment. It was not published until 1936 (by the National Palace Museum, Peiping). For a photo-reproduction of the letter and K'ang-hsi's notation, see *CKTP*, pp. 20-21.

9. *Eminent Chinese*, pp. 606-607; *Ch'ing-shih*, p. 5234.

10. For a photo-reproduction of the original letter, see *CKTP*, p. 21.

11. *CSL*, 277:6b; *Eminent Chinese*, p. 251.

12. For Fu-ch'uan's recommendation, see Ch'ing Tao-jan's deposition in *WHTP*, p. 4.

13. K'ang-hsi on Yin-ssu: *CSL*, 235:25; Pao-t'ai: *Ch'ing-shih*, p. 3553, and *Eminent Chinese*, p. 252.

14. See *CSL:YC*, 44:29; Ho T'u's deposition in *WHTP*, p. 4.

15. Ho Yü-chu: Ch'in Tao-jan's deposition, in *WHTP*, pp. 15 and 18; *Yung-*

hsien lu, p. 62. An San was a Korean who became a bond servant under Mingju. While Mingju was in power, An San was accused of committing serious crimes in Peking, but before the emperor could punish him, Mingju had already sent him to the South, giving him a huge sum of money to engage in the salt monopoly in Yangchow. His region of monopoly covered four prefectures, involving 300,000 *yin* (a certificate that authorized the merchant to buy a prescribed amount of salt from the government, an amount ranging from a few hundred catties—1.1 pounds per catty—to more than two thousand). (For the *yin* system, see *Ch'ing-shih*, p. 1497.) The monopoly enabled An San to reap great annual profits, making him one of the wealthiest men in the South; as the popular saying of the day went, "It was An from the North as K'ang from the West" —the K'ang family being the wealthiest in Shansi. The financial influence of the An family perhaps reached the realm of foreign trade in Canton, as well. In the East India Company's account, there was a certain Mr. An (Anqua: *qua* in Cantonese means Mr. or Sir) whom the English captain Alexander Hamilton referred to in 1703 as one of the "three Villains" who had acquired the exclusive right to China's trade with that company and who refused to pay a fair price for the goods. (See Morse, pp. 102-104.) For An San, see *Eminent Chinese*, pp. 11-13; *Yung-hsien lu*, p. 260; Chao Hung-hsieh's memorial dated 48/4/19, in *WHTP*, p. 306; Shao Yuan-lung's deposition in *WHTP*, p. 15; Bradley Smith and Wan-go Weng, *China: A History in Art* (New York, 1974), p. 248 (An's portrait).

As far as the Fan P'u affair was concerned, Yin-t'ang—much less his eunuch Ho Yü-chu or the salt magnate An San—could not be described as "the number-one man before the Emperor." In contrast, Ho Yü-chu felt the need to conceal his identity and pretended to be the son of the wealthy salt merchant An San, whereas Fan P'u boldly "ordered" local officials to issue warrants to "demand" that girls and boys be sold to him. (Wang Hung-hsü's memorial no. 20, in *WHTP*, p. 90.)

16. See Ch'in Tao-jan's deposition, in *WHTP*, p. 5. Yin-t'ang also told Father Mourao that he "had to feign illness, thus rendering myself a useless person" in order to avoid being designated his father's successor. See Mourao's deposition in *WHTP*, p. 1. This deposition was given by Mourao to the Board of Punishments after he was arrested, in 1726, under the orders of the Emperor Yung-cheng, for alleged collusion with Yin-t'ang in a conspiracy against the emperor. Mourao's statement was quoted in a memorial submitted to the throne by the Board of Punishments and was subsequently published in the *Peking Gazette*, a sort of newspaper; a copy of the memorial was apparently made from the *Gazette* and sent to Europe by the missionaries, and it is now preserved in the Biblioteca Apostolica Vaticana (see Rosso, pp. 408-416). The essence of the memorial also appeared in *CSL*. By comparing the Vatican copy with the texts in *WHTP* and *CSL*, one finds that the Vatican version contains miswritten characters. For a recent study of Mourao, see Pascal M. d'Elia, *Il lontano confino e la tragica morte del P. João Mourão, S.I., Missionario in Cina 1681-1726*. This study, however, sheds little light on the role he played in the succession struggle. Professor John W. Witek kindly supplied this reference.

17. Ch'in Tao-jan's deposition, *WHTP*, p. 2.

18. Ho Tu's deposition no. 1, *WHTP*, p. 5.

19. Clerical posts: ibid.; ginseng trade: Wang Hung-hsü's memorial no. 24, *WHTP*, p. 92, and Ch'ing Tao-jan's deposition, *WHTP*, p. 4. Yung-fu was originally an imperial bodyguard of the first rank and advanced to deputy lieutenant general in 1726. See *CSL:YC*, 45:18; *PCTP*, 22:1b-2; *Ch'ing-shih*, pp. 2609 and 4036; *Eminent Chinese*, p. 927. After K'uei-hsü died, in 1717, Yin-

t'ang received 400,000 in silver taels and 300,000 in real estate, bringing his net worth to more than a million taels. (See Ch'in Tao-jan's deposition, *WHTP*, p. 3.) For Yung-shou, see *WHTP*, p. 14; *Ch'ing-shih*, pp. 2614-19.

20. Yin-t'ang was charged by Yung-cheng with having extorted a total of one million taels from Yung-fu and having forcibly taken all of Yung-fu's business enterprises, which were scattered throughout the empire. See *CSL:YC*, 45:18. Additionally, Yin-t'ang extorted money from T'ung Kuo-jang, governor of Kiangsi, in the amount of 10,000 taels; from Chang T'ung-pi, 5,000 taels; from Sung Ta-yeh, a subchancellor, 500 taels; and from Li T'ing-ch'en, a prefect, 120 taels. See Ch'ing Tao-jan's deposition in *WHTP*, p. 3.

Yin-t'ang used his wealth to promote the cause of the Yin-ssu faction. Sometime before 1720 he invested 300,000 taels to obtain the governor-generalship of Hu-Kuang for Man-p'ei, a member of the faction—even though earlier he had extorted money (at least 10,000 taels) from this man. Cf. Ch'in Tao-jan's deposition, *WHTP*, p. 3, and *Yung-hsien lu*, p. 70.

21. In his *Shui-hu chuan yü Chung-kuo she-hui* (Nanking, 1934), Sa Meng-wu analyzed the origin of *hsiao* from a strictly materialistic viewpoint (p. 7); his discussion of the values of *chung* (loyalty to the throne) and *i* (or *i-ch'i*) is more convincing (pp. 150-151). Aware of the power of this novel to inspire popular rebellions against Manchu rule, K'ang-hsi's grandson, the Ch'ien-lung Emperor, banned it. Cf. Yen Tun-i, *Shui-hu chuan ti yen-pien* (Peking, 1957), p. 257.

22. Ch'in Tao-jan's deposition, *WHTP*, p. 15.

23. Ibid., p. 4.

24. For Yin-ssu's contemplation of assassination, see *CSL*, 235:3b-5b.

25. Ibid.

26. Yin-shih's report: *CSL*, 235:4.

27. For the origin of New Manchu, see *Ch'ing-shih lieh-chuan* (Biographies in Ch'ing history), 10:366; *CSL*, 235:3b-5b; *T'ing-hsün ko-yen*, 25-25b; Robert H. G. Lee, *The Manchurian Frontier in Ch'ing History* (Cambridge, Mass., 1970), p. 18; Chao Ch'i-na, "Ch'ing ch'u tung-pei chu-tang pa-ch'i chih chien-chih yen-chiu," *KKWH*, vol. 5, no. 1, p. 27 (December, 1973).

28. *CSL*, 235:3b-5b.

12. Reversals

1. *CSL*, 235:22.

2. *CSL*, 234:23b.

3. *CSL*, 234:20b.

4. *CSL*, 236:4b; 234:10b-11.

5. *CSL*, 234:9b-10.

6. *CSL*, 234:10b.

7. *CSL*, 234:11b.

8. Yin-jeng was later transferred to Hsien-an Palace, his residence, for "recuperation." (*CSL*, 234:11; 235:14.)

9. Ch'in Tao-jan's deposition, *WHTP*, p. 4.

10. Discussion of madness: *Li Kuang-ti nien-p'u*, II, 39a-b. For a defender of Yin-jeng, see *HTTL*, 5:36b-37, and *CSL*, 235:19.

11. *CSL*, 234:23.

12. *CSL*, 234:24; Ch'in Tao-jan's deposition, *WHTP*, p. 15b. It was said that they were determined to display an unswerving loyalty to Yin-ssu, even to commit suicide with poison, which they concealed in their clothing (*CSL:YC*, 45:17b).

13. *CSL*, 235:3b-5b.

14. *CSL*, 235:12, 14a-b. K'ang-hsi said the effigies were discovered on 47/10/17 (October 28, 1748); see *CSL*, 235:17.

15. *CSL*, 235:17.

16. Hunting: *CSL*, 235:13b-14. A Jesuit in Peking wrote about the emperor's physical condition both before and after the hunting expedition. He first related that K'ang-hsi's suspicion of an assassination attempt during the hunt had already caused him "great pain" and was responsible for such "deep melancholy, accompanied by severe palpitations, that one had to be afraid for his life." Then the emperor fell ill: "The Emperor's sickness, which grew more severe each day, had reduced him to a state of weakness and his Chinese doctors began to lose hope. Having exhausted all their medical means and methods, they turned to the Europeans. They had heard that Brother Rhodés was well versed in pharmacy and they decided that he was in a position to heal the Emperor." It was through the care of Brother Rhodés that "the violent palpitations" that ordinarily agitated the emperor's heart were stopped. Rhodés suggested that the emperor take canary wine, used for liturgical purposes by the Jesuits. The letter also stated that K'ang-hsi had fully regained his health by July 1709. See *Lettres édifiantes*, III, 163.

17. *CSL*, 235:14.

18. For the division of Yin-shih's retainers, see *CSL*, 235:15. All bannermen from the Upper Three Banners were given to Yin-t'i; the unit from the Bordered Blue Banners was given to Hung-wang. Household *pao-i* units and other personnel were divided evenly between Yin-t'i and Hung-wang. For Yin-shih's imprisonment and death, see *CSL*, 235:14b-15b, and *Lettres édifiantes*, III, 163; *Eminent Chinese*, p. 930.

19. *CSL*, 234:14b, 22; *SYNK* 2/8/22.

20. *CSL*, 237:16b.

21. *CSL*, 237:14b.

22. *CSL*, 235:15b-16b.

23. *CSL*, 235:18b-19.

24. *Lettres édifiantes*, III, 163.

25. Ch'ing Tao-jan's deposition, in *WHTP*, p. 4.

26. *CSL*, 235:21-22.

27. *CSL*, 235:24-26.

28. For the ensuing discussion of K'ang-hsi's reaction to the Yin-ssu nomination, see *CSL*, 236:4-14b.

29. Three years later, after definitively deposing Yin-jeng, K'ang-hsi rebuked his ministers for their lack of courage to disagree with him, referring to T'ung Kuo-wei's courageous objection: "If I should decide to release Yin-jeng again on the grounds that he has become morally sound, would any one among you [ministers] dare to follow the example of the Imperial Uncle [T'ung Kuo-wei] who feared not even the death penalty by objecting to my opinion, in contending that [Yin-jeng] was absolutely not releasable? If you ministers don't dare to do the same, then what good would you be to me? I am terribly disappointed with you people." (CCC 51/10/11.) In the *CSL*, this self-indicting passage was de-emphasized and the reference to T'ung Kuo-wei deleted.

30. *Chŏson wangjo sillok*, 47:20. See partial translation in Silas Wu, *Communication and Imperial Control*, p. 59.

31. *CSL*, 236:8b, 25; *Eminent Chinese*, pp. 794-795.

32. *CSL*, 236:9.

33. Brunnert, pp. 98-99; *Ta-Ch'ing hui-tien* (1899), chüan 82.

34. His name is given elsewhere as Pa-hun-tai; compare *CSL*, 236:2 and 237:18b; for Pa-hun-te's role in nominating Yin-ssu, see *CSL*, 236:5-6b.

35. For quotation, see *CSL*, 236:25b (also cf. 236:27b); for Olondai's connection with Yin-ssu, see *CSL:YC*, 29:24-31b; *SYNK* 3/2/29; and *Ch'ing-shih*, p. 4029, which contains an error (Olondai was the son of Kuo-wei, not Kuo-kang).

36. Olondai: *CSL:YC*, 29:28a-b; *SYNK* 3/2/29.

37. For O-fei, see *CSL*, 236:2 and 237:18b. For Alingga, see *CSL*, 235:19b, and *SYNK* 3/2/19; and for his family connection with· the emperor, see his father, Ebilun's, biography in *Eminent Chinese*, p. 220. Alingga died in 1716. His son Arsungga succeeded him, rose to political prominence, and became a chamberlain of the Imperial Bodyguard, and later he was named president of the Board of Punishments. Arsungga was executed by a decree of the Yung-cheng Emperor in 1726. Alingga was posthumously dishonored by a tablet placed before his tombs, which reads: "THIS IS THE TOMB OF ALINGGA, THE DIS-LOYAL, UNBROTHERLY, VIOLENT, AND CORRUPT." See *Ch'ing-shih*, p. 4028, and *Eminent Chinese*, p. 430.

38. *CSL*, 236:5a-b.

39. For Lungkodo, see *Ch'ing-shih*, p. 4081; *CSL*, 248:11, 21. The role of Sunggayan was probably marginal in the Yin-ssu faction. See *CSL*, 236:25.

40. For K'uei-hsü, see *Eminent Chinese*, p. 430; *Ch'ing-shih*, pp. 4028-29. For his role in Yin-ssu's recommendation, see *CSL*, 235:19b.

41. See *Ch'ing-shih*, p. 4028.

42. For Maci, see *Ch'ing-shih*, p. 4027; *Eminent Chinese*, p. 560.

43. *CSL*, 236:14.

44. *CSL*, 235:20.

45. *CSL*, 235:20b.

46. For Sunu's biography, see *Eminent Chinese*, pp. 692-694; *CSL*, 235:4b; and *Yung-hsien lu*, p. 279. For the number of clansmen, see *CSL:YC*, 30:18 (*SYNK* 3/3/13).

47. *CSL*, 235:8.

48. *CSL:YC*, 20:12.

49. *Yü-tieh*: see *Ta-Ch'ing hui-tien* (1899), 1:2-5, 93:1; *HTSL*, 1:28-38; *CSL*, 235:19b-21; 254:18b-20; and Brunnert, p. 56.

50. For Yung-cheng's charge, see *SYNK* 3/5/26 and 5/1/9; for contemporary evidence, see Wang Hung-hsü's memorial no. 24, in *WHTP*, p. 92, and Ch'in Tao-jan's deposition, in *WHTP*, p. 15.

51. *CSL*, 261:9a-b.

52. Yin-ssu's imprisonment: *CSL*, 236:17, and 237:4b; *Ch'ing huang-shih ssu-p'u*, 3:14. For Maci, see *CSL*, 236:11-14b.

53. Ts'ai Sheng-yuan: *CSL*, 60:21, and *Man-Han Ming-ch'en chuan*, 9:2.

54. Leniency toward Yin-ssu: *CSL*, 236:17; 237:4; and 237:19b-20; *Ch'ing huang-shih ssu-p'u*, 3:14.

55. *CSL*, 237:4-5, and 235:27.

56. *CSL*, 237:4-7.

57. *Lettres édifiantes*, III, 103.

13. Life Confinement

1. For the Korean report on Yin-jeng's immorality and complaints, see *Chŏson wangjo sillok*, 52:42 and 54:36; for K'ang-hsi's confession, see *CSL*, 251:7-12b.

2. *CSL*, 250:6-7b.

3. For the ensuing description of the general commandant's office, see *HTSL*, chüan 1156-1157, 1159-1160, and 1162-1163; for the law-and-order structure of the capital city, see Brunnert, pp. 97-102.

4. See *Ch'ing-shih*, p. 3874, where it is recorded that in 1706 "T'ao-ho-ch'i [Tohoci] had just become a new favorite in court."

5. *CSL*, 219:6b; 234:17b-20 (Ling-p'u).

6. For Tohoci's biographical information, see *PCTP*, 56:15; for his sister Ting-fei, see *Ch'ing huang-shih ssu-p'u*, 2:14.

7. Wang Hung-hsü's memorial of 1708 (no. 24), in *WHTP*, p. 92.

8. *Ch'ing-shih*, p. 3974.

9. *CSL*, 235:8b-9; 202:24b-25. For Tohoci's lawlessness and his trial, see CCC 52/1/23 and 51/4/12 (*CSL*, 250:5-6). Though homophones, the original Chinese characters in the CCC used to spell Ching-hsi differed from those used in the *CSL*. (For another variation of the spelling, see *SYNK* 1/3/13.)

10. *SLHK*, p. 7b.

11. *Ch'ing-shih*, p. 4006.

12. Wang Hung-hsü's memorial of 1708 (no. 26), in *WHTP*, p. 93. Wang's other memorials revealed that the heir apparent's adherents in the Six Boards included Ch'ao K'o-t'o, the Manchu president of the Board of Punishments, and a relative of Tohoci (no. 27, *WHTP*, p. 94). Another adherent was Hsü Ch'ao, the Chinese president of Civil Appointments, who was friendly with Asan, one of the heir apparent's chief adherents (no. 27, *WHTP*, p. 94). Of all the Manchu presidents on the Six Boards, Fu-ning-an, president of the Board of Rites, was "the only one . . . who was not an adherent of the Commandant." (No. 25, *WHTP*, p. 93.) On the Boards of Civil Appointments and War "all Manchu presidents and vice-presidents were afraid of the Commandant," hence during the trial, "if at all possible, they were reluctant to utter a single word." (No. 24, *WHTP*, p. 92.) On the Board of Works, the assistant director, Sung Wo-chiao (whose real name was Li Yueh-shan), was originally found guilty of corruption charges and now had "become a member of the Commandant's household staff, functioning as the liaison between the Commandant and the Boards that performed other services for him." (No. 26, *WHTP*, p. 93.)

13. Wang Hung-hsü's memorial (no. 25), in *WHTP*, p. 93.

14. *CSL*, 233:18, 20b-22.

15. CCC 52/2/2.

16. *CSL*, 251:10b-11.

17. *CSL*, 242:17; *Fang Wang-ch'i*, pp. 347-348.

18. *CSL*, 249:5b; CCC, 51/1/28.

19. *CSL*, 248:11 and 21.

20. *CSL*, 248:14 (filial sons); CCC 50/10/27 (*CSL*, 248:15-18b) (denouncing the heir apparent's faction). In the CCC, the emperor also said, "Some have formed a faction for my sake," which was deleted in the *CSL*.

21. CCC 51/1/28 (*CSL*, 249:5-6b). Here the name for Tohoci is T'ao-ho-ch'i. The text in the CCC is not polished and is more explicit.

22. For the court's verification of Wang I's charges against Tohoci, see CCC 51/4/10 (*CSL*, 250:4b); for further investigations, see CCC 51/4/12 (*CSL*, 250:5-6); for punishments, see *CSL*, 250:6-7b.

23. *CSL*, 252:8a-b.

24. *CSL*, 251:7b-12b.

25. Ripa, p. 83.

26. CCC 51/10/1 (*CSL*, 251:8-12b). These frank confessions are omitted in the *CSL*.

27. *CSL*, 252:8. For these charges, which were proven to be true, see CCC 51/11/4 (for example, the accusation made by Ho-tzu, a censor, against Tohoci for extortion); for other charges against Tohoci and Ling-p'u concerning their evil conduct and lawlessness, see CCC 52/1/23 and 52/2/25.

28. For the deaths of Tohoci and his notorious household servants, see *CSL*,

253:10b, and CCC 52/2/25 (*CSL*, 253:18a-b). Some of the heir apparent's adherents were sentenced to death by slow slicing (for instance, Te-lin, nephew of Fu-pao: see *CSL*, 205:25b, and Sung Lao, *Hsi-po lei-kao*, 37:1).

14. The New Contenders

1. CCC 52/2/2 (*CSL*, 253:8-10). At this juncture, court officials continued to believe that K'ang-hsi would reinstate Yin-jeng as heir apparent, and they avoided offending Yin-jeng's henchmen, fearing reprisals. For example, they did not dare report to the emperor that Ling-p'u, Yin-jeng's most trusted confidant, had secretly returned to Peking after being banished to the Amur River region on the Manchurian frontier. When the emperor learned of this, he summoned the Manchu president of the Board of Punishments and asked him why he did not order Ling-p'u's apprehension and trial. The president answered, "Who dares to put him on trial?," at which point K'ang-hsi ordered Ling-p'u captured and executed immediately. See CCC 52/2/25.

2. CCC 50/12/20 (*CSL*, 257:16).

3. *CSL*, 266:5a-b; *Eminent Chinese*, p. 925. P'u-ch'i was among the seven "mad" people mentioned by the emperor during the trial of Chu-t'ien-pao in 1718 (*CSL*, 277:7a-b). Ablan was a great-great-grandson of Cuyen, hence a nephew of the Yin-ssu adherent Sunu; he was later found to have been close to Lungkodo and Yin-t'i.

4. *CSL*, 291:28. See Wang Shan's memorial (undated, but undoubtedly in 56/11/-) no. 3, in *WHTP*, pp. 107-108. Simultaneously, eight censors—including Ch'en Chia-yu and Ch'eng Lien (see chap. 8, note 50)—submitted a joint memorial (dated 56/11/23) echoing Wang Shan's petition. (*WHTP*, pp. 108-109).

5. *Lettres édifiantes*, III, 287.

6. For the dowager empress's death, see *CSL*, 276-8; for the emperor's illness, see *CSL*, 276:5b-6b; for the valediction, see *CSL*, 276:11, 16. For a complete translation of the valediction, see Spence, *Emperor of China*, chap. 4.

7. For the Chu-t'ien-pao case, see *CSL*, 277:6-14; *Ch'ing-shih*, p. 4024.

8. *CSL*, 237:7a-b, 12-13.

9. *CSL*, 277:12. As early as 1701, Chu-tu-na was dismissed from his ministerial position for improper conduct (*CSL*, 204:21).

10. *CSL*, 277:30b.

11. *CSL*, 277:9-10b.

12. *CSL*, 277:20. See Wang Shan's memorial dated 60/3/-, no. 4, in *WHTP*, p. 108; also see Wang Hung-hsü's secret memorial (no. 29), in *WHTP*, p. 95.

13. Court officials had also speculated that the emperor might want to establish Yin-jeng's son as his successor. See *Chosŏn wojo sillok*, 59:25.

14. Actually, the emperor did not reveal this episode with Yin-ssu until January 3, 1715 (*CSL*, 261:10b-11). The emperor's charges against Yin-ssu were later referred to by the Yung-cheng Emperor, who related another event that had occurred in 1708 as proof of Yin-ssu's lack of filial devotion to K'ang-hsi (*CSL:YC*, 40:8a-b).

15. According to Ch'in Tao-jan's deposition, in *WHTP*, p. 14.

16. For the entire incident, see *CSL*, 261:8b-10.

17. *CSL*, 262:5b; 266:7.

18. *CSL*, 269:14b-16b, 20a-b, 22; 270:3; *SYNK* 4/6/3.

19. *Yung-hsien lu*, p. 83.

20. See *Eminent Chinese*, pp. 93-95, 235-237, 283-285.

21. *Yung-hsien lu*, p. 83; *CSL*, 261:6b; *Ch'ing-shih*, p. 3558; *Eminent Chinese*, p. 285.

22. According to the Emperor Yung-cheng (see *CSL:YC*, 94:19b).

23. The earliest reference to an invitation extended by Yin-chen to the emperor for a garden feast occurred on 46/11/11 (December 4, 1707), and nine days later (46/11/20) the emperor was invited to a feast given by Yin-chih; both parties were held in Peking. (*CSL*, 231:14, 16.) For other feasts given for the emperor by Yin-chen and Yin-chih, see *CSL*, 250:3 (Yin-chih); 250:24b (Yin-chen); 258:14b (Yin-chih); 268:25 (Yin-chih); 269:6 (Yin-chen); and *passim*. For Yin-chih's lack of filial piety, see *CSL*, 147:24; *Ch'ing-shih*, p. 3557.

24. For the Meng Kuang-tsu scandal, see *CSL*, 271:11b, 17b-18b; 272:11-12b; 273:2; 280:11.

25. In his secret memorial, Chao wrote to the emperor, "This is to memorialize that I have dispatched agents to investigate the origin and details of the roaming around of the Third Prince throughout the five provinces." The impostor, whose real name was Meng Yü-te, was captured on 56/4/15. See Chao Hung-hsieh Archives, undated, no. 2; Chao's memorials dated 55/12/16 and 56/4/16, *KHTC*, pp. 720, 901.

26. See Nien's memorial dated 56/5/26, in *CKTP*, 89b-190.

27. *Yung-hsien lu*, p. 83.

28. For Yen's biography, see *Eminent Chinese*, p. 908. This encounter between Yin-chen and Yen has been interpreted by several historians as a sign of Yin-chen's intention to form a faction of his own with Southern literati in order to enhance his chances for the heir apparentship. (See, for example, Wang Chung-han, "Ch'ing Shih-tsung to-ti k'ao-shih," *Yen-ching hsüeh-pao*, 36.62:224-225 [June 1949].) But this interpretation is merely conjecture. In the first place, the meeting occurred before the Songgotu incident, which was the first open confrontation between the emperor and the heir apparent's faction: Yen arrived in Peking on May 12, 1703, and the arrest of Songgotu did not take place until June 21. As noted, before the arrest the emperor had received a recommendation of Yin-ssu from his dying brother, Prince Yü. For Yen's meeting with Yin-chen, see *Yen Ch'ien-chiu hsien-sheng nien-p'u*, comp. Chang Mu (1847), 101b-102b, 103-107; *I-men hsien-sheng chi*, 7:9.

29. For K'ang-hsi's scrolls allegedly written by Yin-chen, see *Yang-chi-ch'ai yü-lu* (preface, 1896), 3:3b. This traditional tale seems to be corroborated by palace-archive documents: one of K'ang-hsi's rescripts that he sent to Liang-nai, governor-general of Fukien and Chekiang, in response to Liang's palace memorial of 47/3/4, was not in K'ang-hsi's handwriting at all; it closely resembles Yin-chen's. Compare this rescript attached to Liang-nai's memorial—photoreproduced in *KKWH*, vol. 2, no. 2, p. 154 (also printed in *CKTP*, p. 40)—with the handwritten endorsements of the Emperor Yung-cheng (Yin-chen), either in *CKTP*, pp. 26-33, or in his preface to the *CPYC*. For the shabby style of Yin-ssu's calligraphy, see his letter to Ho Cho in *CKTP*, p. 20.

30. *CSL*, 235:24b-26b.

31. *CSL*, 235:25.

32. *CSL:YC*, 23:15-16; Ch'ing Tao-jan's deposition, *WHTP*, p. 14.

33. *CSL*, 235:27b.

34. For this eyewitness account, see Ripa, p. 83; for his "release," see Hung-wang, "Huang Ch'ing T'ung-chih kang-yao," quoted in Wang Chung-chan, "Ch'ing Shih-tsung," p. 255. That Yin-chen had also been arrested by his father might have been because he had "secretly pleaded for mercy for Yin-jeng," causing the emperor to suspect that he, too, perhaps belonged to the Yin-jeng faction. Cf. *CSL*, 235:27b-28; 269:20.

35. *CSL:YC*, 23:15.

36. *CSL*, 237:4b-5b; Ch'in Tao-jan's deposition, *WHTP*, p. 14.

37. For Yin-t'ang's testimony to Yin-chen's noble attitude toward him, see

Ch'in Tao-jan's deposition, *WHTP*, p. 14. Later in 1714, when Yin-ssu was charged with conspiracy, Yin-chen again begged the emperor for mercy. (*CSL: YC*, 18:7.)

38. The purchasing of offices was not only official but also prevalent during the K'ang-hsi period: see Hsü Ta-ling, *Ch'ing-tai chuan-na chih-tu* (Peking, 1950), pp. 33-35.

39. Tai To's memorial no. 1, in *WHTP*, pp. 101a-b. We find only fragmentary information about the life of Tai To. In governmental service, he was a department magistrate and was promoted to subprefect in Chihli province in 1712: circuit intendant in Fukien in 1713 (which corresponds to the date that he sent his first memorial to Yin-chen); judicial commissioner of Kwangsi; and finally financial commissioner of Szechwan in 1722. He was purged by Yin-chen after Yin-chen's accession to the throne, in 1722. Yin-chen charged Tai To with "fabricating rumors" and "deception." Cf. CCC 50/12/20; *CSL*, 297:3; his deposition in *WHTP*, pp. 110-112; and Yung-cheng's endorsement in Kao Ch'i-cho Archives, no. 6218, dated YC 1/5/12, NPM(T).

40. Others who were asked to go were Yin-shih, Yin-yü, Yin-wu, Yin-lu, and Yin-li; see *CSL*, 263:18b-19, and *Eminent Chinese*, p. 328.

41. Tai To's memorial no. 3, in *WHTP*, pp. 101b-102.

42. The first part of the memorial reads: "Your slave Tai To extends his hearty greetings to his master. My life here in the Fukien yamen is very hard. Unfortunately, after Ch'en Pin became the governor of Fukien, he eliminated all the customary fees. At the same time, my health is very poor. I have sent petitions several times [to the Board of Civil Appointments], asking that I be released from my office and allowed to return to the capital, but I have been rejected by the Board each time. I have therefore contributed two thousand taels to the government in order to obtain permission to serve at the campaign front. I hope that I shall be able to see you in the capital and report to you in detail."

The remainder of the memorial describes why he used an ingenious method for the transmittal of his memorial to his master (this perhaps contributed to the modification of the transmittal system of the palace memorials, instituted after Yin-chen became emperor). He writes: "Seeing that the distance between Fukien and the capital is quite great, I hid this letter inside the double-layer bottom of the box in which I enclosed a set of books as one of the local presents I am sending along to Your Excellency. This is intended to facilitate your reading the letter [secretly]."

43. Tai To's memorial no. 4, in *WHTP*, p. 102.

44. Tai To's memorial no. 7, in *WHTP*, p. 102.

45. *Li Kuang-ti nien-p'u*, pp. 71-72. Li's influence with the emperor was shown by the way K'ang-hsi treated him before Li left the Jehol summer palace in late 1715. Honors and gifts were showered on him, and a farewell banquet was held in his honor. The emperor composed poems of tribute to Li: princes of all degrees as well as court officials were asked to "match verses" with the emperor, and Yin-chen, attending his father, also composed a laudatory poem. At the banquet, the emperor conversed secretly with Li; fearing that the palace attendants would overhear his conversation with the slightly deaf Li, the emperor "wrote his words on slips of paper, and after Li had read them, the Emperor immediately ripped them up or burned them." The mysterious aura surrounding the tête-à-tête undoubtedly enhanced Li's prestige. Finally, K'ang-hsi bid him farewell with a "shaking of hands"—an extraordinary honor bestowed by an emperor upon an official. (Ibid., pp. 62-64.)

46. Tai To's memorial no. 9, in *WHTP*, p. 103.

47. *CSL:YC*, 23:15b.

48. While he was with the emperor during the annual retreat in Jehol, Yin-chen composed poems and sent them to his brothers in Peking, to show his concern for them. For example, see *Yung-cheng ti yü-chih wen-chi* (1897), 24: 12a-b.

49. For examples, see *CSL*, 295:12; 300:5b. As has been mentioned, K'ang-hsi's appreciation for Yin-chen's filialness had been consistent since the late 1690s, when he began to ask Yin-chen to perform pious functions on his behalf. In 1711, when K'ang-hsi rejected the recommendation of his Imperial Household that Prince Hsien (Yen-huang) represent the emperor at his grandmother's tomb, K'ang-hsi instead ordered Yin-chen to serve as his substitute. He justified his decision on the grounds that Prince Hsien was "ignorant"; he also ordered that "hereafter, Prince Hsien be excluded from all sacrificial missions and other weighty assignments." The implication was clear: K'ang-hsi believed Yin-chen was worthy of representing him on such important occasions. See CCC 50/10/ 26.

50. *CSL*, 282:10b-11.

51. *CSL*, 281:16b; 282:11; *Eminent Chinese*, p. 930. For his supporters' speculation, see *CSL:YC*, 44:30.

52. Ch'in Tao-jan's deposition, in *WHTP.* p. 3.

53. Jean Mourao's deposition, in *WHTP*, p. 1.

54. Ch'in Tao-jan's deposition, in *WHTP*, p. 4.

55. *SYNK* 4/6/3.

56. *CSL:YC*, 45:18; *Yung-hsien lu*, p. 143.

57. For Sung-chu, see *CSL*, 268:18b. For Yin-t'i and Li Kung, see Tai To's deposition, in *WHTP*, p. 103, and Feng Ch'en et al., *Li Shu-ku hsien-sheng nien-p'u* (preface, 1730), 5:25b-26, 29.

58. For an example of Nien's influence on the emperor, see Nien's memorial dated 57/10/1, in *CKTP*, p. 202; for Mourao, see his deposition, in *WHTP*, p. 1. K'ang-hsi originally had doubts about Nien's administrative ability as well as about his honesty, and only after an audience with Nien in 1721 did he begin to trust him. The emperor's new confidence in Nien was probably the result of favorable recommendations given him by Nien's lord, Yin-chen. See *CSL*, 256: 8-9, and K'ang-hsi's endorsement, quoted in Nien's memorial dated 61/6/22, in *CKTP*, p. 219 (cf. photo-reproduction copy of Yin-chen's letter to Nien, in *WHTP*, "t'u-hsiang," p. 1).

59. Chang Hsia-tzu's deposition, in *WHTP*, p. 5b.

60. For bribery, see Ch'in Tao-jan's deposition, in *WHTP*, p. 3; for presents to Yin-ssu and Yin-t'ang, as well as debauchery, see *CSL:YC*, 44:30b; 46:16b.

61. For Yin-t'i's recall to Peking, see *CSL*, 295:6b; *Yung-hsien lu*, p. 28. For Yin-t'ang's suspicion, see Ch'in Tao-jan's deposition, in *WHTP*, p. 4.

62. *CSL*, 297:10. The date in *Yung-hsien lu* (p. 28) is apparently an error.

63. CCC 52/2/2 (*CSL*, 253:9); *Kuo-ch'ao ch'i-hsien*, 11:26b-37.

15. The New Emperor

1. *CSL*, 299:1b-2b, 8, 18b, 24b; 300:1-5. The hunting exercise at Nan-yuan was institutionalized under K'ang-hsi. Therefore, although our description of K'ang-hsi's hunt is based on Bell's account, from 1721, the ritual must have been conducted in the same way in 1722. See Bell, pp. 168-172. For the breakfast schedule, see Bell, p. 168. See also *Shih-ch'ao sheng-hsün* (KH), 5:2-3b; 6:3b.

2. Du Halde, I, 497. The *Yung-hsien lu* (p. 48) contains an entry that must have been a summary of an imperial edict published in the *Peking Gazette* at

that time. It reads: "The Emperor fell ill. An imperial instruction was given: I have caught a cold; I have already tried to expel it by sweating [a traditional method in China to cure a cold]. From the tenth to the fifteenth, I shall take complete rest while fasting and praying; it is not necessary to present any memorials to me."

3. Ripa, p. 118. Since Du Halde's account was also based on Jesuit reports, these two sources complement each other and shed light on the exact nature of the illness.

4. K'ang-hsi mentioned all the symptoms of his ill health in his "valediction" (*CSL*, 275:5b-13). Cf. Ripa, p. 114 (K'ang-hsi's 1721 illness).

5. *CSL*, 284:3-4.

6. Yin-ch'i was sent to the tomb of the Dowager Empress Hsiao-hui to perform sacrifical rites before the winter solstice. He was sent on 61/10/1 (November 9, 1722) and K'ang-hsi died on 61/11/13 (December 20). Cf. *CSL*, 299:8b, and Yung-cheng's edict of 1730, included in *Ta-i chüeh-mi lu* (1730), 1:17.

7. The original entry in the *Yung-hsien lu* (p. 20) reads: "Since the sixtieth year of the K'ang-hsi reign [1721], twice on the occasion of the Emperor's birthday, Prince Yung [Yin-chen] had invited the Emperor to visit his garden residence. He entertained the Emperor with opera performances, and personally served wine to the Emperor at the feast. His purpose was to express his good wishes to the Emperor for a long and healthy life. The Emperor's countenance frequently beamed and showed contentment, and in front of the imperial consorts he commended Prince Yung's filial affection and care for his imperial father." That this source referred to Yin-chen as Prince Yung suggests the entry was made shortly after he had given his father a celebration for his sixty-ninth birthday, in early 1722. Cf. *CSL*, 297:3.

8. For Ma-erh-sai's appointments as the emperor's representative, see *CSL*, 235:18 (1708); 275:4 (1717); 282:1b (1718); and 290:9b (1720). The only other official to represent the emperor in this capacity was Alingga, also a chamberlain; he did this only once, in 1709 (*CSL*, 240:13b).

9. *CSL*, 291:22b-23b.

10. For Yin-chen's appointment as the emperor's representative in the last two years of K'ang-hsi's reign, see *CSL*, 295:12 (1721), and 300:5b (1722).

11. For the ensuing events, see *CSL*, 300:5-7; entries in *Tung-hua lu* (1911) are identical with those in *CSL*; those in *Tung-hua lu* (1765) are too sketchy to be useful.

12. According to Yin-chen, four of the emperor's younger sons were waiting outside the emperor's bedroom after the seven older ones had been called in to receive his final words. Among those absent were Yin-t'i (now the eldest) and Yin-jeng (the second), who were both under confinement, and Yin-ch'i (the fifth), who, as mentioned, was at the Imperial Mausolea. The rest had either died or were too young to be summoned. See *Ch'ing huang-shih ssu-p'u*, chüan 3, *Ch'ing-shih*, p. 3555.

13. *Yung-hsien lu*, p. 49, quoting *Ta-i chüeh mi-lu*, 1:17a-b.

14. For the rosary, see *Yung-hsien lu*, p. 49.

15. On the role of Lungkodo, see *Ta-i chüeh mi-lu*, 1:16b-17. Yin-chen's succession was reported to Japan through Chinese merchants: *Ka i hentai*, p. 2955; cf. Du Halde, I, 501.

Epilogue

1. After Yin-chen's enthronement, he made Yin-ssu Prince of the Blood of the First Degree and the leading member of the four Imperial Assistants Plenipotentiary, as well as granting him and his family other favors. In his memorial

to the new emperor, Yin-ssu addressed himself as "Prince Lien . . . your minister"; see Yin-ssu Archives, no. 04623, undated. For Yin-ssu's biography, see *Eminent Chinese*, pp. 926-927.

2. The most influential article on Yung-cheng's "usurpation" of his father's throne is Meng Sen's "Shih-tsung ju-ch'eng ta-t'ung k'ao-shih" in his *Ch'ing-tai shih*, ed. Wu Hsiang-hsiang (Taipei, 1960), pp. 477-510. This was originally published in 1934 as one of the three case studies that composed his *Ch'ing-ch'u san-ta i-an k'ao-shih*, NPM(P). Other scholars who have studied the problem of Yung-cheng's succession have simply tried to support Meng Sen's thesis with more "evidence," such as Wang Chung-han's "Ch'ing Shih-tsung to-ti k'ao-shih," in *Yen-ching hsüeh-pao*, 36.62:205-261 (June 1949), and, most recently, Chin Ch'eng-i's speculative articles entitled "Ts'ung 'Yin-t'i' wen-t'i k'an Ch'ing-shih tsung to-wei" and "Yin-chen[g]: I-ko ti-meng ch'eng-k'ung ti huang-tzu," which appeared respectively in *Chung-yang yen-chiu yuan chin-tai shih yen-chiu-so chi-k'an*, 5:189-222 (June 1976) and 6:95-122 (June 1967). The biographies of Yin-chen and his brothers in the Yin-ssu faction that are contained in the influential *Eminent Chinese* are largely responsible for the acceptance of the Meng Sen thesis in the West. My critical examination of the Meng Sen thesis will be presented in a separate volume on the Yung-cheng Emperor.

Bibliography

Original Sources and the Veritable Records:
Evaluation and Interpretation

I would like to explain the nature of the various kinds of original sources used for my study and their relationship to the *CSL* (*Veritable Records of the K'ang-hsi Reign*). Of all the sources, the palace memorials are the most important, because of both their rich content and their vast quantity. Initially these memorials were stored in the imperial palace, but after 1911 they were absorbed by the archives of the National Palace Museum at Peking (or, from 1928 to 1948, "Peiping"), abbreviated as NPM(P). In 1937, a great number of the NPM(P) archives—including palace memorials; the CCC (Ch'i-chü chu, Imperial Diary, or "Diary of the Emperor's movements and utterances") of all the Ch'ing emperors since the K'ang-hsi reign; and many other kinds of documents and books—were transferred to Chungking, where they were kept in trunks during the War of Resistance against Japan (1937-1945). After the war, these materials were moved to Taiwan and placed in the custody of the National Palace Museum in Taipei, abbreviated as NPM(T).

1. Archival Materials from the NPM(T)

There are approximately three thousand palace memorials from the K'ang-hsi period (1661-1722) in the NPM(T) (about one-third of these are greetings memorials [*ch'ing-an-che*], which, with a few exceptions, contain little substantive information). In conjunction with the palace memorials from the K'ang-hsi period, some from the Yung-cheng period (1723-1735) were consulted when relevant to the present study. The NPM(T) archivists have assigned a four-digit number to a palace memorial submitted during the K'ang-hsi period (for example, Chao Hung-hsieh Archives: 0001 to 1117), and a five-digit number to a palace memorial submitted during the Yung-cheng period (Yueh Chung-ch'i Archives: 00001 to 00728). Some palace memorials were undated; some contain enclosures, supplementary documents such as lists, maps, and so forth.

Since 1969 the NPM(T) has published, in Chinese, the palace memorials of the K'ang-hsi period; these appear, by photo-reproduction, in installments in the *Ku-kung wen-hsien* (*KKWH*; Ch'ing documents at the National Palace Museum), a quarterly of the NPM(T). In 1976 the NPM(T) made available its entire holding of K'ang-hsi palace memorials, in nine volumes under the title *Kung-chung-tang K'ang-hsi ch'ao tsou-che* (Secret palace memorials of the K'ang-hsi reign). This treasure chest contains palace memorials that have already been published in the *KKWH*, greetings memorials (all in Chinese), and all the Manchu memorials and edicts (volumes 8 and 9). For the rare omissions from these two publications, I have cited them according to their dates, if any, and catalogue numbers.

The CCC entries I have used in my study include the emperor's statements made at audiences with his officials, on which the diarists took notes, and the emperor's written instructions, which were transcribed from copies sent to the diarists from other central offices. Copies of the CCC were handwritten and bound in volumes by lunar month (twelve volumes annually, with thirteen for a leap year). The NPM(T) archives contain all volumes written in Chinese for the years KH 29 to KH 42 and KH 50 to KH 52. The NPM(T) archives also contain CCC entries in Manchu, translations of the Chinese entries, with complete sets for KH 11 to KH 12, KH 14 to KH 17, KH 19 to KH 42, and KH 50 to KH 52, and incomplete sets for KH 10 (four volumes), KH 13 (one volume), and KH 18 (seven volumes). This study cites only the Chinese versions.

The documentary importance of the CCC is at least twofold: First, it supplements information in the *CSL*. Second, whenever identical documents can be found in the two sources, the authenticity of the *CSL* may be tested. One must, of course, use the CCC with caution, applying one's best judgment in light of other contemporary documentation: sometimes the diarists may have misunderstood the emperor's words; sometimes they made errors when copying edicts into the CCC. But this is nevertheless an invaluable complement to the *CSL*.

2. Archival Materials from the NPM(P)

In the early 1930s, the NPM(P) published a significant quantity of original documents from the Palace Archives of the K'ang-hsi reign, including palace memorials, imperial instructions written in K'ang-hsi's own hand, and trial depositions. These materials were published in various collections under the titles *Chang-ku ts'ung-pien* (*CKTP*, Collected historical documents from the National Palace Museum Archives); *Shih-liao hsün-k'an* (*SLHK*, Historical materials published every ten days); and *Wen-hsien ts'ung-pien* (*WHTP*, Miscellaneous Ch'ing historical documents).

Some of the material from both the Palace Archives and the Archives of the Grand Secretariat drifted into private hands during the early decades of the twentieth century and was published by individuals such as Lo Chen-yü. He compiled the *Shih-liao ts'ung-k'an ch'u-pien* (*SLTKCP*, Miscellaneous historical documents, first series); and the *Shih-liao ts'ung-pien* (*SLTP*; Miscellaneous records from Ch'ing imperial archives). The *SLTKCP* (pp. 337-575) contains CCC of the K'ang-hsi reign (incomplete volumes of KH

12, KH 19, and KH 42), and the *SLTP* contains incomplete volumes for KH 10. There are also indexes of the Ch'ing archives, which can add to the credibility of the *CSL*. For example, in Lo Chen-yü's *Ta-k'u shih-liao mu-lu: ssu-pien* (Index to historical materials in the Grand Secretariat Archives, sixth series, 1935), one finds an entry entitled "*Chiang-chih Huang t'ai-tzu chu-tsai tang*" (Archives [files] that contain Emperor K'ang-hsi's personal edicts issued to the Heir Apparent) (p. 2, no. 29). This file is dated KH 47/9/-, that is, the very month in which K'ang-hsi deposed the Heir Apparent Yin-jeng. It therefore substantively supports Ch'in Tao-jan's deposition that the emperor had issued edicts to Yin-jeng and had ordered his instructions recorded in a particular file.

Recently the NPM(P) published a special collection of archival materials on the Ts'ao Yin family, entitled *Kuan-yü Chiang-ning chih-tsao Ts'ao-chia tang-an shih-liao* (Collection of archival materials concerning the Ts'ao family, whose members had successively held the position of textile commissioner at Chiang-ning [during the K'ang-hsi and Yung-cheng reigns]), abbreviated as *TCTA* (compiled by NPM[P], Chung-hua shu-chü, 1975). In addition to palace memorials that have already appeared in *WHTP* and *KKWH*, it contains valuable documents from the Grand Secretariat Archives and the Imperial Household Archives, which include Chinese translations of sixty-one Manchu memorials. It also contains a valuable portion of the CCC, KH 53/8/12 (p. 124), pertaining to the emperor's discussion with his grand secretaries of Gali's impeachment of Ts'ao Yin and Li Hsü.

3. Original Foreign-Language Sources

Original sources in foreign languages (that is, neither Chinese nor Manchu) on the K'ang-hsi reign resemble reports produced today by "China watchers." These sources include documents from both within and without China. The *Lettres édifiantes et curieuses* contains detailed information on Ch'ing court politics relayed back to Europe by many Jesuit missionaries. Father Matteo Ripa's *Memoirs* is a closely observed account of K'ang-hsi's private life and the deposition of the heir apparent. The *Chosŏn wangjo sillok* records the Korean envoys' oral reports to their king on Peking politics and social unrest in the empire. Though Korea recognized the Manchu regime's suzerainty and submitted to the status of "tributory state," it was hostile to the "barbarian" Manchu regime, and these reports repeat hearsay unflattering to the K'ang-hsi court. The Japanese source used here, *Ka i hentai* (Intelligence reports on China under the [Manchu] barbarians), includes the debriefings of Chinese merchants who went to Nagasaki to trade Chinese goods for Japanese copper: suspicious of the Ch'ing regime's intentions in Japan, the Tokugawa shogunate made it a function of the Interpreters' Office at Nagasaki to interrogate every shipowner or captain coming from China. These merchants were mostly Southerners with a hatred of the Manchu conquerors, and so part of their "merchandise" consisted of information on the deployment of the Manchu military, geography books, and imperial edicts. In English, the *Kent* supercargoes' account of 1704 of "The Emperor's Merchant" at Canton—as quoted in Hosea B. Morse's _The Chronicles of the East India Company Trading to China, 1635-1834_ (Oxford, 1926-29)—independently attests to the pervasive corruption—penetrating even the Canton trade—engendered by the Heir Apparent Yin-jeng.

4. Miscellaneous Sources

Other original sources include such eyewitness accounts as _Sheng-tsu wu-hsing Chiang-nan ch'üan-lu_ (_WHCN_, An anonymous diary of the K'ang-hsi Emperor's fifth Southern tour, in 1705); personal reports in Li Kuang-ti's _Jung-ts'un yü-lu hsü-chi_ (Recorded sayings of Li Kuang-ti; supplement); and family letters in T'ang Pin's _T'ang-tzu i-shu_ (Collected works of T'ang Pin) and in Ho Cho's _I-men hsien-sheng chi_ (Collected works of Ho Cho). Finally, the _Yung-hsien lu_ (Historical records of the Yung-cheng period) comprises imperial edicts that the compiler, Hsiao Shih, copied from the _ti-ch'ao_ (_Peking Gazette_, a sort of daily newspaper containing imperial edicts and memorials, issued in Peking and distributed throughout China).

These various primary sources are all valuable in that they illuminate details, verify specific points, expose motives, and clarify relations between the major characters in the story. Yet the _CSL_ remains the single most essential source. It embodies countless crucial documents and it provides the chronological thread of the story that I have pursued.

All other sources either supplement the _CSL_ or testify to its authenticity. The suspicion that all of the crimes of Yin-jeng that appear in the _CSL_ were fabricated by the Emperor Yung-cheng is simply not supported by these divers sources; it would be ridiculous to claim, for example, that the _Kent_ supercargoes conspired with Yung-cheng to defame the heir apparent. The charge of tampering with _CSL_ by the Yung-cheng Emperor has been refuted by Fang Su-sheng, an archivist and historian at the NPM(P), in his article "Ch'ing shih-lu hsiu-kai wen-t'i" (Concerning the question of frequent revisions of the _Veritable Records_ of the Ch'ing dynasty), in _Fu-jen hsüeh-chih_ (Fu-jen journal) (vol. 8, no. 2, reprinted in _Chung-kuo chin-tai shih lun-ts'ung_ [Essays on modern Chinese history], vol. 1, pp. 181-196).

Attwater, Rachel. *Adam Schall: A Jesuit at the Court of China, 1592–1666.* Milwaukee, Bruce Publishing Company, 1963; adapted from the French (Paris, 1936) of Joseph Duhr, S. J.

Bell, John. *A Journey from St. Petersburg to Pekin, 1719–1722,* ed. J. L. Stevenson. Edinburgh, Edinburgh University Press, 1965.

Bouvet, Joachim. *Histoire de l'empereur de la Chine.* The Hague, 1699. Citations according to the English translation, *The History of Cang-Hy the Present Emperor of China,* by Jodocus Crull. London, 1699.

Brunnert, H. S., and V. V. Hagelstrom. *Present Day Political Organization of China,* tr. A. Beltchenko and E. E. Moran. Shanghai, Kelly and Walsh, 1912.

CCC: Sheng-tsu Jen Huang-ti ch'i-chü chu 聖祖仁皇帝起居注 (Imperial diary, or Diary of the movements and utterances of the K'ang-hsi Emperor). Manuscript copies at the NPM(T). (The museum contains vols. for KH 29–KH 42, KH 50–KH 52.)

CCC: Sheng-tsu Jen Huang-ti ch'i-chü chu 聖祖仁皇帝起居注 (Diary of the Movements and utterances of the K'ang-hsi Emperor: KH 12/1, 5, 6, 10, 11, 12; KH 19/9; KH 42/7, 8, 9), in *SLTKCP,* vol. 1, pp. 335–578.

Ch'a T'a-shan nien-p'u 查他山年譜 (Chronological biography of Ch'a Shen-hsing). Comp. Ch'en Ching-chang 陳敬璋. 1913. Also in *Chia-yeh t'ang ts'ung-shu* 嘉業堂叢書. 1918.

Chang Ch'ing-k'o kung nien-p'u 張清恪公年譜 (A chronological biography of Chang Po-hsing). 1738.

Chang Hsün-yü 張遜玉. *Chung-tou hsin-shu* 種痘新書 (A new handbook on smallpox variolation). Revised ed., Shanghai, 1912.

Chang Ying 張英. *Nan-hsün hu-ts'ung chi-lüeh* 南巡扈從紀略 (A brief account of my accompanying the K'ang-hsi Emperor on his Southern tour, 1689). In *Hsiao-fang-hu chai yü-ti ts'ung-ch'ao* 小房壺齋輿地叢鈔 (Miscellaneous accounts of geography from the Hsiao-fang-hu Study), t'se 4, pp. 280–284b (1877).

Chang Yü-shu 張玉書 *Hu-ts'ung tz'u-yu chi* 扈從賜遊記 (A tour of the K'ang-hsi Emperor's suburban villa, 1708). In *Hsiao-fang-hu chai yü-ti ts'ung-ch'ao* 小房壺齋輿地叢鈔 (Miscellaneous accounts of geography form the Hsiao-fang-hu Study), ts'e 4, pp. 298–299b (1877).

Chang Yü-shu 張玉書. *P'ing-ting shu-mo fang-lüeh* 平定溯漠方略 (The official account of the pacification of the northern deserts, 1696). 1708.

Ch'ang-lu yen-fa chih 長蘆鹽法志 (The salt Gazetteer of Ch'ang-lu), comp. Lu Chih-yü 魯之裕. 1926 edn.

Chao Ch'i-na 趙綺娜. "Ch'ing ch'u tung-pei chu-fang pa-ch'i chih chien-chih yen-chiu" 清初東北駐防八旗之建置研究 (A study of the establishment of the Eight Banners Garrison system in Manchuria during the early-Ch'ing period). In *KKWH*, vol. 5, no. 1, pp. 23–26 (December 1973).

Chao Hung-hsieh Archives (The original memorials of Chao Hung-hsieh) 趙宏燮 Undated, no. 2. NPM(T).

Chao Kuang-hsien 趙光賢. "Ch'ing-ch'u chu-wang cheng-kuo chi" 清初諸王爭國記. (The succession struggle of the Manchu princes in the early-Ch'ing times). *Fu-jen Hsüeh-chih*, 輔仁學誌 (Fu-jen journal of Chinese studies), vol. 12, nos. 1 and 2, pp. 1–9 (1944).

Chen-wu chiang-chün Shan-Kan t'i-tu Sun kung Ssu-k'o hsing-shu 振武將軍陝甘提督孫公思克行述 (The life story of General Sun Ssu-k'o). In *SLTKCP*, vol. 2, pp. 961–1013.

Ch'en Chieh-hsien 陳捷先. "To-erh-kun ch'eng 'Huang-fu she-cheng wang' chih yen-chiu" 多爾袞稱「皇父攝政王」之研究 (A study of the question of Dorgon's being entitled as the Shun-chih Emperor's "Imperial Father the Prince-Regent"), in *KKWH*, vol. 1, no. 2, pp. 1–19 (March 1970).

Ch'en Chieh-hsien 陳捷先. "Ch'ing-ch'ao huang-ti ti Man-wen pen-chi" 清朝皇帝的滿文本記 (Notes on the Manchu edition of the Ch'ing emperors' *Pen-chi* [Imperial Annals]). In *KKWH*, vol. 3, no. 2, pp. 1–29 (March 1972).

Ch'en Wan-nai 陳萬鼐. *Yüan-Ming-Ch'ing hsi-ch'ü shih* 元明清戲曲史 (A history of Chinese drama during the Yuan, Ming, and Ch'ing dynasties). Taipei, 1966.

Cheng T'ien-t'ing 鄭天挺. *Ch'ing-shih t'an-wei* 清史探微 (Studies in Ch'ing history), K'un-ming, 1936.

Ch'eng-shih tsu-p'u ssu-chung 程氏族譜四種 (Four genealogies of the Ch'eng clan). Tōyō Bunko edn., 1895.

Chiang-nan t'ung-chih 江南通志 (General gazetteer of Chiang-nan), comp. Huang Chih-chien 黃之雋 and Yin-chi-shan 尹繼善. 1736 edn.

Chiang-nan wen-chien lu 江南聞見錄 (Heard and seen in Chiang-nan). Taipei, 1967.

Ch'in-ting Ku-chin ch'u-erh chin-chien 欽定古今儲貳金鑑 (Precedents of establishing the heir apparent in Chinese history). Palace edn., 1783; also photo-reproduction edn., Taipei, 1974.

Ch'ing huang-shih ssu-p'u 清皇室四譜 (Four genealogies of the Ch'ing imperial family: emperors, consorts, princes, princesses), comp. T'ang Pang-chih 唐邦治. 4 chüan. Shanghai, 1923.

Ch'ing lieh-ch'ao hou-fei chuan kao 清列朝后妃傳稿 (Draft biographies of Ch'ing-dynasty empresses and consorts), comp. Chang Ts'ai-t'ien 張采田. 2 chüan. 1929.

Ch'ing-pai lei-ch'ao 清稗類鈔 (Unofficial sources on the Ch'ing, arranged by categories). 48 ts'e. Shanghai, last preface, 1917.

Ch'ing-pi shu-wen 清秘述聞 (Civil-service examination registers under the Ch'ing), comp. Fa-shih-shan 法式善. 1799.

Ch'ing Sheng-tsu yü-chih 清聖祖諭旨 (Instructions of the K'ang-hsi Emperor). In *CKTP*, pp. 35–45.

Ch'ing shih 清史 (History of the Ch'ing dynasty), 8 vols. Revision of *Ch'ing-shih kao* 清史稿 (Draft history of the Ch'ing). Taipei, 1961.

Ch'ing-shih kao 清史稿 (Draft history of the Ch'ing). Hong Kong, n.d.

Ch'ing-shih lieh-chuan 清史列傳 (Historical biographies of the Ch'ing dynasty). 80 chüan. Shanghai, 1928.

Ch'ing-tai ti-hou hsiang 清代帝后像 (Portraits of the emperors and empresses of the Ch'ing dynasty). Ts'e 1. NPM(P), 1935.

Chosŏn wangjo sillok 朝鮮王朝實錄 (Annals of the Yi dynasty), Sukchong reign, comp. Kuksa P'yŏnch'an Wiwŏnhoe 國史編纂委員會 (The Compilation Committee of the National [Korean] History). A facsimile reproduction of the T'aebaek-san 太白山 edn. Seoul, 1955–58.

CKTP: Chang-ku ts'ung-pien 掌故叢編 (Collected historical documents from the National Palace Museum Archives). As of the eleventh issue the title was changed to *Wen-hsien ts'ung-pien*. Published by the Wen-hsien kuan 文獻館 (Department of historical records), NPM(P), 1928–29; 1964 Taipei reprint with continuous pagination used.

CPYC: Chu-p'i yü-chih 硃批諭旨 (Vermilion endorsements of the Yung-cheng Emperor, including memorials concerned). 112 vols. 1738; 1964 Taipei reprint with continuous pagination used.

CSL: Ta-Ch'ing Sheng-tsu Jen-huang-ti shih-lu 大清聖祖仁皇帝實錄 (Veritable records of the K'ang-hsi reign). 300 chüan. Tokyo, 1937.

CSL: YC: Ta-Ch'ing Shih-tsung Hsien-huang-ti shih-lu 大清世宗憲皇帝實錄 (Veritable records of the Yung-cheng reign). 159 chüan. Tokyo, 1937.

Doolittle, The Reverend Justus. *Social Life of the Chinese.* 2 vols. New York, Harper & Brothers, 1865; 1966 Taipei reprint used.

Du Halde, P. J. B. *The General History of China,* tr. R. Brookes. 4 vols. London, 1741. From the French edition: *Description géographique, historique, chronologique, politique, et physique de l'empire de la Chine,* 4 vols. Paris, 1735.

Ecke, Betty Tseng. "Emperor Hui-tsung, The Artist: 1082–1136." Ph.D. dissertation, New York University, 1972. For a précis, see *Sung Newsletter,* no. 8, pp. 302–303 (1973).

d'Elia, Pascal M., *Il lontano confino e la tragica morte del P. João Mourão, S. I., missionario in Cina, 1681–1726.* Lisboa, Agência-Geral do Ultramar, 1963.

Eminent Chinese of the Ch'ing Period (1644–1912), ed. Arthur W. Hummel. Washington, U.S. Government Printing Office, 1943–44.

Fang Wang-ch'i ch'üan-chi 方望溪全集 (Collected works of Fang Pao). Ssu-pu ts'ung-k'an edn. Shanghai, 1936.

Four Books, The, tr. and notes by James Legge. New York, Paragon Book Reprint Corp., 1966.

Gamble, Sidney D. *Ting Hsien: A North China Rural Community.* New York, Institute of Pacific Relations, 1954.

Gerbillon, P. P. *The Second Journey of P. P. Gerbillon and Pereyra in Tartary, in 1689.* In Jean B. Du Halde, *A Description of the Empire of China and Chinese Tartary,* 2 vols. London, 1738–41.

Giles, Herbert A. *A History of Chinese Literature.* New York, D. Appleton and Co., 1923.

Hang-chou pa-ch'i chu-fang ying chih-lüeh 杭州八旗駐防營志略 (A brief history of the Eight Banners Garrison at Hangchow), comp. Chang Ta-ch'ang 張大昌. Taipei reprint, n.d.

Hightower, James R. "Yuan Chen and the Story of Ying-Ying," *Harvard Journal of Asiatic Studies* 33: 93–103 (1973).

Ho, Ping-ti. "The Salt Merchants of Yang-chou: A Study of Commercial Capitalism in Eighteenth-Century China," *Harvard Journal of Asiatic Studies* 18: 130–168 (1954).

Hsiao I-shan 蕭一山. *Ch'ing-tai t'ung-shih* 清代通史 (A general history of the Ch'ing dynasty). Revised ed., 5 vols. Taipei, 1962–63.

Hsiao-t'ing hsü-lu 嘯亭續錄 (Miscellaneous notes on Ch'ing history: Supplements), by Chi-hsiu chu-jen 汲修主人 [Chao-lien 昭槤]. 3 chüan (completed 1817–1826). Shanghai, 1880.

Hsü Ch'ien-hsüeh 徐乾學. *Tan-yüan wen-chi* 憺園文集 (Collected literary works from the Tan Garden). 37 chüan. Taipei, 1971.

"Hsü Ch'ien-hsüeh teng pei-k'ung chuang" 徐乾學等被控狀 (Complaints filed against Hsü Ch'ien-hsüeh and others). In *WHTP*, pp. 112–129.

Hsü, Francis L. K. *Americans and Chinese*. New York, Doubleday, 1970.

Hsü Ta-ling 徐大齡. *Ch'ing-tai chüan-na chih-tu* 清代捐納制度 (The system of purchasing offices by donations under the Ch'ing). Peking, 1950.

HTSL: Ta-Ch'ing hui-tien shih-li 大清會典事例 (Precedents and edicts pertaining to the collected statutes of the Ch'ing dynasty). 1220 chüan. Shanghai, 1899; Taipei reprint (19 vols.) used.

HTTL: Hsiao-t'ing tsa-lu 嘯亭雜錄 (Miscellaneous notes on Ch'ing history), by Chi-hsiu chu-jen [Chao-lien]. 10 chüan (completed ca. 1814–1815). Shanghai, 1880.

(Huang-Ch'ing) K'ai-kuo fang-lüeh (Berlin, 1926), tr. Erich Hauser.

Huang-ch'ao wen-hsien t'ung-k'ao 皇朝文獻通考 (Encyclopedia of the historical records of the Ch'ing dynasty). 300 chüan. N.d. Taipei reprint with continuous pagination (pp. 4857–7489 of *t'ung-kao* series).

Hui-chou fu-chih 徽州府志 (Gazetteer of Hui-chou), comp. Hsia Lien 夏鑾. 16 chüan. 1827.

Hung Yeh 洪業. "Yen Cheng-hsien hsien-sheng i-kao wu-chung" 閻貞獻先生遺稿五種 (Five manuscripts of the late Mr. Yen Cheng-hsien), *Shih-hsüeh nien-pao* 史學年報 (Historical Annual), 2.5: 1–15 (1938).

Ides, E. Ysbrants. *Three Years Travels from Moscow Over-land to China*. London, W. Freeman, 1706.

I-men hsien-sheng chi 義門先生集 (Collected works of Ho Cho), comp. Wu Yin-p'ei 吳蔭培. 12 chüan and *fu-lu* 附錄 (Appendix) 4 chüan, P'ing-chiang 平江 1909.

Je-ho chih 熱河志 (Gazetteer of Jehol). Imperial preface, 1781.

Ka i hentai 華夷變態 (Intelligence reports on China under the [Manchu] barbarians, 1674–1724), comp. Hayashi Shunsai 林春勝 and Hayashi Hōkō 林春篤 Tokyo, Tōyō Bunko, 1958–60.

Kao Ch'i-cho Archives (The original palace memorials of Kao Ch'i-cho) 高其倬. No. 06218. NPM(T).

Kao Shih-ch'i 高士奇. *Hu-ts'ung tung-hsün jih-lu* 扈從東巡日錄 (Diary of a follower of the imperial eastern tour [of 1683]). In *Hsiao-fang-hu chai yü-ti ts'ung-ch'ao* 小房壺齋輿地叢鈔. 1st ser., ts'e 4, pp. 253–264 (1877).

Kao Shih-ch'i 高士奇. *P'eng-shan mi-chi* 篷山密記 (A secret account of meetings with the K'ang-hsi Emperor in 1703), in *Ku-hsüeh hui-k'an* 古學彙刊 (Collected works of eminent scholars), comp. Teng Shih 鄧實. 1st ser., no. 12. Shanghai. Kuo-sui hsüeh-pao she, 1912.

Kessler, Lawrence D. *K'ang-hsi and the Consolidation of Ch'ing Rule, 1661–1684.* Chicago, The University of Chicago Press, 1976.

KHHT: Ta-Ch'ing hui-tien 大清會典 (Collected statutes of the Ch'ing dynasty). 162 chüan. 1690 edn.

KHTC: Kung-chung tang K'ang-hsi ch'ao tsou-che 宮中檔康熙朝奏摺 (Secret palace memorials of the K'ang-hsi period). 9 vols. (documents in vols. 8 and 9 are in Manchu). NPM(T), 1976–77.

KHWC: K'ang-hsi ti yü-chih wen-chi 康熙帝御制文集 (Collected literary works, edicts, and so forth of the K'ang-hsi Emperor). 4 vols., with continuous pagination. Taipei reprint, 1966.

KKWH: Ku-kung wen-hsien 故宮文獻 (Ch'ing documents at the National Palace Museum). NPM(T); the sequence from vol. 1, no. 1 (December 1969) to vol. 3, no. 1 (December 1971) contains photo-offset reproductions of the palace memorials submitted during the K'ang-hsi reign.

K'o-she ou-wen 客舍偶聞 (Random news items), anonymous. In *Chen-ch'i t'ang ts'ung-shu* 振綺堂叢書 (Miscellaneous publications from the Chen-ch'i Hall). N.d.

Ku-kung po-wu yuan yuan-k'an 故宮博物院院刊 (Bulletin of the National Palace Museum). Peiping, 1935.

Kuo-ch'ao ch'i-hsien lei-cheng ch'u-pien 國朝耆獻類徵初編 (Classified biographies of eminent men of the Ch'ing period), comp. Li Huan 李桓. 720 chüan with appendixes (12 chüan). 1884–1890.

Kuo Hua-yeh hsien-sheng shu-kao 郭華野先生疏稿 (Draft memorials of Mr. Kuo Hsiu), by Kuo Hsiu; 4 ts'e. N.d.

Lasswell, Harold D. *Power and Personality.* New York, Viking, 1963.

Le Comte, Louis Daniel. *Memoirs and Observation, Topographical, Physical, Mathematical, Mechanical, Natural, Civil and Ecclesiastical Made in a Late Journey through the Empire of China.* London, 1697.

Lee, Robert H. G. *The Manchurian Frontier in Ch'ing History.* Cambridge, Mass., Harvard University Press, 1970.

Lettres édifiantes et curieuses concernant l'Asie, l'Afrique et l'Amérique, published under the direction of De M. L. Aimé-Martin. Vol. 3 (China). Paris, Société du Panthéon Littéraire, 1843.

Li Hsü Tsou-che 李煦奏摺 (Li Hsü's memorials). Peking, 1976.

Li Kuang-t'ao 李光濤. "Ch'ing T'ai-tsung to-wei k'ao" 清太宗奪位考 (A study of Ch'ing T'ai-tsung's struggle for imperial succession), in his *Ming-Ch'ing-shih lun-chi* 明清史論集 (Essays on Ming-Ch'ing history). Taipei, 1970.

Li Kuang-ti 李光地. *Jung-ts'un yü-lu hsü-chi* 榕村語錄續集 (Recorded sayings of Li Kuang-ti; supplement), 20 chüan, 1894.

Li Shu-ku hsien-sheng nien-p'u 李恕谷先生年譜 (A chronological biography of Li Kung), comp. Feng Ch'en 馮辰 et al., revised by Sun K'ai 孫鍇. Preface, 1730.

Li Wei Archives (The original palace memorials of Li Wei) 李衞. No. 07722. NPM(T).

Li Wen-cheng kung nien-p'u 李文貞公年譜 (A chronological biography of Li Kuang-ti); 2 ts'e, 1825.

Liang-Huai yen-fa chih 兩淮鹽法誌 (Salt gazetteer of Liang-Huai). 1869.

Liu Ch'eng-fu 劉誠甫, ed. *Yin-yüeh tz'u-tien* 音樂辭典 (A dictionary of music). Shanghai, 1935.

Malone, Carroll Brown. *History of the Peking Summer Palaces under the Ch'ing Dynasty.* Urbana, University of Illinois Press, 1934.

Mancall, Mark. *Russia and China: Their Diplomatic Relations to 1728.* Cambridge, Mass., Harvard University Press, 1971.

Man-Han ming-ch'en chuan 滿漢名臣傳 (Biographies of eminent Manchu and Chinese officials), Chü-hua shu-shih 菊花書室 edn. 90 chüan. N.d.

Meng Sen 孟森. "Ming Lieh-huang hsün-kuo hou-chi" 明列皇殉國後記 (An account of the death of the Emperor Lieh of the Ming dynasty), in *Ming Ch'ing shih lun-chu chi-k'an* 明清史論著集刊 (Collected essays by Meng Sen on Ming and Ch'ing histories). Peking, 1959.

Meng Sen 孟森. *Ch'ing-tai shih* 清代史 (A history of the Ch'ing dynasty). Taipei, 1960.

Miyazaki Ichisada 宮崎市定. *Kakyo* 科擧 (The civil-service examination in imperial China). Osaka, 1946.

Miyazaki Ichisada 宮崎市定. *Ajia shi kenkyū* アジア史研究 (Asiatic). 4 vols. Kyoto, 1964.

Mo Tung-yin 莫東寅. *Man-tsu shih lun-ts'ung* 滿族史論叢 (Essays on the history of the Manchus). Peking, 1958.

Morse, Hosea Ballous. *The Chronicles of the East India Company Trading to China, 1635–1834.* Oxford, The Clarendon Press, 1926–29.

NWF Manchu Archives: Nei-wu fu Man-wen tsou-hsiao tang 內務府滿文奏銷檔 (Manchu archives of the Imperial Household pertaining to financial reports to the throne on expenditures). Cited in this book are the following:

(1) "Chuang Ch'in-wang Yun-lu tsou shen-hsün Sui-ho-te tsuan-yin lao P'ing chün-wang che" 莊親王允祿奏審訊綏和德鑽營老平郡王摺 (Palace memorial submitted by Prince Chuang, Yun-lu [Yin-lu], concerning the trial of Sui-ho-te for his bribing the old Prince P'ing [Na-erh-su] for a personal favor), dated YC 11/10/7. Chinese translation in *TCTA*, pp. 192–196.

(2) "Nei-wu fu teng ya-men tsou Ts'ao Yin and Li Hsü chüan-hsiu hsing-kung i-chi ching-t'ang hsien che" 內務府等衙門奏曹寅李煦等捐修行宮擬給京堂銜摺 (Palace memorial submitted jointly by the Imperial Household and other offices [the Grand Secretariat and the Board of Civil Appointment], which recommends that Ts'ao Yin and Li Hsü be given metropolitan honorary titles for their contributions for the construction of temporary imperial palaces [at Yangchow]), dated KH 44/intercalary 4/5. Chinese translation in *TCTA*, pp. 30–31.

(3) "Nei-wu fu tsung-kuan Yun-lu teng tsou hsün-kuo Li Hsü chi Ho-shou

chia-jen wei Yin-ssu mai nü-tzu ping sung yin-liang ch'ing-hsing che," 內務府總管允祿等奏訊過李煦及赫壽家人爲胤禩買女子並送銀兩情形摺 (Palace memorial submitted by Yun-lu, minister of the Imperial Household, and others reporting on the trial of the household servants of Li Hsü and Ho-shou who had purchased [Soochow] women for, and had presented silver to Yin-ssu), dated YC 5/2/23. Chinese translation in *TCTA*, pp. 210–213.

(4) "Pa pei-le teng tsou ch'a-hsün Ts'ao Yin Li Hsü chia-jen teng ch ü-fu k'uan-hsiang ch'ing-hsing che" 八貝勒等奏查訊曹寅李煦家人等取付款項情形摺 (Palace memorial submitted by Yin-ssu, reporting on the trial of the household servants of Ts'ao Yin and Li Hsü for their appropriating public funds as payoffs [to Ling-p'u and others]), dated KH 47/9/23. Chinese translation in *TCTA*, pp. 60–61.

Okada Hidehiro 岡田英弘. "Ch'ing T'ai-tsung chi-wei k'ao-shih" 清太宗卽位考實 (A study of Hong Taiji's succession to the throne), *KKWH*, vol. 3, no. 2, pp. 31–38 (March 1972).

Orléans, Pierre Joseph d'. *History of the Two Tartar Conquerors of China*, tr. and ed. the Earl of Ellesmere. London, Hakluyt Society, 1854; reprinted in China, 1939.

Oxnam, Robert B. *Ruling from Horseback: Manchu Politics in the Oboi Regency, 1661–1669*. Chicago, University of Chicago Press, 1975.

PCTP: Pa-ch'i Man-chou shih-tsu t'ung-p'u 八旗滿洲氏族通譜 (Genealogy of the Manchu clans in the Eight Banners). 80 chüan. 1745.

Poe, Dison Hsüeh-feng. "Imperial Succession and Attendant Crisis in Dynastic China," *Tsing Hua Journal of Chinese Studies*, New Series, vol. 8, nos. 1 and 2, pp. 84–153 (August 1970).

Ripa, Matteo. *Memoirs of Father Ripa*. London, John Murray, 1846.

Rosso, Antonio Sisto, O. F. M., *Apostolic Legations to China of the Eighteenth Century*. South Pasadena, P. D. and Ione Perkins, 1948.

Sa Meng-wu 薩孟武. *Shui-hu-chuan yü chung-kuo she-hui* 水滸傳與中國社會 (The novel *All Men Are Brothers* and Chinese society). Nanking, 1934.

Saeki Tomi 佐伯富. *Shindai ensei no kenkyū* 清代鹽政の研究 (The salt administration under the Ch'ing dynasty). Kyoto, 1962.

Saeki Tomi 佐伯富. "Shincho no kōki to Sansei shōnin" 清朝の興起と山西商人 (The rise of the Ch'ing dynasty and Shansi merchants), in *Shakai bunka shigaku* 社會文化史學 1: 11–41. Tokyo, 1966.

Schwartz, Benjamin I. "On Filial Piety and Revolution: China" (A review of Richard H. Solomon's book *Mao's Revolution and the Chinese Political Culture*), *Journal* of Interdisciplinary History, vol. 3, no. 3, pp. 569–580 (winter 1973).

Shan Shih-yuan 單士元. "Kuan-yü Ch'ing-kung chih hsiu-nü ho kung-nü" 關於清宮之秀女和宮女 (Concerning the palace ladies in the Ch'ing court), in *Ku-kung po-wu yuan yuan-k'an* 故宮博物院院刊 (Bulletin of the NPM), pp. 97–103. Peiping, 1935.

Shang Yen-liu 商衍鎏. *Ch'ing-tai k'o-chü k'ao-shih shu-lu* 清代科舉考試述錄 (The examination system in the Ch'ing dynasty). Peking, 1958.

Shih-ch'ao sheng-hsün 十朝聖訓 (Sacred instructions of ten reigns [1616–

1874]): K'ang-hsi reign (1661–1722), 60 chüan; Ch'ien-lung reign (1736–1795), 300 chüan. Taipei reprint, 1965.

SLHK: Shih-liao hsün-k'an 史料旬刊 (Historical materials published every ten days), 40 ts'e, NPM(P), 1930–31; 1963 Taipei reprint with continuous pagination.

SLTKCP: Shih-liao ts'ung-k'an ch'u-pien 史料叢刊初編 (Miscellaneous historical documents; 1st ser.). 2 vols. Peiping, 1924 preface by Lo Chen-yü 羅振玉.

SLTP: Shih-liao ts'ung-pien 史料叢編 (Miscellaneous records from the Ch'ing Imperial Archives), comp. Lo Chen-yü 羅振玉, Port Arthur, China, 1935. 1st ser. (I), 12 ts'e, and 2nd ser. (II), 6 ts'e, including

(1)   *Sheng-tsu ch'in-cheng shu-mo jih-lu* 聖祖親征溯漠日錄 (A daily account of the K'ang-hsi Emperor's campaign against the Western Mongols, 1696), in I, ts'e 1.

(2)   *Sheng-tsu hsi-hsün jih-lu* 聖祖西巡日錄 (A daily account of Emperor K'ang-hsi's western tour, 1703), in I, ts'e 1.

(3)   *Sheng-tsu Jen Huang-ti ch'i-chü chu* 聖祖仁皇帝起居注 (Diary of the movements and utterances of the K'ang-hsi Emperor), I, ts'e 1, and II, ts'e 7.

Spence, Jonathan D. *Ts'ao Yin and the K'ang-hsi Emperor. Bondservant and Master.* New Haven, Yale University Press, 1966.

Spence, Jonathan D. *Emperor of China: Self-portrait of K'ang-hsi.* New York, Alfred A. Knopf, 1974.

Su-chou chih-tsao Li Hsü tsou-che 蘇州織造李煦奏摺 (Palace memorials of the Soochow Textile Commissioner Li Hsü). NPM(P), 1937. The 1964 reprint of *Wen-hsien ts'ung-pien* (pp. 1–116), which includes Li Hsü's palace memorials contained in this volume, omits the last eleven pages of Li's memorials.

Su-chou fu-chih 蘇州府志 (Gazetteer of Soochow). 80 chüan. 1748.

Sung Lao 宋犖. *Hsi-po lei-kao* 西坡類稿 (Classified essays of Sung Lao). 1917.

Sung-shih 宋史 (Sung history), in *Nien-ssu-shih* 廿四史 (The twenty-four dynastic histories). K'ai-ming shu-tien edn. N.d.

SYNK: Shang-yü Nei-ko 上諭內閣 (Imperial edicts of the Yung-cheng Emperor issued through the Grand Secretariat), 34 ts'e, 1741. Citations according to date of edict.

Ta-Ch'ing hui-tien 大清會典 (Collected statutes of the Ch'ing dynasty). 100 chüan, 1899 edn.

Ta-i chüeh-mi lu 大義覺迷錄 (A record of awakening to the truth [conerning Tseng Ching's trial records and confessions]). 1730.

Ta-Ming hui-tien 大明會典 (Collected Statutes of the Ming dynasty), 1505.

Tai To tsou-che 戴鐸奏摺 (Tai To's palace memorials to his lord Prince Yung, Yin-chen), in *WHTP*, pp. 101–103.

T'ao Chün-ch'i 陶君起. *Ching-chü chü-mu ch'u-t'an* 京劇劇目初探 (A preliminary study of the themes in Peking opera). Peking, 1963.

T'ang-tzu i-shu 唐子遺書 (Collected works of T'ang Pin). Ai-jih-t'ang edn., 1870.

TCTA: Kuan-yü Chiang-ning chih-tsao Ts'ao-chia tang-an shih-liao 關于江寧織造曹家檔案史料 (Archival materials concerning the Ts'ao family, whose members had successively held the position of textile commissioner at Chiang-ning), comp. NPM(P). Peking, Chung-hua shu-chü, 1975.

T'ing-hsün ko-yen 庭訓格言 (Family instructions of the K'ang-hsi Emperor); preface by the Yung-cheng Emperor, 1730.

Ts'ao Yin Archives (The original palace memorials of Ts'ao Yin) 曹寅. Nos. 2757–2759, 2760, 2762. NPM(T).

Ts'ao Yin tsou-che. 曹寅奏摺 (107 palace memorials submitted by Ts'ao Yin to the K'ang-hsi Emperor). In *KKWH*, vol. 2, no. 1, pp. 128–188 (December 1970).

Tung-hua lu 東華錄 (Tung-hua records), comp. Chiang Liang-ch'i 蔣良騏. 37 chüan. Chü-hua shu-shih edn., 1765.

Tung-hua lu 東華錄 (Tung-hua records), comp. Wang Hsien-ch'ien 王先謙, 30 vols. Shanghai, 1911.

Tung-p'ing chou chih 東平州志 (Gazetteer of Tung-p'ing subprefecture). 1771 edn.

Wang Ching-ch'i 王景祺. *Tu-shu t'ang hsi-cheng sui-pi* 讀書堂西征隨筆(Jottings on a western journey). In *CKTP*, pp. 114–142.

Wang Chung-han 王鐘翰."Ch'ing Shih-tsung to-ti k'ao-shih," 清世宗奪嫡考實 (The Yung-cheng Emperor's struggle for the right of succession), in *Yen-ching hsüeh-pao* 燕京學報 (Yenching journal of Chinese studies) 36.62: 205–261 (June 1949).

Wang Hao 王灝. *Sui-lien chi-en* 隨鑾紀恩 (Memoir on imperial favors received in the 1703 visit of Jehol), in *Hsiao-fang-hu chai yü-ti ts'ung-ch'ao* 小房壺齋輿地叢鈔 1st ser., ts'e 4, pp. 286–297.

Wang Hung-hsü mi-shan hsiao-che 王鴻緒密繕小摺 (Tiny secret palace memorials submitted to the K'ang-hsi Emperor from Wang Hung-hsü). In *WHTP*, pp. 78–95.

Wang Shih-cheng 王士禎. *Chü-i lu* (Chü-i records) 居易錄. In *Yü-yang san-shih liu chung* 漁洋三十六種 (Collected works of Wang Shih-cheng). N.d.

Wang Shu-nu 王書奴. *Chung-kuo ch'ang-chi shih* 中國娼妓史 (A history of prostitution in China). Shanghai, 1935.

WHCN: Sheng-tsu wu-hsing Chiang-nan ch'üan-lu 聖祖五幸江南全錄 (An anonymous diary of the K'ang-hsi Emperor's fifth Southern tour, in 1705). In *Chen-ch'i t'ang ts'ung-shu* 振綺堂叢書, ed. Wang K'ang-nien 汪康年. 1st series. N.d.

WHTP: Wen-hsien ts'ing pien 文獻叢編 (Miscellaneous Ch'ing historical documents). NPM(P), 1930 ff; 1964 Taipei reprint (2 vols.) used.

Wright, Arthur F. "Sui Yang-ti: Personality and Stereotype," in his (ed.) *Confucian Persuasion*. Stanford, Stanford University Press, 1960.

Wright, G. N. *China. In a Series of Views, Displaying the Scenery, Architecture, and Social Habit, of That Ancient Empire*. 4 vols. London, Fisher Son & Co., 1843.

Wu Chen-yü 吳振域. *Yang-chi-chai ts'ung-lu* 養吉齋叢錄 (Miscellaneous notes from the Yang-chi study). 35 chüan, including *Yang-chi-chai yü-lu* 養吉齋餘錄 (Additional notes from the Yang-chi study), 10 chüan. Preface, 1896.

Wu Hsiu-liang 吳秀良 (Silas H. L. Wu). "Nan-shu-fang chih chien-chih chi ch'i ch'ien-ch'i chih fa-chan" 南書房之建置及其前期之發展 (The founding of the South Library and its early development), in *Ssu yü yen* 思與言 (Thought and word), 5: 6–12 (March 1968).

Wu, Silas H. L. "Value Demands and Value Fulfillment: An Approach to the Study of the Ch'ing Emperor-Official Relationship," *Ch'ing-shih wen-t'i* (Bulletin of the Society for Ch'ing Studies), 1.8: 27–37 (May 1968).

Wu, Silas H. L. *Communication and Imperial Control in China: Evolution of the Palace Memorial System, 1693–1735.* Cambridge, Mass., Harvard University Press, 1970.

Wu, Silas H. L. "Emperors at Work: The Daily Schedules of the K'ang-hsi and Yung-cheng Emperors, 1661–1735," *Tsing Hua Journal of Chinese Studies*, New Series, vol. 8, nos. 1 and 2, pp. 210–227 (August 1970).

Wu, Silas H. L. "A Note on the Proper Use of Documents for Historical Studies: A Rejoinder," *Harvard Journal of Asiatic Studies* 32: 230–239 (1972).

Yamawaki Teizirō 山脇悌二郎. *Nagasaki to Tōjin* bōeki 長崎と唐人貿易 (Nagasaki and the China trade). Tokyo, 1964.

Yang-chi-chai ts'ung-lu. See Wu Chen-yü.

Yang-chi-chai yü-lu. See Wu Chen-yü.

Yang-chou fu-chih 揚州府志 (Gazetteer of Yangchow). 1733.

Yang-chou hua-fang lu 揚州畫舫錄 (An account of the "gay boats" at Yangchow in eighteenth-century China), by Li Tou 李斗. Peking, 1960.

Yen Ch'ien-chiu hsien-sheng nien-p'u 閻潛丘先生年譜 (A chronological biography of Yen Jo-chü [1636–1704]). comp. Chang Mu 張穆. 1847.

Yen Tun-i 嚴敦易. *Shui-hu-chuan ti yen-pien* 水滸傳的演變 (Evolution of the [novel] *All Men Are Brothers*). Peking, 1957.

Yin-chi-shan Archives (The original palace memorials of Yin-chih-shan) 尹繼善. No. 02284; undated (submitted in 1723 or 1724). NPM(T).

Yin Hua-hsing 殷化行. *Hsi-cheng chi-lüeh* 西征紀略 (A brief account of the Western Campaign, 1696), in *Chao-tai ts'ung-shu* 昭代叢書 (The Chao-tai series). Ts'e 47.

Yin-ssu Archives. No. 04623. "Tsung-li shih-wu wang ta-ch'en Lien ch'in-wang ch'en Yun-ssu teng tsou-che" 總理事務王大臣廉親王臣允禩等奏摺 (A palace memorial submitted by the imperial assistants plenipotentiary, your subject Prince Lien, Yin-ssu, and others [dated 1723]). NPM(T).

Yoshio Hosoya 細谷良夫. "Ch'ing-tai pa-ch'i chih-tu chih yen-pien" 清代八旗制度之演變 (Evolution of the Ch'ing Eight Banner system). In *KKWH* 3.3: 37–60 (June 1972).

"Yu-kuan Na-erh-su ti shih-hsi chi-ch'i sheng-p'ing chien-li shih-liao" 有關納爾蘇(素)的世系及其生平簡歷史料(Historical sources concerning the genealogy and the brief life history of Na-erh-su." In *TCTA*, Appendix 2, pp. 218–222.

Yung-cheng ti yü-chih wen-chi 雍正帝御制文集 (Collected literary works, edicts, and so forth of the Yung-cheng Emperor). 30 chüan. Palace edn., 1897.

Yung-hsien lu 永憲錄 (Historical records of the Yung-cheng period), comp. Hsiao Shih 蕭奭. Shanghai, 1959.

Zucker, Adolf Eduard. *The Chinese Theater.* Boston, Little, Brown, 1925.

Glossary

amba fujin 大福晉

Ch'ang-sheng tien ch'uan ch'i 長生殿傳奇

ch'i-chü-chu kuan 起居注官

chia-jen 家人

chiang-t'ien i-lan 江天一覽

chien-sheng 監生

chih 制

chih-tao liao 知道了

chin-feng 謹封

chin-shih 進士

ch'in-wang 親王

ching-t'ien 敬天

ching-yen 經筵

ch'ing-ming 清明

ch'u-pao an-liang 除暴安良

ch'uan-hsin tien 傳心殿

chü-jen 舉人

chün-wang 郡王

chung-kung 中宮

fa-tsu 法祖

fang-kuan 坊官

fei 妃

fei-tse 飛賊

ha-ha chu-tzu 哈哈珠子

ho-chin yen 合卺筵

hsiao 孝

hsiao-shou 小手

Hsin-che-k'u 辛者庫

hsün-tsang 殉葬

huang-kuei fei 皇貴妃

huang-ti 皇帝

Hui-chen chi 會眞記

I-cheng ch'u 議政處

I ching 易經

i-ch'i 義氣

i-jen 異人

jih-chiang (kuan) 日講（官）

kuang-shan k'u 廣善庫

k'un-ch'ü 崑曲

liang 兩

Mai-kung 邁公

na-ts'ai 納采

Nan-shan chi 南山集

Nan shu-fang shou 南書房收

Nei-wu fu 內務府

Pao-ho tien 保和殿

Pao-i 包衣

Pao-t'a wan 寶塔灣

pei-le 貝勒

Po-hsüeh hung-tz'u 博學鴻詞

San-kuo yen-i 三國演義

shang-kang 商綱

Shang-shu fan 上書房

sheng-yuan 生員

shih 是

shu-chi shih 庶吉士

shu-pan 書辦

Shui-hu chuan 水湖傳

Sin jeku (Manchu for Hsin-che-k'u)

ssu-k'u 司庫

ssu-kuan 司官

ta-cheng 大徵

ta fu-chin 大福晉

Tai'-ho tien 太和殿

t'ai-miao 太廟

T'ai-p'ing lo 太平樂

T'ao-ho-ch'i 陶和氣

T'ao-hua shan 桃花扇

t'i-t'ien hsing-t'ao 替天行道

tien-shih 殿試

t'ing-li 聽理

T'o-ho-ch'i 託和齊

Tz'u-ning kung 慈寧宮

wan-shou wu-chiang 萬壽無疆

wan-sui 萬歲

wu-ch'eng 五城

Wu-i tien 無逸殿

wu tz'u ming jen 無此名人

yin 引

yin-tz'u 淫辭

yü-ch'ien jen-yüan 御前人員

yü-tieh 玉牒

yü-yung 玉蛹

Index

HARVARD EAST ASIAN SERIES

By Lloyd E. Eastman.

*Out of print. Most of these titles can be ordered through University Microfilms.